Ade Bozzay

THE MOANING OF LOAF

THE MOANING OF LOAF

"It is a truth seldom acknowledge that if life gives you lemons, it is probably because you live near a lemon tree." **Jacob Spittledock, professional misery guts** 1892-1960

by

Ade Bozzay

2017

First Printing: 2017

ISBN: 978-0-244-30316-7

Dedication

To my wife, Joanne, and children Aidan and Bethanie,
for supporting me and not letting the beer run out.

IN THE BEGINNING

"It is true money will not buy you real happiness, but as a personal preference, I would much rather have an angry strangle wank in the comfort of a private jet en route to Monte Carlo than in a broom closet in the basement of a seedy crack house in Bangkok"
Archbishop Jessop Week-Bladdar 1925-1992

In the beginning was the word, and that word was probably misconstrued by someone who then made it into a personal issue and started a fight causing people to be miserable. It happens a lot, the history of the human race is probably littered with misery caused by the wrong interpretation of words or actions. "Brother Abbot...I have just looked at the original parchments we are copying from, it says we should celebrate, not be celibate" followed swiftly by "Oh for fu…" and so on.

Long before mankind found untold misery in money and all the trappings of wealth, they were still miserable. It is just the way we are, get used to it. Even early man suffered from fire envy as he watched the dim yet cosy glow of his neighbour's cave from the dank darkness of his own sparse stony dwelling, surrounded by soggy wood and broken dreams of warmth. I reckon many of our early counterparts burnt to death in the foolish act of trying to carry a fire home. I guess early man was never destined to have it easy, if it wasn't his significantly clubbed other moaning that Mrs Cro-Magnon across the way always got a new sabre tooth wrap every season, it was Mr. Cro-Magnon flaunting the size of his flint to all and sundry, causing jealousy all around.

We just can't be pleased, if someone gave us a gold pig, we would complain that it didn't crap diamonds. If we were impoverished and destitute living rough in a wheelie bin and found a warm boot, we would grumble and curse at the fact we had two feet to cover or that it clashed with our urine stained nylon trousers. We are just never happy.

Give a man a fish, he will eat for a day, give him the ability to fish for himself and he will find a way to strip the natural fishy resources right out of his local environment, causing him to stray into someone else's territory for more fishy goodness and subsequently causing a territorial dispute that will end up with thousands killed in a massive sea battle over the last remaining fish finger filling.

We try to be happy, but we aren't really very good at it. Everyone pretends to be happy, on the outside at least, before locking themselves up for the night in front of the telly box with a five kilo tub of ice cream and watching other people pretending to be even more unhappy than you in TV programs designed to make you forget how really miserable you are whilst trying to entice you to buy things you don't need, that will probably add to your overall misery, in between scenes. We are the same with social media, we use it to lie and deceive people we really neither know well or care about to convince them our lives are so much better than theirs. We all have great lives on social media, eat great food, share inspiring statuses and feel good stories from the gloom of our laptops and tablets, wrapped in a duvet eating cold baked beans straight from the can with a spoon you stole from a café.

"Living the dream" we type from our squalid nightmare existence of fear of debt collectors and payday loan repayments that have calculations even NASA can't compute. Reposting pictures from your last holiday, "Happy times", you type with a multitude of smiley faces as you push away the long overdue credit card final reminder demanding repayment for that very holiday. Happy times indeed as we borrow a small sliver of happiness from the promises of tomorrow. Face it, we just can't help ourselves, we are addicted to being miserable at any cost.

Occasionally, every century or so, someone is born, someone who despite adversity, hardship and every ill the universe can bestow upon them keep smiling and striving forward without a moment of regret, without a second of self-pity or sense of defeat. Someone who rises tall stands proud and faces the world head on and makes everything they have the greatest it can be.

Nobby Loaf is not one of those people.

CHAPTER ONE

"My god, they are wearing the same outfit as me, I must hate them instantly and forever" **No Man, ever**!

In all fairness, Nobby Loaf is not a miserable person, but at the same time, he isn't a happy person either. He is the sort of person whose glass is neither too full nor too empty, just as it is. If he found a gold bar he would be pleased with the wealth it would give but equally perturbed at the thought of having to carry it and the responsibility that comes with it to such a degree one would cancel out the other and he would be left in a state of facial torpor that gave the impression he couldn't give a wet slap either way. Mother Nature had not been kind Nobby in many ways, he was tall, 6 foot 9 inches although due to the way his shoulders hunched and his legs bowed as he walked, he averaged around 5 foot 11. He was allergic to most things, including sun light, sea water and foreign foods, so the one time he ever went abroad on holiday consisted of one day of sun bathing and swimming on one of the many golden beaches of the Costa del Sol, followed by three weeks in a local Spanish hospital. It would have only been a week, but after his first hospital meal there, a dish of Spanish fame, things went, as they say in the medical profession, tits up for him.

Nobby Loaf liked to laugh but somehow until recently his life never seemed to offer him much to laugh at, although he often found he offered other much to laugh at. He regularly found himself to be the butt of other peoples humour, mainly due to his slightly unusual gait and appearance and inept ability in even the most routine tasks. Jokes tended to get lost on Nobby, his sense of humour appeared to inhabit a separate time zone, often taking several days to catch up. On many occasions, punch lines suddenly revealed their meanings to him at very inopportune moments. He had often been reduced to gales of uncontrollable laughter whilst sat on a bus. This scenario usually caused old ladies to panic and get off several stops early and walk despite their false hips, or it instinctively made mothers gather their children nearer and quickly scan for any available escape routes. The delay in comprehension of jokes had always been a constant problem for Nobby and many spiteful people would tell him a joke on purpose knowing full well that it would probably cause him untold amounts of embarrassment and trouble at a later date. Like the time the significance of a joke dawned on him three days after being told it, causing him to break out into whoops of unrelenting laughter which brought tears to his eyes and almost stained his trousers. After several minutes the whoops had reduced to persistent giggling. He couldn't help himself and he tried desperately to explain to everyone the reason for his actions, but alas the congregation of Aunt Mavis' funeral were not amused.

Nobby enjoyed simple things, walks in the country, supermarket muzak, masturbating to internet porn and making farty noises on his old battered leather settee. In fact, that is what he was doing as we join him in this tale.

Nobby raised himself from the settee and let his body drop back down again, producing another leathery fart and another fit of giggles. When this fresh set of giggles had abated, he toyed with the idea of jumping up and down a bit, thus creating a string of farts or a fart symphony as he likes to call them, but ultimately decided against it on the grounds that this was exactly what he did only half an hour ago. In retrospect, he realised that he had more or less done it almost every hour for the past few days. God, he was bored.

Nobby swung his legs up onto the settee and laid down to relax. He began to think of the new friends, well, one friend he had made recently. He closed his eyes and began to daydream of more exciting times. He was just settling into a pleasant bout of nostalgia when abruptly an unpleasant thought sprung to mind,
"You are all alone and you have no friends left", his mind told him quite bluntly. Nobby pondered the thought for a moment and he was intending to argue with himself but realised that he was absolutely right. Sadly he recognised the fact that he indeed didn't have a single friend in the whole world, well not anyone who would call him up and ask him out for a pint or two, no real friends. Now to be honest it completely escaped his notice that he never had any real friends anyway until recently that is, and they've gone now. Truth be told he was never what could be described as popular, in all fairness an old syphilitic, pus ridden leper, wearing rags, whilst ringing a bell and shouting "unclean, unclean", probably had a larger circle of friends than Nobby. He never really noticed his apparent lack of friends before, after all, you don't miss what you never had. Nobby was the sort of person who would quite happily begin talking

to complete strangers at bus stops and describe in graphic detail the current state of his piles or whip off his sock for you to examine his festering verruca or gamey bunion. Sparkling conversation and Noel Coward style wit were not Nobby's strong point; in fact, any type of conversation with Nobby should carry some kind of health warning and be avoided at all costs. Fortunately, his outward appearance usually caused people to cross the road when they saw him coming anyway, so verbal contact was a rare occurrence. People sort of sensed Nobby in the way wild animals sensed approaching danger. Nobby didn't look, nor indeed was he, dangerous. Quite the opposite, in fact, he more resembled the kid at school who at fifteen still held his mother’s hand and never did games because of some mysterious illness which, despite multiples of rumours and several bullying’s, still remained a secret. He looked like the kid that wore the same uniform as everyone else, yet still managed to stick out in a crowd because it seemed that his uniform was trying its hardest not to be associated with him.

As mentioned he was tall, although stooped, so had the gait of a wizened old man. His hair had a certain greasy lankness to it which is only usually found on people who have just spent the past several hours in a night club, during a heatwave, dancing like frenzied loonies with a swarm of killer hornets in their grotty nylon Y fronts. Even when Nobby had washed it, his hair never quite seemed to dry.

His eyes were something else again, being both long and short sighted at once. The lenses of his glasses were so thick it took sunlight an extra few seconds to penetrate them. His glasses would have put Jack Duckworth to shame; hardly a single piece of the frames could be seen beneath the sticky plasters and tape. They were held to his head by his ears, which individually were fairly normal as far as ears go, but from face on it became apparent that they were not level, causing his glasses to slope slightly to the left, which in turn gave the impression that his eyes were also uneven. The cockeyed glasses were supported by his nose, which was almost completely normal, except for the way they flared constantly as he spoke. Just below his nose, you could find his mouth, a conspicuous mishap of evolution. He had unusually large upper front teeth which his top lip strained in vain to cover, thus causing them to continually poke out in a dangerous manner. Nobby didn't appear to possess a chin, his neck just seemed to bypass the normal formalities of forming such trivial things as chins and consequently just grew outwards slightly and disappeared behind his oversized upper teeth.

His body was thin and gangly but due to his pronounced forward stoop that he had whilst walking these features were normally hidden by his ill-fitting clothes. His stoop gave his arms the optical illusion of being far too long. So instead of reaching around waist level, they reached mid-thigh and just hung there limply flapping as he walked.
This gave the impression to anyone who cared to take notice or give him a second glance that his upper body was stood still while only his legs were going somewhere.

Nobby wasn't blessed with good looks or even average looks, but it was fair to say they were pretty unique and though many people may have forgotten his name few ever forgot his face, regardless of how much they tried. If God had fashioned Nobby in his own image, then it is little wonder that he doesn't wish to be seen.

Nobby lay silently on the settee, brooding moodily over his loneliness when a random thought entered his head. "At least I'm not a virgin!" he told himself.
Now for most people this would be considered a straight forward and normal thought.
Coming as it did from Nobby it suddenly became a thought that would send a shiver down the spine of the most street wise and unfussy prostitute. As far as thoughts go, it was one that should be sealed in concrete and dumped in some undisclosed coordinates in the North Sea.

Before venturing any further two important facts need to be pointed out;

1, Nobby has never had a girlfriend,

2, Nobby cannot actually remember losing his virginity, although consequential events made him believe he had.

The events surrounding the loss of his virginity are as bizarre as the fact that anyone like Nobby could lose their virginity in the first place.

Several years earlier Nobby found himself at a party, not that anyone invited him; somehow he just happened to be there. It is fair to state that Nobby often got invited to parties, although he was usually invited towards the end of a party as the hosts were trying to clear their homes so they could go to bed. This particular occasion Nobby had found himself there by accident, some drunken reveller who didn't know him had seen him in the street and dragged him in thinking Nobby was in fancy dress. The party was banging away like a bunny rabbit on speed, and everyone was having a great time, even the guy throwing up in the potted plant was enjoying himself.
Everyone except the DJ that is, Nobby had found his way to the DJ.
In normal daylight, Nobby was a ghastly sight to behold at best, but in a darkened room illuminated only by the flicker of strobe lighting his demeanour took on the appearance of a greasy haired Orang-utan with bad eyesight and ill-fitting clothes.
When the DJ, a slightly balding 40+-year-old with a pronounced middle age spread, first spotted Nobby lurching towards him he damn near soiled his nylon Y-fronts. He froze in panic as Nobby shuffled closer and closer, staring in open mouthed disbelief at the unnatural collection of bodily parts and mismatched clothing that made up the thing which approached.
The DJ suddenly became aware that there was silence in the room, he blinked for what seemed like the first time in hours and scanned the rest of the room. Everyone was looking at him, confused expressions on the faces of those who were sober enough and capable of giving a

damn. He looked down and realised that his equipment had fallen silent.
"Music" he suddenly thought and pressed the button to start the next track. He mumbled a quick apology about faulty wiring into his microphone and increased the volume of the record slightly.
The room filled with music once more, and almost as quickly as they had stopped, the people started dancing again.
The D.J let out a deep breath, ran his hand over his fore head to remove the sudden sweaty moisture that had gathered there, careful not to dislodge his toupee, and took a moment to collect his thoughts, he scanned the dance floor for the hideous being he had seen, or at least thought he had seen. His mouth had become pretty dry following the experience, he needed a drink, he reached for his orange juice and noticed, disturbingly that his hands were trembling slightly, "not surprising really" he muttered to himself whilst carefully sniffing his orange juice just in case someone had spiked it. After a quick drink and a couple of moments to recollect himself he got back down to business, selecting the next few records to be played, once that was sorted he decided a quick crafty puff on his special cigarette would steady his nerves. He was just about to enjoy a blast on his special cigarette when he was tapped on the shoulder. He turned hoping it was some young girl he could impress with his hairy chest and jet black toupee/hair. It wasn't, it was Nobby, and close up at that.
This time the D.J did shit himself.

Nobby had seen many strange things during his life, mainly because one way or another he was usually responsible for them, but he couldn't understand why the D.J had dived under the table and was at present tearing up his home made cigarettes and sobbing the words "I'll never touch the stuff again, I promise, just take it away" and then laughing like that bloke outside the fun house at Blackpool. After a couple of moments, Nobby realised that perhaps this was not the best time to request the chicken song. Meanwhile, unperturbed by all the ongoing events, Nobby's bladder made its presence felt, informing him that the three glasses of warm cider he had drank needed to be released, and being a dutiful host to his bodily organs Nobby wandered off in search of relief. From beneath the disco turntables the D.J gibbered with joy as he watched Nobby turn and walk away, he was so ecstatic in fact he damn well pissed himself out of sheer bliss.

Nobby wasn't used to drinking, so the cider he had managed to procure and subsequently down rather rapidly was beginning to strain his bladder and the urgency to empty it was becoming greater by the minute. To make matters worse, Nobby found his coordination somewhat impaired and his vision even more blurred than usual. Nobby was drunk, a condition he was unfamiliar with having been drunk only once before after a particularly unsuccessful attempt at home brewing, which resulted in him spending several weeks in hospital suffering from toxic poisoning and his home brew being disarmed in a controlled explosion by the bomb squad, after two bottles had exploded and partially destroyed his shed. Nobby had only opened one bottle and sniffed at the contents and as a consequence remained totally rat arsed for the next four days. And now he was drunk again, swaying slightly as he lumbered towards the hallway that led to the stairs and hopefully the toilets. As he entered the hallway he came to a halt and squinted with what he considered to be his myopic good eye. "This is not good." he said to himself as he eyed the multitude of people sitting all over the stairs he needed to desperately navigate. Nobby took a final look at the stairs, noting a narrow but relatively unobstructed path between the people, taking a deep breath he set off towards the stairs. At the very bottom of the stairs Nobby made his way past a man of about forty, but judging by his toupee, gold medallion and obviously painfully tight trousers, he was trying to look twenty. He gave Nobby a passing glance as he lurched by but quickly returned his attention back to the blind drunk and highly impressionable teenage girl wearing little more than a few square inches of dress. Slightly further up Nobby passed a young man staring dejectedly at nothing in particular whilst clinging to a half full bottle of Newcastle brown ale. He was mumbling to any one in earshot that he would never go to a party again, although apparently he always does because the sad case is at every single party going, clogging up the stairs and whining to himself. A few more steps further up and Nobby struggled passed two young women, one of which was sobbing her heart out and the other was trying to console her, while scowling at any man came near enough, occasionally saying comforting words to her companion such as "don't trust 'em" and "they're all bastards" to which the sobbing girl would predictably

bawl "but I love him" and carry on crying with even more gusto than before.
Nobby winked at them as he passed and for a few moments their troubles were forgotten as they both eyed this strange looking man with a twitching eyelid as he stumbled past.

A few steps more and Nobby had to stride over a young man who appeared to be unconscious and covered in vomit, not necessarily his own. At the top of the stairs was a young couple, who seemed to have had their mouths glued together,

Nobby had to grip the bannister to pull himself around them, but they didn't seem to notice, but there again as they were, they could have missed Nagasaki if they were in the epicentre.

Finally, after his treacherous ascent, Nobby reached the top landing and was glad to find that this was the first piece of floor that wasn't covered in people. He quickly scanned the landing, and found himself confronted by four unmarked doors; he decided to try pot luck and hope to find the pot he was looking for. As chance would have it the first door he tried was the right one, unfortunately it was locked, a man's voice from inside informed Nobby to "piss off I'm having a crap" followed by a females giggle. Nobby's bladders threaten to give way there and then. He quickly tried the next door, it was unlocked, and he stepped inside and switched on the light. It was a bedroom and thankfully unoccupied. He looked around in desperation for some kind of receptacle, anything, a vase, a bottle, even a waste basket. Nothing usable or slightly waterproof presented itself. Nobby's bladder quivered violently and painfully, things were not looking rosy. He opened the wardrobe but it was chock full of kids clothes and stuffed toys. Nobby, being a decent bloke and caring person, did not want to be responsible for the tears of a young child as it discovers someone has pissed on "Mr Snuggly" the teddy bear. He closed the wardrobe doors and turned away and found himself staring at the window. He looked at the window for a few moments before a spark of inspiration hit him, "the window" he thought "I'll pee out of the window". He opened the window and was glad to see that it over looked the rear garden and not the street, he was half way undoing his zipper when he realised that with the light on he could quite clearly be seen by anybody from outside. So still clutching his zipper and tensing the muscles around his bladder exit he recrossed the room and turned out the light. In the resulting darkness, Nobby edged towards the window, all the time keeping close to the bed, using it as a guide. Approximately three-quarters of the way around the bed Nobby trod on something soft, normally under the circumstances he would have paid little, if no notice of it, but a moment later that soft something bit him.

It had been a uniquely bad day for Tiddles the cat, if it had not been for his quick thinking and lightning reflexes many of his nine lives would have no doubt been chalked up on some celestial black board. Earlier in the day Tiddles had a narrow escape whilst scrounging in the dustbins at the rear of the local Chinese take away, he had been drawn there by the smell of chicken emanating from within the buildings enclosed yard, the smell had interrupted his daily grooming session normally carried out in the relative safety of behind the bus shelter. The aroma had wafted in-between the bus shelter and the building behind it, down through the narrow passage it created and directly into Tiddles nostrils, and from that point his belly practically dragged him in the direction of the smell. From the top of the wall which bordered the rear yard Tiddles was disappointed to find that the chicken that had guided him there was inside the building, well out of his reach. He wasn't disappointed for long though as his nose detected something just as pleasant wafting over from the large metal bins. Tiddles walked carefully along the wall until he was overlooking one of the large bins, he peered downwards into it and there just below him lay a mountainous heap of chicken frames, many of them still had their wings on. Tiddles thought he had died and gone to heaven, the aroma of the still warm frames drifted up his nostrils and he drew the odour deep into his lungs, his mouth began to salivate, and his stomach put in its penny's worth as well with a low but audible rumble. Without much further ado he hopped down from the wall and into the bin. As far as Tiddles was concerned this was what made life worthwhile, there was nothing he enjoyed more than eating chicken, or any type of bird really because birds were stupid and deserved to be eaten. He held his nose above the pile of frames letting the full tantalising aroma play around his olfactory senses, his mouth was drooling persistently, his belly growling expectantly. He selected a tasty looking piece of wing and opened his mouth wide to accept it. He could almost taste it and he would have done if he

hadn't been yanked upwards tail first by a bulky Chinese bloke with a great big whopping knife.
It cost Tiddles a handful of hair off his tail but he managed to scratch his way free from the man's grasp and narrowly avoided being impaled on the knife as he was dropped to the floor. Tiddles was up the wall in a flash, all thoughts of chicken gone from his mind, survival was the "in" word for the foreseeable future. Tiddles quickly put as much distance as possible between himself and that take-away.

Disappointed, hungry and totally hacked off, but fortunately not hacked up, Tiddles found solace beneath an old gardeners shed in nearby allotments and hid there sulking for a couple of hours.

Eventually, his hunger forced him out of his retreat and dejectedly Tiddles headed home. Only he didn't get that far, because on his way from the allotments Tiddles had to cross the public park and feeling sorry for himself as he was, failed to notice until the last moment the stupid mongrel dog that almost bit off a chunk of his arse. Tiddles spent the next two and a half hours stuck up a tree whilst being barked at by a mange ridden sack of flea's that has the cheek to call itself a dog and then just to add insult to injury it began to rain. Tiddles absolutely abhorred rain; he hated rain even more than being outwitted by mice. There is nothing more miserable looking than a wet moggy, and Tiddles felt like he looked, in fact, he cursed the day his father jumped on his unsuspecting mother, had his wicked way before disappearing into the night without so much as an introduction. It had been raining for about half an hour before the dog finally buggered off and it was about another fifteen minutes after that before Tiddles decided the coast was clear enough to venture down again. Finally after a quick and undisturbed dash he arrived back in his own territory to find his favourite bit of kitty totty being rogered stupid by a rival Tom , Tiddles was having none of it and launched into attack mode, swiping out with a well-aimed claw into his love rivals, or rather lust rivals, furry plums. All hell broke loose, both Tiddles and the stray tom fighting tooth and claw, scratching and biting each other where ever possible. Tiddles' pent up anger from the day's events had found a release, and he used it to his advantage. He was winning, his body was racing with adrenaline, and he felt unstoppable. So it came as a nasty surprise to find himself being beaten over the head with a broom, wielded by the old lady whose garden they happened to be in. It was times like this that he wished he was a tiger and just eat the fucking lot of them, but seeing as he wasn't, instead, beat yet another hasty retreat and hid behind the next door neighbours green house. Tired, beaten, bruised, humiliated and angry Tiddles snuggled down in some fallen leaves that had blown around the green house and in a short while was fast asleep, dreaming of ripping to pieces Chinese men, tatty mongrels, scabby toms and cute grey haired old ladies.

Later when Tiddles awoke the sky had turned dark and a bracing wind was blowing around the greenhouse, he shivered and gingerly stretched his tired and aching body. His stomach rumbled menacingly as a reminder that it still needed filling, so after a quick perfunctory lick all over, he headed off towards the house he shared with a couple of Humans whose company he tolerated mainly because they fed him. After a short walk home, stopping on occasion to mark his territory, he arrived not at the quiet sanctuary he had expected to find, but a house full of people, noise, flashing lights and empty beer cans. Normally it such situations Tiddles would have turned tail and returned later when the commotion had abated, but after the day he had endured nothing was going to prevent him from finding somewhere warm to curl up in his own home. With this resolve in mind Tiddles prepared himself for the obstacle course to come, he darted swiftly up the garden towards the back door, his eyes constantly scanning the surrounding area, it appeared all clear. He reached the back door and stopped to listen, a myriad of sounds reached his ears but too many at once to make sense of, there was no way of telling just what the situation was beyond the door. Tiddles sat for a few moments still listening and thinking, his only option was to take a look through the catflap. He nudged the flap open with his head and sneaked a quick look around the kitchen, the room was full of people milling about some singing and dancing, others talking and laughing. Everybody was preoccupied and so far Tiddles had been unseen, this was good but the tricky bit was still to come, how to get from here to where he wanted to be, which was upstairs safely ensconced under a bed, without attracting any one's attention. It wasn't that Tiddles didn't like people; it's just that they always want to stroke him with their greasy finger, and as Tiddles would tell you it's not easy trying to lick your own back clean. His best plan of action he thought was to dash as quickly as possible from where he was, to the side of the fridge, along the wall, into the living room, behind the sofa, into the hall and then one final mad dash upstairs and hey presto, sweet dreams of three legged mice with no sense of direction. The coast was clear and he made his first move as fast as lightning over to the fridge, keeping low as he went. Once there he pressed himself up against the wall keeping his eyes on the entrance to the living room, waiting for the right moment to resume his progress. He waited silently, evaluating the situation, biding his time for the right moment when as few as possible obstacles stood in his path. Shortly the right instant came, Tiddles muscles tensed, his legs twitched in anticipation, his heart beat increased, he inhaled a lung full of air, he rose from his crouched position, his eyes fixed rigidly on his goal, he could make it, he sprang forward and surprisingly to him, instead of landing in the living room, he was hauled upwards in to the arms of a drunken man.

Moments later he narrowly avoided being pushed into the washing machine, it was only by baring his teeth and claws, and lashing out in all directions at once (not for the first time that day) that he was ungracefully dropped on the floor. Instinct took over and caution was forgotten,
Tiddles ran like buggery, weaving between furniture and feet, straight upstairs, stopping for nobody until he was safely tucked under the largest bed he could find.
Once safe Tiddles cowered beneath the bed panting, his body shaking, adrenaline still coursing through his veins,

all his senses were on edge and his muscles were coiled ready for attack. Thankfully attack didn't follow and gradually Tiddles began to relax in the familiar surroundings, he lay down, his body exhausted from the day, slowly tension began to leave his body and he snuggled down in the darkness of the room, underneath the shelter of the bed. Presently Tiddles was once again fast asleep and knocking the shit out of a gang of dogs in his dreams.

At least he was until Nobby trod on his tail. The pain jolted Tiddles into instant overdrive, although still half asleep, the cat's instincts went into action finding something on which to vent the day's anger and frustrations, big style. Tiddles spun around, his tail was still pinned down as he bared his teeth and extended his claws, in the darkness Tiddles located his "attacker" and in one swift movement sank both teeth and claws into Nobby's ankle, with a joyous exhilaration which made life seem worthwhile for Tiddles. On the other hand, Nobby felt neither joyous nor exhilarated, what he did feel was his bladder forgetting its manners and rapidly ejecting its contents down his leg instead. Nobby tried to scream but failed; the normally ever present moisture in his mouth had suddenly turned to Velcro and had currently adhered his tongue firmly to the roof of his mouth. He stood rigid with panic, fear preventing him from moving, the room's darkness adding to the terror. The pain only registered slightly a numbing paralysis had overcome his nervous system dulling the sensations of feeling, although he was highly aware that something hideous was still attached to his ankle and even now mauling it vigorously. Nobby's mind was in confusion, as a small boy he had nightmares about monsters that lived under the bed but as he grew older such things became nonsense. Yet here he was being attacked by something ghastly from under a bed, he suddenly felt very dizzy and sick, and to make matters worse the thing on his ankle felt as though it was trying to drag him under the bed. He could feel his leg being physically yanked closer and closer to the edge of the bed. Nobby sensed something warm trickling down his leg and a renegade thought ran through his mind "Oh my god, I'm bleeding to death". It was this thought and the basic instinct of survival that spurred Nobby's body into action. He swung his unmolested leg as far backwards as he could before thrusting it forwards again with all the strength he could muster at his unseen assailant.

Tiddles was starting to panic himself, he had done such a fine job of sinking his fangs into Nobby's ankle, he now found that he was unable to remove himself from it, and was frenziedly trying his damnedest to wrench himself free. Just to make things worse Tiddles could smell Nobby's urine getting rapidly closer. Tiddles tugged and yanked desperately against Nobby's ankle but his teeth were too firmly embedded. His earlier joy had quickly dissolved into despair, causing him once more to wish he was a tiger so he could just eat the damn thing and have done with. Just as things seemed unable to get any worse, it did, Nobby's premature bladder ejection reached Tiddles mouth. Tiddles went ballistic and with a final last ditch attempt to dislodge himself, semi dislocating his jaw in a never before experienced dimension, releasing its hold on Nobby's ankle. Tiddles sprang backwards in disgust, just in time to see Nobby's now unstopped leg go hurtling past, and it carried on hurtling upwards in an arc that would have made the most experienced can-can dancer wince. Tiddles slunk back under the bed out of harm's way, he tried to close his mouth but found he couldn't, at least not fully. From that day on everyone who encountered Tiddles always remarked about how he appeared to be smiling all the time and how cute he looked with his tongue permanently hanging from the side of his mouth. Tiddles was going to regret the day he ever met Nobby, but for the moment took perverse pleasure in the unravelling events.

Nobby's only concern at present was the momentum of his unstopped leg, which right now was about head level and showing little sign of slowing. This action, in turn, was causing the rest of his body to over balance, all to his dismay. Without telling him, his body decided not to put up a struggle against his airborne leg and befittingly collapsed backwards into what would have been a perfect back flip, that is, if the door which joined this room to the next hadn't intervened. Some two-thirds through his impromptu display of gymnastics Nobby's shoulder struck the door and even though he didn't weigh nine stones fully dressed and dripping wet through, the door swung open, allowing Nobby and his now dramatically altered somersault to complete their journey otherwise unhindered. His legs carried on over his head and his body followed with little argument, causing him to land in the adjoining room with a resounding thud on his arse. Stunned and winded he sat there in the dark facing the way he had just come. His heart was beating faster than a woodpecker on amphetamines, his chest heaved, panting for breath, his body was covered in a cold sweat, his trousers were covered in warm piss. The glint of Tiddles eyes, watching from under the bed in the other room, renewed his sense of urgency. Nobby rose quickly to his feet and instantly remembered his chewed ankle and a wave of nausea made its presence felt. With most of his senses still scrambled Nobby tried to turn and run but sadly only succeeded in treading on his own foot and once more Nobby found himself falling, this time forwards for a change. Unfortunately for Nobby, there was no door to break his fall this time, so he landed fair and square onto the room's bed. He lay there for a moment panting heavily, thanking God for a soft, if somewhat lumpy landing. Slowly he began to gather his thoughts and not forgetting the eerie and sinister glowing eyes in the next room. Nobby realised that hanging, or rather lying around, waiting to be eaten was not an option he wished to experience. He pushed himself upwards from the bed and was just about to regain his feet when he was grabbed by the neck and forcefully pulled him back towards the bed. Once again Nobby found his body unwilling to cooperate as he collapsed feebly on to the bed.

Something under him moved on the bed and the grip on his neck loosened slightly,

Nobby was about to use his remaining strength in an attempt to jerk free of his captor when a low husky voice pierced the darkness "And where do you think you are going" it said. At this Nobby's nerves went twang in a most unpleasant manner, and in one last attempt to try and avoid any unsavoury repercussions of his predicament, Nobby fainted.

It was extremely unfortunate that Nobby chose this of all times to pass out, as it would have been the greatest high points of his otherwise sad and lonely life, because it just happens that the husky voice belonged to quite a fit bit of prime rumping totty, who had been dumped on the bed unconscious several hours earlier. Until Nobby's fortuitous arrival she had been sleeping off the accumulative effects of eleven Gin & oranges, three rum & blackcurrants, several cans of warm lager, two headache tablets and a suspiciously ropy kebab that didn't quite appear as dead as it should be. This incomparable cocktail of ingredients was, in turn, having some rather strange effects on the girl, for at present, as far as she was concerned, she was soaping down the entire English rugby team, and to top it all she had just bagged the hunkiest of the lot (enter Nobby). Now nobody really knows what exactly did happen in the next couple of hours, although Nobby did briefly regain consciousness during this time but promptly re-fainted in horror as he realised something was having a damn good chew on his manhood.

CHAPTER TWO

"Sod this for a lark, I am off to stay with my sister in Nagasaki"
Hayato Miyamoto, 6th August 1945

As the light of a new day filtered softly through the thin summer curtains, catching flitting particles of dust in its brilliance and sending shadows back into hiding amid the deepest nooks and crannies of the room. The warmth and sense of living that radiated from the light spread slowly but with unstoppable purpose, throughout the room and over its occupants. The suns radiance crept steadily over the bed, seemingly winding a lazy path through the ruffles and folds of the duvet, carrying with it the warmth of the morning. The light fell across the face of one of the beds occupants, a young woman. She stirred slightly as the sunlight played across her closed eyelids, her mind rising sluggishly from the realms of her dreams, sending the fluttering remains of her already forgotten night time fantasies back into the deepest corners of her subconscious, stored away ready to be recalled when the time was right. She was beginning to wake, already aware of the light within the room, her body tensed slightly in a subdued stretch, a small yawn escaping her lips. She tentatively opened one eye and squinted unfocused about the room, at first she was a little confused as it wasn't familiar but slowly fragment by fragment memories of the party returned and with it the realisation that she didn't make it home last night. She re-closed her eye and tried to recall how she got to bed but the memory eluded her, she remembered arriving at the party already well drunk and heading straight for the kitchen, because that was where all the drinks were usually kept at parties, but little after that. She vaguely recollected dancing with some really gorgeous hunk, which was good; she also recollected throwing up all over him, which wasn't good. After that everything else was blank. She was suddenly startled when something behind her moved in the bed, and she quickly realised the fact that she had not slept alone. This realisation didn't shock her, only intrigued her, she had lost count of the times she has awoke to a similar scenario. She smiled to herself and carved another imaginary notch on the bed post, the little black dress she had been wearing was worth its weight in gold, she had yet to fail to pull when wearing it, it was a definite cock magnet. It was just a shame she couldn't remember a damn thing about last night's conquest. “Perhaps it was that barman from the pub?" she thought dreamily to herself, after all she had spent ages trying to convince him to come to the party when his shift ended and he did say he would think about it. The suspense was killing her; she was dying to know who the lucky fellow had been. She turned her head to one side and peeked out of one eye at her bed mate.

Two seconds later she was sat bolt upright in bed and wide awake, staring open mouthed in bewildered horror at Nobby. She began to tremble; a cold clammy sweat coated her skin,
"NO," she thought to herself "I didn't, I couldn't, I wouldn't, never, ever, no way, nope, no". She looked again at Nobby, "No, we probably both got totally wrecked and passed out and some body put us here to

sleep it off that's all" she reasoned to herself, "nothing happened, just got dumped on the same bed".
She sat for several moments letting her mind convince her that this was the case, they were both just dumped there and that was all. Nothing happened, just ended up here she told herself. Her cold sweat subsided and she felt as though a huge terrible weight had been lifted from her mind. She looked about the room and spotted an alarm clock on the bedside table on her side of the bed, 07:35 a.m. it informed her. "Jesus, I'd better get home before my dad gets in from work" she whispered quietly to herself, as not to wake Nobby. She yawned deeply and had a good hard stretch, she felt a little better. She grabbed her side of the duvet and pulled it back, suddenly she felt a lot worse. Her now exposed legs revealed that she was naked from the waist down, her lovely slinky cock magnet dress now no more than a stained and crumpled piece of fabric gathered about her waist. The trembles and cold sweat that had so recently left returned and they brought their friends with them; nausea & panic. With a shaking hand, she reached tentatively over and moved the duvet covering Nobby to one side, and was rewarded with the ghastly sight of his bare spotty arse. She dropped the duvet and began praying desperately to herself.
"Oh, God please no, no, please God no, don't do this to me, tell me it's a joke, it's not true, it's a mistake, a lie, a dream, a nightmare, anything just tell me it's not real, please God please" and as if expecting some miracle to occur she rubbed both her eyes vigorously, opened them again and took another look at Nobby, sadly for her he was refusing not to be there. She began to cry, her body

shaking with uncontrollable sobs, big fat tears streaked down her face smudging her mascara. She began to pray again.
"Oh good lord, please don't do this to me, tell me we didn't, not with him, anything but that, just tell me we never did, I'll promise never to do it again, ever, honest, please God, not him !" she pleaded. For over thirty minutes she sat like this praying and crying, she felt so ashamed, everyone would get to find out and because of it no other man would ever want her, and she would probably end up having to marry Nobby simply because no one else would want her.
Then out of the blue, the answer came to her, the only thing that could save what little reputation she had to begin with, it wasn't going to be easy but if she played her cards right it should work out okay. The time for brooding had stopped, now was time for stage one of her plan.
She began screaming rape.

The next three months of Nobby's life were spent in prison awaiting trial. To most people this would be a daunting prospect at best, being locked away, alone, apart from their friends and family, no one to talk to, nothing to do but while away your time miserably. So as far as Nobby was concerned life went on as comparatively normal.
Even in prison other inmates chose to ignore him and the vicious convicted twenty stone twisted and totally unfussy sodomite with whom Nobby shared a cell, kept his distance. No one wanted Nobby as their "Bitch".
Eventually, Nobby was released without charge, not that

anyone believed his story of the night's events, despite offering his ankle as exhibit A.
After seeing Nobby for himself, the judge decided that the girls story of being charmed to bed by Nobby after he got her drunk and then forcing himself upon her was a "collection of fabricated unbelievable nonsense" he also stated that he found it impossible to accept that Nobby could charm anybody no matter how drunk they were and also that it stretched the bounds of credibility to even consider Nobby capable of overpowering anybody who wasn't already in a coma. At this, the case was dismissed and Nobby found himself free to go home, the girl, on the other hand, left for another part of the country in shame, joined a nunnery and took an oath of celibacy and silence and indulging in daily baths with a wire brush and bleach.

Nobby returned home basically none the worse for his experience, although he did vow never to go to another party. The imprisonment, accusations, the trial and the local press coverage of the events didn't really worry Nobby too much, he knew his innocence and as far as he was concerned that's all that mattered. For most people life after what Nobby had recently experienced would have been intolerable, even after being found not guilty the social stigma of having been accused of rape would have no doubt lost them a few so called friends and set tongues wagging with half-truths and unashamed fantasised gossip. For Nobby, though nothing really changed, seeing as everyone went to great pains to avoid him anyhow, the fact that everyone was now going to even greater pains to avoid him for different reasons was completely lost on Nobby.

But all that was in the past and Nobby wasn't one for dwelling on the past, it offered little in the way of fond memories. Nobby positioned himself in front of his settee and flopped backwards with all the grace of a hippopotamus falling off a skateboard. The settee farted and Nobby giggled, but not for long "perhaps the novelty is wearing off a bit" he thought to himself, and then tested his theory by jumping up and down on the settee, producing a fart Symphony which disproved his hypothesis as it caused a spasm of untold merriment to him. After this latest bout of giggles stopped and Nobby had wiped the resulting tears from his eyes, he found himself staring at a familiar shape under the table across the room. A smile spread across his face, an unfamiliar sight on Nobby as life tended to give him little to smile at, but when he did smile anyone in the vicinity started to panic.

Nobby's face wasn't used to smiling, therefore the facial muscles responsible for lifting the corners of his mouth were pretty weak and the effort required to raise a smile tended to also pull his eyebrows downwards. When he did actually manage to smile the corners of his mouth twitched frenetically under the strain and if he smiled for more than ten seconds he began to drool. So if you ever found yourself in the unfortunate predicament of being smiled at by Nobby, instead of the warm and sincere expression of friendship it is meant to display, what you actually get is the feeling that you are only moments away from being hacked to death with a spoon, wielded by a rabid, psychotic chain saw lover who was having a very bad day, in short Nobby's smile made Charles Manson, Hannibal Lecter, Norman Bates and Jack the Ripper look like the Teletubbies. In fact, the only thing that was really unaffected by Nobby's smile (apart from the occasional inanimate object that didn't flinch) was his dog, Rambo. In truth Rambo didn't give a squashed moggy about Nobby's smile, Rambo didn't really give a squashed moggy about Nobby. To be honest Rambo wished that Nobby would just fuck off and die in some freak accident involving an abandoned fridge, some high voltage electrical cable and a swimming pool. Suffice to say, as yet his wishes had not come true, but he was working on it.

Nobby had had several pets over the past few years, in an attempt to have a companion with which to share his life, only none of them (except Rambo) lived that long. Nobby's first choice of a pet was a goldfish, not the most stimulating of pets but there again Nobby wasn't the most stimulating of people either. Nobby had won the fish at a fun fair although he didn't realise it was a pet at first, he assumed it was some sort of boil in the bag prize he had won on the hook a duck. He named the fish Moby in an attempt to be amusing. Moby, being a goldfish had no complaints about living with Nobby, as every ten seconds or so its tiny mind forgot everything and therefore it never became bored. Although it wasn't exactly ecstatic when Nobby knocked his bowl over and he was suddenly introduced to the floor. Nobby panicked as Moby flapped around feebly on the damp patch of carpet, dangerously close to several sharp shards of glass. He scooped Moby up into his hand and rushed into the kitchen in search of a temporary home for him. As per usual Nobby's kitchen sink was chock full of washing up which had been waiting since a week last Thursday to be attended to. Nobby searched frantically for anything that was clean enough into which Moby could be placed. Moby's flapping about had become more feeble, his gills dilating spasmodically attempting to inhale oxygen, Nobby had become increasingly aware of his fish's decreasing activity and a new urgency spurred on his search. His eyes found the kettle and without even thinking about it filled it with cold water and plopped Moby inside. Nobby then went out to purchase a replacement bowl.

It was several hours later when Nobby returned home from his shopping expedition, as it had not been as easy as he'd expected. He had been forcefully ejected from two separate pet shops due to a misunderstanding caused by his over bite and virtually none existent chin which meant that his pronunciation of some words when a bit of centre. This is what occurred when he had asked the shop assistants if it was possible to have a look at their bowls. Eventually, he was able to procure the item he required by drawing the article in question and playing dumb. He was exhausted when he finally made it back home, so he decided to have a nice cup of tea before doing anything else.

Exit Moby, enter fish flavoured tea.

Nobby then bought himself a budgie, which he named Albert Ross, to the amusement of no one at all. Nobby attempted to teach Albert to speak, but each time Nobby went near the cage Albert fell off his perch and hid his head under his wing. Sadly Albert mysteriously vanished without a trace one day while Nobby was hoovering out the bottom of his cage. Undaunted by his lack of success as animal custodian, Nobby decided that perhaps something a little bigger, such as a cat, would be easier to look after and with this thought in mind he duly purchased himself a kitten. And like the twat he is, he called it Rover.

Nobby followed the advice given to him by the pet shop owner who said that the new cat should not be allowed to leave the house for several weeks until it had settled down and accepted its new home. So in accordance with this advice, Nobby accordingly kept Rover imprisoned in the spare bedroom for ten weeks. At first, Rover would try and escape the bedroom whenever possible but never succeeded and after ten weeks stopped trying. Nobby noticed the cat no longer attempted to escape and took this as a sign of settling in, so began to leave the bedroom door open so that Rover could begin to explore the rest of the house. To begin with, Rover would only venture beyond the doorway for short periods of time staying upstairs and hiding behind the bed if Nobby came up. Rover finally decided to explore downstairs, he had seen everything there was to see upstairs and curiosity got the better of him. He padded down the stairs silently, stopping when he reached the door to the living room and a couple of quick furtive glances around the door jamb showed him that the coast was clear. He entered the room vigilantly, constantly looking and listening for anything that posed a threat, circling the room, keeping the right side of his body next to the wall. Rover eventually found himself at another door way, this one leading to the kitchen. Again he took a couple of quick glances into the adjoining room, Rover spotted Nobby sat at a table with his back to the door. Under normal circumstances, Rover would probably have turned tail and shot off back upstairs, but these were not normal circumstances, for he had spotted a chance of freedom. He peeked into the kitchen again, Nobby still had his back to Rover so he was unaware of the cat's presence, which was just the way Rover wanted it. Just beyond Nobby was another door, which had been left slightly ajar and through the three to four inch gap Rover could see the outside world which he had only previously seen through the bedroom window. He estimated that he could easily fit through the gap in the door and without any further ado Rover sped past Nobby's legs and out of the door. Once beyond the door way Rover felt liberated and a new sense of euphoria filled his body and soul, he ran across the garden with joyous bounds, scaled the garden fence with a rapturous leap and ended up, with a sickening crunch, in a Doberman's mouth.

Nobby was still smiling at Rambo under the table; he wiped the drool from his chin and leaned forward
"At least I've still got you, Rambo old friend." he said softly.

Nobby's dog shuddered awake at the mention of that infernal named that he had had thrust upon him, not that he had anything against a good thrust every now and then, but being called Rambo was intolerable. Ok, so it may be a bit of a compliment in human terms, but it amounted to the equivalent of being called a small and dripping testicle wart in dog terms. He looked up at the sound of his name and after realising that it was only Nobby speaking, he closed his eyes again and farted in response.
Nobby's smile faded and his eyes stared at nothing in particular, his mind wandering backwards retracing the events of the past few weeks. In fact, his mind tried to keep on wandering hoping to leave Nobby behind, but the physical link kept pulling it back with the gentleness of an over enthusiastic bungee rope.

Just less than a month earlier on a typical wet Saturday summer evening, where the clouds hung limply in the skies with all the allure of a dirty dishcloth, emitting a continual and persistent soggy dampness ordinarily only witnessed by early morning joggers and postmen. The sun itself had given up its struggle to spread a little warmth and happiness many hours earlier, and at present was just biding its time until it could shine elsewhere with perhaps a little more success. Light rarely shone in Nobby's life and tonight was no exception; with the curtains drawn the only light in his living room came from the television which filled the room with an eerie bluish tinge, casting sporadic shadows around the room. Nobby himself was, as usual for a Saturday evening, sat in his favourite armchair that matched the farting settee, staring blank eyed and open-mouthed, in a semi aware state at the t.v. The reason for his present state of being was due to the fact that he had had his usual masturbation session over an episode from his DVD box set of Baywatch and now existed on a spiritual plane which is beyond most men, a place known as the five fingered post ejaculative temporal coma. Nobby had never actually seen a full episode of Baywatch; he seldom lasted past the opening credits and then usually spent the next two hours dancing with angels (with silicone implants) in swimsuits. At this particular moment, Nobby was about half way through his post elbow jerking trance when a crashing noise from the kitchen dragged him by the throat back to reality, Nobby and reality didn't always see eye to eye so they tended to avoid each other whenever possible. Today they were thrust upon each other with an abrupt jolt. Nobby was somewhat confused and disorientated, he glanced downwards at his lap and found himself holding his penis tightly. Nobby panicked and fell to the floor, wrestling his own cock in the mistaken belief that it was a snake(although a rather small one) having a crafty munch on his prized plums, he was even more shocked to find that he was actually trying to strangulate his own tallywhacker.

"What the hell's going on ?" he thought, trying to make some sense of the situation, normally he drifted back to consciousness gently, but for some reason today something had disturbed his visions of plastic surgery perfected Amazon women in bikini's just begging for him to rub in their sun tan lotion. He lay motionless on the floor in front of the TV., sweating and panting with his trousers around his ankles, unsure as to why he had been disturbed. Just then as if to remind him another crash emitted from the kitchen.

"Oh great!" thought Nobby "I'm being burgled and all I can do is roll around the floor with my trolleys down whilst fighting a losing battle with my own pork sword". Nobby wasn't a brave man by any description, he always hid behind the sofa during the nasty bits in horror films and now his first instinct was to hide somewhere until the burglars had gone, but he felt that under the circumstances the prospect of being discovered by an intruder whilst grappling his pecker into three falls and a submission was not the type of thing he cared to share with the world. He stood up slowly and pulled up his trousers, it was at this point that he realised that he hadn't mopped up, so to speak, after his bishop bashing session and now it was all over his hands and trousers.

"Brilliant," he thought "when the police come and ask me if I can describe the person who attacked me, I can say yes officer, he was about six foot tall and covered in spunk". He regarded the sticky knob juice on his hands; "shit" he said quietly to himself and wiped his hands on his jumper. Another crash sounded from the kitchen and Nobby's ring piece threatened to give way, his whole body was visibly shaking and his heartbeat was pounding in his ears. "I need a weapon" he suddenly thought, although in truth at the first sign of trouble he would most probably drop it and run.

He scanned his living room for anything with which he could defend himself, but sadly Nobby's living room was no well-stocked arsenal, it contained little more than an armchair, an old battered sofa, a television set, a radio/cassette player and a few odds and ends. The most fearsome weapon he could lay his hands on was a broken shoe horn, so armed as he was, he moved silently towards the kitchen which had been very quiet for the past minute or so, as he reached the door he looked at his shoe horn and hoped to God that the intruder had already gone. He stood before the door, straining to hear any sounds from within. He couldn't hear anything, all seemed quiet, and he steeled himself and placed a hand on the door knob. At that moment something inside the kitchen thudded noisily against the door sending a vibration up Nobby's arm. This time his anal sphincter gave way.

In the kitchen Rambo had been sat looking at the door which led into the living room, he was getting a bit desperate now, he really should have gone earlier but with it raining he didn't want to get wet, so refused to go for a walk when Nobby tried to take him. Now though, he really needed to go. He continued staring at the door, "where is he?" Rambo thought to himself, surely Nobby had heard him especially considering a number of pots and pans he had knocked off the draining board to attract his attention. Rambo usually slept in the living room, but on certain days he was locked in the kitchen for several hours before being let out again by an unusually cheerful Nobby. Not that Rambo really cared what mood Nobby was in or for that admit he didn't have a bad life, he was fed regularly, had a warm place to sleep and Nobby never really mistreated him. It was just that Nobby had an unnatural knack of causing accidents whenever he was around. Rambo had barely survived quite a few. For example, last summer, Nobby decided to have a barbecue in the back garden, which was fine and dandy until he attempted to erect a deckchair next to the barbecue, just so he could keep an eye on it. Nobby spent the next five minutes on the floor wrestling with the damn thing after it had collapsed when he sat on it, trapping himself in the mechanism. During his struggles with the deck chair Nobby failed to get free, but he did manage to knock the barbecue over, which would have landed on top of Rambo if he hadn't, seconds earlier, got up to have a better look at Nobby. Instead, the contents of the barbecue, a few burnt sausages and a large amount of glowing red charcoal, spilt out onto the path and under the freshly creosoted shed, which burst into flames almost instantly.

Rambo shuddered at the memory, but the shudder made his plight a little more desperate, where was Nobby when you actually needed him. Rambo stood before the door, "perhaps", he thought, "if I jump up at the door, I could open it and find Nobby". He took several steps back, eyed up the door and ran as hard as he dared into it, the door refused to budge, although the jolt had loosened his bladder somewhat. He looked balefully at the door again, no sign of Nobby. Rambo couldn't wait any longer, he had no other choice, he'd probably get a bollocking later but he couldn't help himself. Rambo let out a sigh of relief as he, indeed, relieved himself on the lino.

Nobby couldn't help himself either as he stood on the other side of the door. The front of his trousers were

covered in man wax, the back were covered in more skid marks than the starting grid of the Grand Prix. With what little dignity he ever possessed gone, his feeble resolve reached new heights. A sudden calm overcame him, enough was enough, no one had the right to enter his home and terrorise him this way, and someone was going to pay for this. With this notion in mind, coupled with the fact that he realised how bad he must smell would most likely prevent anyone from grabbing him, Nobby turned the door knob, flung open the door, jumped into the kitchen, slid on Rambo's urine, glided across the lino and knocked himself out cold on the fridge.
Rambo regarded Nobby’s prone body,
"Oh, now you come!" he thought bitterly.

Approximately an hour and a half later Rambo found himself being dragged around the local park in the drizzle, he wasn't a happy doggy. Nobby was an even less happy human, he had awoken to find himself covered in all manner of bodily waste, not all of which was his own. He had stood up slowly, still a little dizzy, his head began to pound fiercely and on examination, he found a lump equal in size to a golf ball smack in the middle of his forehead. He looked about the kitchen, taking in the disarray which presented itself. Nobby turned and left the kitchen in silence, he walked through the living room, into the small hallway and up the stairs. He entered the bathroom and stepped into the shower still fully clothed, turned on the taps and let the water run over him. After several minutes of just standing there, he removed his glasses and began to wash himself down, taking off items of clothing as he went, washing each piece thoroughly before placing them in the linen basket. He washed twice before stepping out of the shower and wrapping a clean towel about his naked body. Nobby then moved to the bedroom and set out a fresh set of clothes on the bed before drying his body, once redressed he returned downstairs to the kitchen and set about cleaning the whole place up. After the pots and pans had been washed and put away and the floor had been scrubbed and disinfected, Nobby gave Rambo a bit of a kicking.

Now Rambo was being hauled around the soggy grass of the park, it was at times like this he wished that he hadn't been as bloody nosey as a pup. When Rambo was very small he had lived with his mother and his brothers and sisters, life was great then, eating and playing, and no one smacked your arse if you pissed on the carpet. His mother had told him and his siblings that soon they would have to leave her and go to live with some humans as pets, and if they were good little doggies they would have a happy life. Rambo had seen humans before, after all his mother lived with some and they were very nice to her and often played with him and his brothers and sisters, so being told that he would soon have to live with some humans of his own seemed a good idea. Eventually, the day came when his mother said that some humans would be arriving shortly to look at them and possibly take some of them home, Rambo was sad that he would probably be leaving his mother and family, but at the same time excited at the thought of starting a new life elsewhere. He spent the following few hours eagerly awaiting the arrival of the humans. Soon he heard voices getting closer and his mother said that somebody was coming, Rambo couldn't hold his excitement any longer, and he ran towards the door and started yapping for all he was worth. After what seemed absolute ages the door opened and in walked his mother's master, Rambo barked like mad, his tail working overtime, he was so excited he didn't see Nobby walk in.

It was pointless complaining now, like it or not he was with Nobby and that was that. The rain was getting worse now and the wind was starting to get up a bit, he looked up at Nobby with pleading eyes, he just wanted to go home, he had been punished enough surely. Unfortunately Nobby wasn't looking, he was staring ahead of himself, a grim expression on his face, his thoughts dark and brooding. Rambo sighed inwardly; he would just have to plod around in the drizzle until Nobby decided it was time to go home. Rambo felt utterly miserable and he wished desperately that he wasn't here, and surprisingly enough just like that, he wasn't.

Nobby felt the lead go slack in his hand and instantly looked down at it. The lead was just dangling there in his hand empty, Rambo had gone. Nobby quickly spun around and scanned the whole area. He was in a large open space, alone with a vacant dog lead. There was nowhere Rambo could have hidden and there was no way he could have run off without Nobby

spotting him. Once again Nobby looked at the lead and the dog that wasn't there anymore,
"I must be cracking up," he muttered to no one in particular, and then without any warning, Nobby wasn't there either.

Three teenage lads who had been hiding in the bushes nearby witnessed the whole disappearing dog and man affair. They all swore from that day forth never to sniff lighter fluid again.

CHAPTER THREE

"Come closer big boy" she purred seductively in soft velvety angelic tones that could stiffen the most flaccid of appendages at 100 yards and did nothing to disguise the wicked mischievousness of her words. She lay naked on a huge plush circular bed with barely more than a wisp of satin blanket protecting what little modesty she cared to conceal. The bed, in turn, lay in the centre of a cavernous circular room. The room was adorned with a wild lavishness that is seldom seen outside high-class French brothels in movies, but this was no brothel, this was a temple, a temple of love, her temple of love and her method of prayer was sex and she was gagging for a damn good praying.

The walls, or rather a single wall, which encompassed the whole room was unbroken by windows, a vivid pink and gold flock wallpaper covered the wall in an apparent seamless splendour which extended from ceiling to floor. The ceiling itself would have made Michael Angelo's work on the Sistine Chapel look like infantile vandalism. It depicted a multitude of chubby cheeked and bare arsed cherubs flitting playfully around a central mural showing several different scenes of the Garden of Eden. Each scene was painted into a segment of the immense circular ceiling. Altogether there were four segments and where they met in the ceilings centre was a large portrait representation of what was presumably God himself, glaring downwards with a stern expression on his face, looking strangely like Brian Blessed suffering from trapped wind. In the first segment of the mural, Adam and Eve were both sat serenely beneath the tree of knowledge, ignorant to their nakedness. Above them in the lush foliage of the tree, a serpents head could be seen poking between the branches, peering down on the unsuspecting couple. An image of God gazed upon his creation from the realm of heaven and was obviously pleased with what he saw judging by the smug look on his holy face. In the next segment of the fresco, Adam and Eve were busy doing Gods bidding to "go forth and multiply" and at present were putting great effort in to going forth and multiplying with each other for all they were worth under the tree. God appeared to be well chuffed in this picture, even the serpent had a smile on its face. The next picture showed Adam and Eve, still sweaty from doing God's work; having a crafty munch on some homemade apple pies and washing it down with home brewed cider while God wasn't looking. Only God was looking, and he didn't seem at all pleased, but on the other hand, the serpent appeared to be well and truly laughing his tiny serpentine testicles off. The final picture was of God sticking his omnipresent almighty boot right into Adams arse and ousting him straight out of the garden to be followed shortly by Eve and a suitcase full of fig leaves. The snake was absolutely pissing himself by now.

In any other location these images would have probably not been tolerated, but here in this cathedral of carnal pleasure, they were right at home. In the borders between each picture hung four elaborately ornate chandeliers cut from the finest crystal that anyone could wish for. When illuminated each individual teardrop of crystal cast a small rainbow somewhere in the room, as a whole the four chandeliers filled the room with seemingly billions of tiny images of refracted light. The whole assemblage of chandeliers and ceiling decoration was suspended by the circular wall which towered up to a mere forty feet overhead. Apart from the flock wallpaper the wall was embellished by all manner of ornamentations, including life sized portraits of well-bred and muscular horses standing majestically amid green pastures, with back ground scenes of hunters and hounds having a jolly wheeze at the expense of a miserable looking fox. Floor to ceiling mirrors surrounded by the most decadent and opulent frames imaginable, some of elaborate gilt roses entwined around climbing brambles, others of hand carved antique wood depicting fearsome native gods or serene ethnic idols. Many mirrors had engraved glass, fancy swirls or scrolls decorating the corners and edges of the reflective surfaces. All categories of aged weaponry from longbows to crossbows, machetes to muskets and spears to swords, all equally dispersed about the wall. Hunting trophies of animal heads from tigers to rhinos and anything in between jutted out haphazardly in various places around the wall, each one looking uniformly despondent at being there. A suit of highly polished armour stood at either side of the rooms' only door, like two ancient warriors guarding the entrance of a forbidden temple, ready to defend the sanctum with their lives if necessary. An immense tapestry covered a large section of one wall, depicting mysterious and mythical beasts, such as Dragons, Unicorns, Phoenix's and Griffins, all in such splendid colours and richness of detail, that they could all be real.

The room's floor was covered in a deep lush of pink carpet, as soft as the fur of a kitten, yet as smooth as the baize of a billiard table. The pile was so thick your feet vanished and household pets could easily be lost. At the centre of the room, the floor raised slightly to form a circular tier on which stood the bed. The bed was adorned with pink and white satin sheets which shone and glimmered at every movement they made, flowing around the bed like a soft and inviting mist, enveloping everything it touched in a subtle coolness. Huge over stuffed pillows of varying pinks and whites were piled against the pink voluptuous velvet covered semi circular headboard which almost encased one half of the bed. Suspended above the bed was a huge circular canopy containing untold amounts of delicate lace curtains, which could be lowered automatically around the bed to afford its occupants a bit, although not a great deal, of privacy.

The most strikingly beautiful object the room had to offer sat on the bed, the most ravishing muse of a woman you could ever dare to dream of. She was a woman who could send a man insane with just a smile or plunge you into rapturous orgasms with a just single word. She was everything which was pure, all that was beautiful, she was Venus goddess of love personified. Her skin was as smooth as the finest silk, unblemished by time or illness, milky white from top to toe. Her body was well toned, her muscles defined in a way that added to her femininity and beauty. She had long blonde hair, which moved and flowed in the same way that a field of golden corn sways and ripples in a gentle breeze, giving it the appearance of its own life. It hung to her shoulders like finely spun gold thread, framing her face in a bright halo which emphasised her already striking features.

Her eyes were the blue of only the purest and deepest lagoons, a sparkle in each one added to this perception. Her lips were full and luscious, a natural deep pinkness in them that could never be matched by any lip stick. Behind her lips lay a set of perfectly even pure white teeth. She wore only a gossamer veil of silk that was the bed sheet, which only just succeeded in not being transparent, in to which her ample bust was thrust and was appearing to try to escape. She leaned forwards on the bed, moving onto her hands and knees, her bust swaying gently below her, a playful twinkle in her eyes, eyes which could haunt your dreams and speak volumes in just one glance, and at present, they were saying "I want you, and I want you now!" She was looking at the only other living thing in the room. Strangely and unbelievably that living thing was Nobby!

She winked slowly whilst licking her lips and crooked a finger towards him; she pouted her lips in a kissing motion and then licked them again, even more erotically. She whispered his name "Nobby" she purred "my Nobby" she added, then licked her lips again as though saying his name had left a sweet taste on them. She lay back on the bed, arching her back, slightly raising her hips at the same time. "It's all yours" she moaned in a purely sexual manner "take me now"

Nobby couldn't believe his luck, here he was in a room bigger than his house, which contained a bed bigger than his front garden, and to top at all there was a blonde bird with massive love jugs that was aching for it and apparently, as far as he could tell, he was it!
He tried to speak, but he found that a lump had developed in his throat; he also had one in his trousers. His knees had turned to jelly and the only coherent thought that ran through his head was "quick, get it while you can" and without any help from Nobby himself his legs began to move towards the bed. At the foot of the bed lay a polar bear skin rug, its white fur in total contrast to the pink of the carpet; it was literally impossible to miss. Nobby was used to the impossible and tended to inevitably achieve it without any effort what so ever. So it’s no surprise that he failed to notice the monstrous thing, complete with snarling mouth and enormous fangs and subsequently placed his foot straight into its gaping cake hole. His foot became instantly lodged.

Momentarily halted in his progress, Nobby looked downwards to see why his foot had stopped. His eyes followed his leg to his ankle and then to the bears head, his gaze lingered there for a few moments while his mind reviewed the situation, and a milli second later he was reminded that he had been in this predicament before, only in the dark. Panic registered and Nobby screamed. He attempted to dislodge the bear from his

foot by shaking his leg, the action causing the body of the rug to hunch forward.
"Oh shit, it's going to pounce" thought Nobby hysterically. He began to turn to run, succeeding only in falling on his backside. As Nobby landed on his arse he rolled backwards causing his legs to rise upwards at his momentum. The polar bear rose up with Nobby's leg and came free of his foot, and fell onto his chest. Nobby, momentarily stunned from his landing, opened his eyes to come face to face with the beast.
"My throat," thought Nobby "it's going for my throat" and with a spurt of bravery not common to him, he grabbed the bears head and pushed it away with all his might. Now only being a rug it wasn't very heavy, so it travelled quite a distance in the direction which it had been thrown and landed on top of one of the suits of armour, which rocked at the impact before toppling over into its companion. All this took place behind Nobby, so he only heard all the crashing, he didn't stop to look back, and he was on his feet and dashed to the bed before the noise had stopped. He found himself in the arms of the woman, he glanced up at her
"Quick," he said breathlessly "we have to get out of here". She held him in her arms, his face pressed against her breasts; she looked down at him, a gentle kindness glowing in her eyes. She brought her lips close to his ear "It's Ok now Nobby, we're safe" she whispered, "I think you've killed it." she hugged him tighter
"You're my hero" she added. Although he didn't particularly want to, he pulled his face from her cleavage and took a quick peek towards the door. The polar bear

rug was laid across the fallen suits of armour, a foot and a half of shiny sword protruded upwards from its body. "Ha, got the bastard!" thought Nobby with a greatly increased sense of bravado; he decided to play it for all it was worth. He looked upwards at the woman who smiled adoringly back at him.
"I only did it to protect you," he said "didn't have time to say anything, that's why I screamed, as a warning to you, my S.A.S training took over, you know, lightning sharp reflexes and all that"
"Yes," she said smiling kindly at him, she pulled him even closer to her chest "you're my big strapping soldier boy, my protector, you killed the big bad wolf" she went on, all the while stroking his hair.
"Huge great bloody bear actually, but it was nothing really, did it all the time in the paras" replied Nobby, ego inflated to bursting point, he was just about to tell her about the imaginary time he wrestled two alligators and knocked out a rampaging silver back gorilla with one punch just for a laugh, when she pushed him away from her. Shocked by her sudden change in tactics he found himself on his back staring at the ceiling. After giving the events a couple of seconds to sink in he was just about to complain when in one swift movement, she straddled his waist and began unbuttoning his shirt, Nobby decided not to complain, this time at least. She lifted his string vest and leant forward, she began to kiss his chest. Once again Nobby found himself staring at the ceiling, this time with a gormless smile on his clock. Surely he had died and gone to porn heaven. After several minutes of chest kissing the woman stopped and sat up, Nobby stared at her, drool running down his

cheek from smiling like an idiot. She ran her hands up and down her body seductively,
"I've waited all my life for you" she purred softly "and now I have something for you" at this she pulled off the satin sheet she had wrapped around her and threw it to one side. Nobby's mouth dropped open, his temperature rose several degrees and he almost popped his cork in his pants. She was now completely naked, her breasts wobbling just inches from his face, he had never seen anything as beautiful in his entire life, she made the top super models look like pissed stained old bag ladies who sit outside railway stations begging for pennies and reeking of methylated spirits.
"I am all yours Nobby, I am your sex toy, use me as you feel fit" she moaned, Nobby's mouth was as dry as a nun's crotch; his hands were shaking as he reached forward towards her breasts. He hesitated centimetres away from them and looked at her face, she smiled and nodded at him, and his hand moved forward and touched her left nipple.
She began to scream rape.

Her screams rang in his ears, echoing throughout his skull, he sat bolt upright and tried to push her away, to get from under her. Only she wasn't there, the circular room wasn't there, the heroically slain rug wasn't there, nor the vanquished armour or all the pink trimmings. They had all disappeared, Nobby was alone. He was sat on a simple bed in a simple room and he simply had a little pee with relief. Seconds later he almost shit his self when he suddenly realised that he didn't have a bloody clue where he was or how he got here. He looked around himself, his head still a little fuzzy and disorientated from his dream or nightmare depending on how you look at it. The sheet of the simple bed was sticking to his body with sweat and urine; he pulled the wet sheet away and dropped it on the floor. Nobby glanced down at his body and was startled to find he was clad in something that alarmingly resembled a hospital gown, the kind that fastens at the back and never actually covers your arse. He turned this information over in his mind and came to the conclusion that he must have had an accident, heaven knows he's had plenty in the past, only this room bore no resemblance to any hospital room he had seen previously. For one thing, it didn't have any windows and more disturbingly, he realised after a second look round, no door.

He turned around on the bed to see behind him, surveying all aspects of the room as his eyes darted from corner to corner and floor to ceiling. It was roughly the same size as Nobby's own bedroom, but that's where any similarity ended. There was no wallpaper, no carpet, no curtains, no wardrobe and most importantly no stash of girlie magazines under the bed. This room resembled, for want of a better description, the inside of a gigantic Tupperware box; the smooth surfaces of the walls had no visible joints where corners occurred. The walls, the floor and ceiling all seemed to be fashioned from one single piece of metal that looked like lead, but on inspection felt almost velvety. Basically, and more to the point, Nobby quickly realised he was in what appeared to be a completely sealed box, and that wasn't a pleasing thought at all.

Even more confused than what was his normal state Nobby rose to his feet and began pacing up and down the room. After a couple of circuits he assessed that apart from the bed there was no other furniture, and more worryingly, he did indeed appear to be well and truly sealed in, not even as much as an air vent or comical mouse hole. Even with his limited intelligence, Nobby guessed that in an apparently sealed room like this one, oxygen, or rather lack of it, would soon become a major problem, so he sat back down on the bed and tried to breathe only when necessary. Another thing that was bothering him was that on his grand tour of the room he hadn't noticed any kind of lighting, all the walls and ceiling were smooth and unbroken by anything that vaguely looked like a bulb, yet the whole room was being brightly illuminated from no discernible source. "Perhaps I'm still dreaming." he thought to himself, after all, it did have several nightmarish qualities. He sighed deeply and rubbed his eyes. He stopped rubbing his eyes and stared at his hand for a moment before rubbing his eyes again. After his second rub, he opened his eyes slowly and peered around the room. What he saw made him keel over and fall off the bed in shock. Once on the floor Nobby got to his knees and scampered beneath the bed and lay there sweating and panting for a while. Shortly after he felt brave enough to he poked his head from his hidey hole and took another look. "Oh my God," thought Nobby "it can't be true.
“It's definitely a dream, this can't be happening". He pulled himself from under the bed and sat on the floor which was pleasantly warm notwithstanding its metallic look, even despite this warmth his body was shaking, but

not from any temperate issues, but in a nervous anticipation, his heart racing as he held up his hand again. He studied it closely, turning it over to examine the other side. Suddenly Nobby began to cry, he wasn't prone to out bursts of such emotions, but he found that he couldn't stop himself and considering that no one was around to see him, Nobby cried out aloud.

Despite the circumstances, Nobby had never felt as happy in his entire life, now for the first time he could ever remember, he was not wearing his glasses, yet he could see perfectly. Normally without his specially designed glasses, he couldn't see a damn thing, everything blurring into one huge spectrum of varying shapes and colours. He recollected one occasion after misplacing his glasses how he had attempted to make himself a cup of coffee. He had felt his way around the kitchen, squinting at jars and bottle trying to see what they were, he had collected all his ingredients and had put them all together in his cup. He added boiling water from the kettle and hey presto! A lovely steaming hot cup of instant gravy, complete with two spoons of salt and just a dash of salad cream.

Nobby wiped the tears from his eyes, he still found it unbelievable, maybe this was a hospital after all, although he still had no idea how he came to be here. The last thing he could remember was walking Rambo in the park, he then vaguely recalled Rambo's strange disappearance. He considered this for a while and toyed with the idea that perhaps he was going mad, but there again if going mad meant having perfect eyesight he was

quite willing to change his name to Napoleon. Nobby also remembered banging his head on the fridge, maybe that has something to do with what's happening, for all he knew he could still be sparked out on the kitchen floor and this is nothing more than a strange dream. He reached upwards to feel the bump on his head, it wasn't there, and just to perplex matters further, neither was his hair. He felt again just in case he had somehow missed it, but it was definitely bald. He stood up quickly and looked at the pillow on the bed somehow hoping he had got up so fast his hair had been left behind and would be there waiting for him to return. It wasn't.
"Brilliant now I look like a prick with ears," he said out loud to no one in particular and funnily enough, some one, in particular, answered back.
"Don't worry, it will soon grow back." a voice said. Nobby spun round to see who had spoken; the room was as empty as before. He crouched down and peered under the bed, all clear. He stood up again and viewed the room; again, it was still empty.
"Now I'm hearing things." Nobby said
"No you're not, Nobby." said the voice. Nobby gazed around the room again, he was still alone, he took a couple of steps backwards until his back reached a wall, he slid down onto his backside, pulled his knees to his chest and wrapped his arms around them. He didn't like this one bit, an empty room had spoken to him, empty rooms didn't normally speak to him, in fact, nobody normally spoke to him. He sat in silence for several minutes trying to make some sense of the situation, perhaps he really had gone mad, after all, he had been through lately it didn't seem impossible, it certainly

would explain a great deal. Also if he was insane, surely it wouldn't matter any if he did speak to none existent people, it was better than sitting in silence, sulking. He guessed that he had nothing to lose and decided to speak. "Er...Hello" he said, not sure if he really wanted a response or not

."Hello Nobby" came the reply "Is everything alright?" the voice asked

"Yep, I've definitely flipped" spoke Nobby to himself and then answered "well seeing as you've asked, no I am not alright, thank you very much"

"What appears to be the problem?" asked the voice. Nobby stood up and began pacing the room as he spoke, "Well to begin with I seemed to be trapped in a sealed box with no obvious oxygen supply or any means of escape, not that I want to escape, oh no not me, I love it here, it's just in case there's a fire or something, it would be nice to have a door or a window, anything really, just call me old fashioned but hey, I just love doors and windows. Another thing, I seemed to have lost my glasses, although I don't appear to require them anymore, it's just that I had them before I got here and I would like them back if that's ok, just as a memento, I'm sure you understand, nothing personal. Oh yeah, were the frigg I'm I? I don't remember how I got here, although I am pretty sure I had a full head of hair when I left home earlier" Nobby paused for a second and rubbed his hand over his head "All I have now is a head full of air, and to top it off nicely I seem to holding a conversation with someone who does not exist, now this may be common place to you, but I'm new here so it's a little peculiar, in

fact on a scale of one to ten, I would give it a peculiarity factor of two hundred"
"There is no need to worry Nobby, the room has its own air supply, and as for everything else, well perhaps it would be better if we were to talk face to face" replied the voice.
"Fine, in that case," said Nobby "could you please bring a first aid kit with you?"
"Yes, certainly" answered the voice "may I enquire why?"
"I have a feeling that you're going to need it!!" shouted Nobby, at this he stomped
over to the bed and flopped on to it, he was getting weary of the day's events, he had grown used to life playing little jokes on him, but today it was seriously taking the piss. He pulled the pillow over his bare bonce, he suddenly felt quite troubled.

Rambo, in contrast to Nobby, was quite enjoying himself, although at first, he had been a bit confused when he awoke in a strange environment. He too like Nobby had experienced an odd dream. To begin with, he had dreamt that he was in a gigantic fur lined kennel which had a faint odour of aniseed about it. The floor of the kennel was strewn with a multitude of squeaky toys of all descriptions, ranging from smiling postmen to stupid looking cats and various rubber bones of numerous shapes and sizes. The walls of the kennel were bedecked with pictures of lamp posts and dead moggies, all tastefully done of course. Towards the rear end of the kennel, Rambo spotted a huge padded dog basket, from which emanated the unmistakable aroma of sex. Rambo followed his nose or rather got dragged along by it, towards the basket, stopping briefly here and there to sniff at particular bits of carpet along the way, but never for long as the alluring scent from the basket seemed to overpower the smell of anything else. He arrived at the basket, the perfume of female dog now stronger than ever, cautiously he stuck his nose over the edge of the basket and filled his lungs with the heady odour of a bitch. He looked over the rim and a sudden urge of pure unadulterated lust filled his shabby, flea bitten body. Inside the cushioned basket sat the most beautiful and totally gorgeous French poodle bitch he had ever seen, and she was panting just for him. Rambo wasted no time and after the indispensable rear end sniffing, he jumped aboard the love rodeo and started banging away like a carpenter on whizz. He closed his eyes in ecstasy and began howling the howl of the blessed, "this is the life" he thought "warm kennel and a hot bitch". Rambo was in heaven or at least he was until he opened his eyes again and found to his horror that his poodle had gone. In its place was the biggest, nastiest looking battle scarred Rottweiler, which was frothing at the mouth. It was growling in obvious displeasure at Rambo’s energetic efforts at playing mister wobbly hides his helmet, especially considering that the Rottweiler was not only very large and extremely ugly; it was also very, extremely male.

Rambo shuddered at the memory, he had been trying not to think about it, but each time he thought about not thinking about it, he thought about it even more. What he

needed was something to take his mind off of the dream, some form of distraction.
"Maybe I could find something to chew," he thought, and promptly hopped off the bed to investigate. He strolled around the room, cocking his leg in each corner as he went, but nothing of any chewability presented itself, so he sat down and had a good scratch instead. His stomach rumbled noisily and Rambo realised that he hadn't seen anything to eat or drink when he had walked around the room, this wasn't good. Something had to be done about the problem, he was hungry, so he did the only thing he knew how to do under such circumstances, he began to howl, letting everybody and anybody know he needed feeding.
"And what would you like to eat?" inquired a voice from nowhere. The unexpected interruption startled Rambo slightly and he instantly stopped in mid howl. He sniffed the air and listened intently for another sound, he was a little confused. It wasn't the fact that even though his senses told him that there was no other presence in the room, yet someone had spoken to him, being a dog he didn't worry about such things, it was the fact that the voice had spoken like a human and surprisingly Rambo had understood every word. Normally he couldn't understand what humans were saying, although over the years he had grasped the meaning of a few often spoken phrases, such as "bad dog", "get down", "walkies" and "come here you little shit" he didn't exactly comprehend the meaning behind the words, he had just learnt to react in a certain way to a certain sound like Pavlov's dogs. But now each word that had been spoken had a meaning.

Rambo considered this for a moment or two before barking again.
"I don't..er .,.understand what's going on" Rambo barked
"What is it that you don't understand, Rambo?" the voice inquired in a friendly manner which set Rambo at ease, he liked friendly voices even if he couldn't see its owner.
"Well ..." began Rambo "how come you are speaking like a human, yet everything you say makes sense to me?"
"Oh that" the voice responded "well while you were asleep we fitted you with a universal matrix brain wave length decoding cyphenator, that is why you can understand me, you will from now on be able to understand anything which is said to you in any language"
"Oh, right...er..Thanks" said Rambo "I'm sure it'll be...er... useful"
"Now you said you were hungry," asked the voice.
"I did?" asked Rambo, lost for a moment "oh, yes I did, didn't I?"
"Yes you did"
"Well, in that case, any chance of some prime steak in gravy and a large bowl of milk?" barked Rambo, his tail wagging in hopeful expectation.
"No problem" came the reply, and several short seconds later a section of flooring opened up, a couple of foot in front of Rambo, and his dinner request rose silently from it.

Three bowls full later Rambo was laying on his side, unable to assume his normal laying down position which was on his stomach due to the fact that it may just explode under the pressure. It had been undoubtedly the finest meal Rambo had ever eaten in his entire life, sure beats the hell out of the reconstituted textured vegetable protein in unnaturally flavoured jellified artificial meat juice which laughingly called itself dog food that Nobby fed him on. He wondered what else he could get while he was here, after all, it may not last for ever. Rambo decided to try another request,

" Er .... hello" he barked

"Hello Rambo, can I help you in some way?" answered the cheery sounding voice

"Well, I was just wondering, if it's not too much trouble that is, just in case I was to get bored or something, would it be possible to have something to play with?"

"I don't see why not, do you have anything particular in mind?" inquired the voice

"Well if you could see your way clear to a toothless, clawless cat that can't run very fast I would be quite happy with that"

"NO" was the stern reply

"Oh, why not?" asked Rambo, it had seemed a reasonable request

"Because it would be cruel," said the voice

"Would it?"

"Yes"

"Who to?" puzzled Rambo

"The cat"

"Really?" Rambo was genuinely surprised at this

"Yes!"

"Oh well, in that case, forget I asked, it's just that I'm new here," said Rambo, he was going to leave it at that

when a sudden thought occurred to him "Er .... Where exactly am I, by the way?"
"At present" began the voice "you are orbiting the Earth at a distance of approximately six thousand miles aboard the United union's starship, The Traveller, a scientific research vessel on an information gathering expedition in and around your solar system" answered the voice with obvious pride.
"Oh, that's nice," said Rambo, and with that little matter cleared up, he decided to have a bit of a kip.

Nobby sat moodily on the bed, contemplating what seemed to be another unexplainable chain of events, to which he had become embroiled as an unwilling passenger and to which he had no control. He had been sat there for quite some time, brooding away happily to himself, when a sudden faint popping sound behind him caught his attention. He turned just in time to see a section of wall impossibly disappearing into itself to reveal a doorway. Nobby remained on the bed, staring intently at the new doorway, through which a section of the corridor could be seen. The corridor was running at a parallel to his room and appeared to be fashioned from the same material that made up the floor, ceiling and walls of this room. He continued to stare at the opening, considering the possibility of venturing out for a look, he was just about to get up when something entered the room and saved him the bother. It floated into the room gracefully and with a total disregard to the laws of gravity, it stopped several feet away from Nobby and hovered there silently. Nobby regarded it closely, weighing up the possibility of it being dangerous. It wasn't very big, only six or seven inches from top to bottom and it looked for all the world like an oversized electric razor with a small aerial sticking out of its top.

"Please follow me," it said in an electrically synthesized voice usually only found in lifts and annoying children's toys, Nobby just stared at it in disbelief as it hung there ominously. He found that despite the absurdity of the situation, he wanted to laugh; lord knows he could do with it.
"Please follow me" the razor thing repeated, this time it turned around and as gracefully as it arrived, it departed. Nobby sat still, he felt somewhat like Alice in wonderland, he'd just been spoken to by an electric razor, what next? He wouldn't be surprised to find himself arguing religion with a microwave oven at some point. He saw the floating shaver re enter the room, "Please follow me" it intoned and moved back towards the door, this time waiting for Nobby to follow, he didn't. He remained where he was, keeping his eyes on the floaty razor. The razor waited a further thirty seconds before moving to within six inches of Nobby's face.
"Please follow me" it ordered, its tone more impatient than previously
"Can't you say anything else?" enquired Nobby
"No!" was the short reply
"Oh!" exclaimed Nobby and got off the bed and did as he was told.

Nobby and the floating razor like gadget worked their way along several corridors, each one as uniformly bland as the last. There were no markings, no doors, no

windows just long expanses of grey walls and little else to break the monotony of it all. Nobby was surprised not to have seen anyone staggering around the corridors, lost and confused as it would have been easy to wander along the same corridor ten times and not realise it. His guide floated ahead of him, moving silently and steadily turning once or twice down adjacent and equally plain corridors. Nobby plodded behind like an obedient dog, willingly following its master into unknown territory, his mind was a jumble of thoughts darting in and out of his perception. Why was he here, where was here and had he turned the gas off. Nobby was so deep in thought he failed to notice his guide had stopped several feet ahead of him, so subsequently walked into it giving his forehead the second good crack of the day.
"Please wait here" intoned the guide before Nobby could say anything, so he folded his arms and leant back against the wall. The guide about turned and began to head back down the corridor, Nobby pushed himself off the wall and started to follow it, the guide stopped and turned to face Nobby.
"Please wait here" it repeated
"Not bloody likely," said Nobby adamantly
"Please wait here" replied the probe "there is no need to worry" it added
"No, of course not" said Nobby " I mean, what is there to worry about, I've only been led around a labyrinth of featureless corridors and identical passages by a floating electric razor, who then tries to dump me at a dead end and then tells me not to worry, how silly of me to even consider complaining" ranted Nobby as sarcastically as he could.

"I am not an electric razor," said the guide, sounding a little hurt.

"Well, you bloody look like one!" snapped Nobby
"I am a mark six ordinance and surveillance probe," said the probe with a touch of pride
"I don't give a monkeys cheesy bell, you still look like an electric razor"
"Look, there is no need to insult me," said the probe "I am just doing my job"
"No, you're not" replied Nobby "if you were doing your job you would be running up and down somebody's face removing stubble and buzzing a lot"
"I am warning you to desist from any further abuse, or I will not be held responsible for my actions" threatened the probe
"Oh buzz off, ha ha, get it, buzz off, it's a joke" laughed Nobby. The probe swung to within an inch of Nobby's face,
"I'm warning you, if you persist I'll ..."
"You'll what?" interrupted Nobby "shave off my eyebrows and de fluff my arse?"
"Right that's it, don't say I didn't warn you" at this the probe moved back several feet and tilted forwards so that it's top faced Nobby. A small opening appeared on the top of the probe and from it, a small metallic tube emerged. It pointed directly at Nobby, who was beginning to suspect that perhaps things had yet again taken a turn for the worse. A high pitched whine could be heard building up from within the body of the probe, the tip of the tube began to glow red, Nobby closed his eyes tightly, he had a rough idea of what was coming but

had no wish to see it. His body tensed, waiting for impact, the whining reached a crescendo, and Nobby took a final deep breath.

"PROBE 6174, what do you think you are doing?" boomed a voice, seemingly from everywhere at once. Nobby quickly opened one eye and peeked at the probe, it was back in its upright position with metallic tube retracted.

"Er … Nothing" the probe said nervously

Don't lie" boomed the voice "you were about to disintegrate our guest, wasn't you?"

"Well ... just a little bit" answered the probe "but it won't happen again, honest" it added hopefully.

"That's right it won't, "said the voice "report to technical lab four to be dismantled"

"Oh, fuck," said the probe and promptly sped off. Once it was out of sight Nobby let out the breath he had been holding.

"Sorry about that Nobby, but some of the probes are having difficulty integrating their new emotions"

"W.. w..what?" spluttered Nobby looking around himself for the source of the voice

"I know, I know, it sounds stupid," said the voice "but some boff in the technical department submitted a thesis on improving the various probes efficiency by giving them feelings. The powers that be thought it would be a good idea, so on a temporary basis all probes now have emotions"

"Oh, smashing," said Nobby for lack of anything else to say

"Not really" returned the voice, mistaking Nobby's comment as a valid contribution to the conversation "thing is, personally, I think that they were given too many feelings at one time, so far we have several probes who have fallen in love and wish to get married and raise children, several more have expressed desires to become artist or poets, some will not do anything unless you say pretty please and one committed suicide because the coffee machine never returned its calls"

Nobby had stood in silence while the voice was speaking but now took the chance to speak himself.

"Er,.Well, I am sorry to hear of your problems, but I have a few of my own which I would like putting right if that's ok with you?"

"I'm sorry Nobby," said the voice "please step into my office, and we shall endeavour to render the situation"

Nobby looked at the blank walls around him,

"Fine," he said, "where is it?"

"Just touch the wall to your right" was the reply; Nobby looked at the wall to his right, which was equally as boring as any other he had seen so far. Tentatively he reached out and touched the wall, instantly a tiny hole appeared where his finger had touched, he quickly withdrew his hand. The hole expanded rapidly and within a second it had become a doorway. Nobby wasn't the slightest bit surprised by it, in fact, if his head suddenly sprouted wing, claimed independence from his body and flew away, he wouldn't have been surprised, not today anyway.

Cautiously Nobby entered the door way, poking his head through first for a quick glance before entering fully. The room was in darkness except for a single column of light which illuminated what, to Nobby, looked ominously very much like a dentist's chair and that alone didn't inspire him to venture any further. He remained at the door way,

"I'll just stop here if that's alright with you?" said Nobby into the darkness, his voice quavering slightly

"Please don't be afraid Nobby, we mean you no harm" replied the voice out of the darkness.

"Look," said Nobby "I'm getting fed up talking to myself, you said we were going to talk face to face"

"You wish for me to show myself?" the voice asked

"Yes" answered Nobby, who wasn't really sure if he did or not. Another column of bright light appeared within the dark room and into it stepped the owner of the voice.

Nobby gave out a small strangulated laugh and collapsed to the floor in a dead faint like a whimsical Victorian lady in a bad melodrama.

CHAPTER FOUR

Fluffy green crocodiles waved goodbye and readjusted their top hats before disappearing gracefully beneath the gently bubbling banana yellow waters of the nearby river. Overly friendly blue gorillas cheered and whooped as they returned to the jungle, swinging hand over hand with practised ease, carrying their toys and comics in their feet, through the sparkling golden leaves of the wild continental quilt trees. A majestic, yet wobbly, herd of jelly textured rhinos whistled happy tunes as they too returned to the marshmallow jungle, weaving their way through the thick foliage of the angel delight bushes on their papier Mache tricycles. A spongy elephant on a translucent pogo stick trumpeted a jolly song as it returned to its burrow in the banks of the chocolate lagoon, checking to make sure the seams in their stockings were straight before they entered. A flock of migrating giraffes on roller skates shouted goodbye from above, as they navigated between pop rock studded candy floss clouds. Tartan zebras frolicked around on their large red space hoppers, gently ribbing each other over their colours depending on their clan, as they headed back towards the monster munch valleys beyond the jam topped sponge pudding mountains. Several purple polka dotted tigers sped off in a see through Ford Cortina, tooting their horn excitedly as they went, driving into the distance towards the great plains of never ending pornography.

Then all was quiet, Nobby stood alone on the open grasslands of his own personal utopia as the sun shone lazily down between the pink speckled confectionery clouds.

Nobby loved it here, he loved his animal friends, and they were always pleased to see him, even if they were only often fleeting and totally imaginary. The latter fact didn't matter to Nobby, they liked him and he thought that was wonderful, in fact, anything more than being completely ignored Nobby considered somewhat wonderful. But now his animal friends had gone, and that meant only one thing, his dreams were over and soon it would be time for reality to encroach harshly and miserably once again. Nobby semi subconsciously decided to make the most of what little time he had left and sat down on the blue feathery grass. He relaxed a little and looked around at the scenery. Everything was perfect, the sky was just the right shade of orange, the sun a particular emerald green which appealed to him, the trees had just the right mixture of silvers and gold's and the air was filled with the heady aroma of baked beans on toast, with just the right measure of kebab. As far as Nobby was concerned this was heaven.

Suddenly and without apology, heaven ceased to exist as the indefatigable nature of reality stumbled in with all the finesse of a squid operating a pneumatic drill. Everything was replaced with a void of impenetrable blackness, total and unyielding. He groaned inwardly as he remembered why he had retreated into his dreams in the first place, and tried

desperately to retreat back again, but, alas, his dreams were not coming out to play.
Nobby was faced with only one real option, and that was open his eyes and get it over and done with. He opened his left eye cautiously, he saw nothing but black. He opened his right eye, everything still black. Nobby toyed with the idea that he had gone blind but thought it unlikely. He decided to hold his hand up in front of his face, but unfortunately, his hand wouldn't move. With a start, he quickly realised that he was most probably sat in the awful looking dentist chair thing he had witnessed earlier and if that wasn't bad enough it felt as though some one had super glued him to it for good measure. He attempted to raise his hand again, but it seemed stuck fast.

He tried his other hand, no joy there either, same went for his legs. Nobby struggled for several moments against the chair, trying desperately to break free, but his efforts proved futile and he soon gave in. The total blackness didn't help, it felt as though the darkness was pressing against him, holding his body down into the chair. Nobby had never been a great fan of the dark, he normally slept with the lamp on at the best of times and this was about as far away from the best times as you could get.
Nobby didn't like this one bit, he wanted to be free, but he quickly realised struggling was pointless. That left him with little choice, and the only possible way out of this dilemma he could see was to ask for help and besides, being at present physically immobile meant that

his mouth was basically the only part of himself he could move.
He called out into the surrounding darkness, "Hello?"
"Ah, I see that you have re-joined us," said the familiar voice
"You're lucky" quipped Nobby "I can't see anything!" instantly a circle of light surrounded him, he squinted against its brightness.
"Is that better?" the voice asked, Nobby's eyes adjusted to the light and he noticed that apart from the circle around him the remainder of the room was still in darkness.
Nobby pulled against the chair, he was still stuck, and he began his struggles once more.
"Please don't be afraid, we mean you no harm, we just want to talk to you," said the voice calmly. Nobby stopped his struggling for a moment,
"If you mean me no harm, why the buggery am I tied to Victor Von Frankenstein's lobotomy chair then?" snapped Nobby
"It was for your own protection"
"Like crap it was"
"It's true, honest. We didn't want you to fall and hurt yourself" replied the voice, sounding a little hurt at the accusation
"Well if you had just left me on the floor, I wouldn't have been able to fall anywhere. I have tried it numerous times and never fallen anywhere" retorted Nobby
"We were only trying to make you comfortable" answered the voice

"Well thank you, you are a real saint," said Nobby sarcastically "but I'm awake now, so how about untying me?"
"Very well," said the voice and at that Nobby felt the bond between him and the chair disappear. He jumped out of the chair and quickly stepped away from it just in case anyone changed their minds. Stood there in the circle of light, with his backside hanging out the back of his gown Nobby suddenly felt very exposed, he hadn't realised it until now but whilst in the chair he had felt somewhat protected. Now surrounded as he was by darkness, with his bum uncovered for probing, he felt very small and vulnerable.
"Where are you?" said Nobby into the encircling shadows, his voice trembling audibly.
"You wish me to show myself?" asked the voice
"Yes ... no .. erm.. I'm not sure...I suppose so, I think!" answered Nobby, wishing he hadn't asked the damn question in the first place. The rest of the room began to illuminate, and Nobby saw that it did indeed resemble an office of some sort. It was fashioned from the same material as everything else. It was considerably larger than the room he had awoken in, but it had the same seamless walls and floor. A few feet before Nobby stood a desk which didn't actually stand on the floor but appeared to grow from it, giving the impression that the floor just channelled upwards to form what was now obviously a desk. Sat upon the desk were several large books, great ancient leather bound tomes looking completely out of character with the rest of the modern, yet, bland room. There were four books piled on top of each other, each one had a series of symbols, which

Nobby didn't recognise, printed on the covers. Next to these was a selection of writing implements of varying size and colour, all bunched together in a ceramic looking pot which seemed designed for that particular purpose. In the centre of the desk was what Nobby guessed to be a computer, but he could only see the rear of it from where he was stood, and beside that was something that resembled an ornate cigar box. On the far side of the desk was another chair similar to the one in which he had been previously sat, only sitting in this one was probably the strangest and most unnerving thing Nobby had ever seen in his life.

Sat in the opposite chair, and looking quite at home in it, was what could only be described as an ugly, off colour, long haired, googly eyed dolphin in a boiler suit.

Nobby wasn't sure whether he should laugh, cry or just wet himself. In the end, he opted for staring open mouthed in disbelief instead. The dolphin like creature regarded Nobby, in turn, giving him the chance to become accustomed to its appearance. Nobby just drooled.

It did indeed resemble a dolphin in outward appearances, especially its head, although its skin colour was a brownish pink rather than the bluey grey of your everyday Flipper. It looked as though it was suffering from severe sun burn. Towards the back of its head sprang a thick mass of black hair, noticeably flecked with a hint of grey, which had been swept back and tied into a rough ponytail. Unlike a dolphin its eyes were not flat on the sides of the head, instead, a small fleshy mound on either side of its head made the eyes face forwards. The rest of its face tapered into a rounded snout which gave it the dolphins bottle nosed appearance. From where Nobby was stood he couldn't actually see its mouth, but if he could he certainly wouldn't have been put at ease by the small but sinister looking teeth contained within, teeth that only a masochistic suicidal maniac with an aversion towards their taste buds would ever consider French kissing. The creatures head didn't as much as taper into a neck, more or less just sprouted shoulders. The upper torso of the creature looked humanoid, to the degree that it had two arms and on the end of each a hand. The hands had the same skin tones as the head and apart from having a pair of opposable thumbs on each one, they were quite, well, normal. The desk obscured anything from the waist down, so it could have had six legs with a castor on each for all Nobby knew. Not that he gave a flying toss at the moment; he was still gaping and slavering at the creatures face.

They continued to stare at each other's visage for several moments longer before the creature broke the silence,

"I suppose you would like to know who I am?" it said.

Nobby blinked for the first time in what seemed days, his mind snapped back from its semi aware dream like state that it usually adopted during times of stress.

"Huh! .. What?" came his stuttered reply, still unsure of what was happening?

"I suppose you would like to know who I am?" it repeated

"Shit to that, I would rather know WHAT the frig you are!!" answered Nobby truthfully

"Ah,... yes, I expect my appearance may seem a little unusual to you," it said "But I am not from around here"
"No shit!" replied Nobby who had worked this one out for him self
"Please be seated and I will endeavour to explain " the alien lifted its hand and gestured towards the chair behind Nobby, who regarded it dubiously before carefully seating himself on the very edge of it.
"My name is quite unpronounceable in your language, so you can call me Bill," said Bill the alien/dolphin man
"Charmed I'm sure" answered Nobby, who expected aliens to have more exotic sounding names, like Zartox or Quargon, even fucking Spock would have done anything other than Bill.
"I come from a distant galaxy many millions of light years away, from a planet identical to yours called Muck," Bill announced
"MUCK!!" snorted Nobby "you call your planet Muck?"
"Yes," said Bill coolly "what's wrong with that?"
"Well, it's a bit of a silly name don't you think?" chided Nobby, who was beginning to relax slightly
"So is Earth," said Bill "it means the same thing." Nobby thought this over for a few moments before answering, "Yeah, I suppose you're right it does doesn't it, sorry. Bit of a coincidence though?"
"Not really Nobby, in our travels over the years we have visited many other civilised planets, the majority of which have been named by their inhabitants after similar base elements such as ground, dirt or rock. In fact, there are several other planets called Earth and Muck, or at least their colloquial equivalents" explained Bill

"Oh right," said Nobby " er... you mentioned that your planet was identical to mine "
"Well it was, not anymore though," said Bill
"Sorry you lost me there," said Nobby holding his hand up like a pupil at school "is it identical or not?"
"What I mean is that your planet is exactly the same as mine was several millions of years ago" clarified Bill
"Look" said Nobby "I'm a bit stupid me, thicker than a rhino's foreskin at best, so is it or isn't it identical?"
Bill sat back in his chair and sighed, this could be a long afternoon.
"Do you know anything about Astrophysical geometric history?" the alien asked
"I did woodwork at school, grade three g.c.s.e" answered Nobby "I could make you a nice spice rack, sort of"
"Ok then," continued Bill "do you know how the universe was formed?"
"Er.. as far as I can remember it wasn't on the syllabus, but there again they could have covered it while I was off sick or something" replied Nobby. Bill sighed again; he knew this wasn't going to be easy,
"Right, in that case, I shall explain it to you," said Bill "and then hopefully you will understand"
"Fine," said Nobby looking at the watch he didn't have on "I don't think I have anything better to do !"
"Right then here goes" began Bill sitting forwards in his chair, "many millions of billions of years ago the universe was nothing more than an infinite vacuum, containing little more than hydrogen gases and varying carbon atoms. Then, for reasons which still remain a mystery, a huge explosion occurred. An explosion so immense that it still rages today, billions of years later, at

the universe's centre. Like all explosions the blast threw debris and matter in all directions, most of this matter consisted of molten gases and carbons, which clung around central sparks of super-heated hydrogen. These sparks are now what we refer to as suns, but they are just mere sparks compared with the catalytically intense fire that burned at the heart of the universe"
"The shock waves of the blast pushed these sparks out into the emptiness of the universe and the further they moved away from the centre, the cooler they became. The molten gases and carbons eventually condensing into solid masses which would eventually form the planets. Now all this didn't happen overnight, it was a slow process taking thousands of millions of years, but at the same time it also didn't happen simultaneously; stars were being thrown out from the explosion continuously over a period of time. So the stars furthest from the centre were the oldest and the older the star was, the more chance that some of them brought forth life. Even now the universe is expanding as the stars continue to move away from the centre, spreading into the empty void of space" Bill sat back in his chair, Nobby realised that the alien was watching him, so he stopped picking his nose and smiled briefly. Bill shook his head and took a deep breath before carrying on with his explanation, "Now approximately thirty million years ago my planet was where yours is at present, and your planet was thousands of billions of miles closer to the universes centre than it is now, but back then your planet was just emerging from an ice age. At the same time, my planet was identical to yours now, the same land masses, the same climate conditions and most importantly the same

life forms." Bill informed Nobby, but most of the excitement which filled Bills words was lost on him, only a few of the more interesting points sank home.
"So what does it all mean?" asked Nobby
"Don't you see..?" exasperated Bill "Don't you understand the implications of such a find?"
"Sorry,..er.. nope. Woodwork, Rhino's foreskin and all that!" said Nobby simply whilst shrugging his shoulders, Bill flopped back into his chair and let out a deep breath. He took a moment to recollect his thoughts before continuing, deciding to evade the more complex theorem regarding the disproval of the long held random universe theory and sticking to something, hopefully, simpler.
"To begin with Nobby.." said Bill slowly "for us, it is the chance to see living history, to discover what our planet was like millions of years ago"
"Oh right," said Nobby "yes there is that, I suppose it would be interesting"
"Yes it is" smiled Bill "it gives us the chance to observe creatures that no longer exist on our planet"
"Hang on a minute" interrupted Nobby "but I thought you just said that the Earth contained all the same life forms as Muck?"
"Nobby, my planet is thirty million years older than yours, a lot of the creatures that exist here now have either become extinct or evolved into different forms due to changing climates and conditions on my planet" explained Bill "for the majority of the life forms that you have here, all we have are fossil's and educated guesses." a sudden thought occurred to Nobby,
"So what you are saying is that the Earth is going to become just like your planet?"

"Yes, that is pretty much exactly it" beamed Bill whilst nodding his head "it's totally
Unbelievable really, but our planets are like twins separated by time, exact carbon copies of each other, virtually clones so to speak "
"So humans are going to evolve into what you are now?" asked Nobby. Bills smile faded too fast for Nobby's liking.
"Er.. no, I'm afraid not," said Bill balefully. Nobby sat upright and squinted at Bill, who shifted uneasily in his seat, being squinted at by Nobby wasn't a pleasant experience at best.
"What do you mean 'no'?" growled Nobby
"I'm sorry, but I mean no, just that," apologised Bill "unfortunately humans became extinct a long time ago" He spoke softly, as though he was a doctor, explaining to a relative that a loved one was now worm food.
"You mean extinct!!!" blurted Nobby incredulously "we rule the bloody world mate, supreme species and all that, how the frig could we be extinct?"
"Listen to me, Nobby," said Bill carefully "Many different life forms have existed on this planet since the beginning of time, but 90% of them no longer exist. Many have evolved into entirely new species, others couldn't keep up and simply died out. Look at the dinosaurs, they ruled the planet for hundreds of millions of years, yet suddenly they died out, sadly the same happened to the humans"
"But dinosaurs were just great big stupid fucking lizards that lumbered about all day eating each other" replied Nobby "Man is different, we have technology and science, we have learnt to make use of tools, we have

overcome illnesses and in some degree postponed death. We have intelligence, we have logical ideas, and we have risen above all other animals"
"And for all that" Bill interrupted "Mankind still managed to destroy itself faster than any other species that ever existed." he let the words find their way to Nobby, who stopped protesting long enough for them to sink in.
"We destroy ourselves, not some natural disaster?"
"Yes, I'm afraid so, and the same is happening here," said Bill.
"Was it a nuclear war?"
"No, not war, it was greed and arrogance"
"Greed and arrogance!! What the chuff that supposed to mean?" snapped Nobby
"Exactly what it says" replied Bill "Mankind was consumed by its own ignorance; they believed that they were more powerful than nature itself, that they could tame the world to obey them. Mankind's population was growing too fast, everybody knew it. People were living longer, less and less was dying from illnesses, a cure had been found for almost everything and the birth rate was soaring. More and more land was being used to cope with the populace overspill, less and less land was available for agricultural use. Scientists and intellectuals warned of the need for population control, but arrogance made mankind believe they were unstoppable, but all to soon the strain of overpopulation began to show. Coal fields were empty, oil wells ran dry, gas supplies diminished and then the unthinkable happened, the food supply began to dwindle. Fragile economic structures collapsed, financial markets crashed, governments

crumbled and law and order ceased to be. It had become everyone for themselves, total anarchy ruled. The strong hoarded food, the weak starved, chaos reigned supreme. Without a structured society sanitation problems were ignored, and with no real medical services, pestilence and famine reared their ugly heads. 90% of the population was wiped out within a decade and it took less than a century to finish off the remainder" Bill sat back and studied Nobby's expression, he could see that Nobby was disturbed by his revelation, He looked withdrawn. Nobby turned over the information in his mind, but no matter how he looked at it the result was the same, what Bill had said all made complete sense, but that didn't make it easier to accept or believe. Despite his own reservations, he recognised a truth in the words that Bill had spoken and it was quite plain to see the way mankind was heading.
"We're all going to die then?" asked Nobby with an air of finality
"Yes, I'm afraid it's inevitable"
"When?" asked Nobby
"Well it's impossible to put an exact date on it, but I would say probably in about half a millennia or so," answered Bill apologetically. Nobby mulled the news over; at least it wasn't going to happen in his life time so there was little point brooding over it. Once again his unique sense of realism sprang into action and put things into perspective for him.
"So if you're not human, what are you?" asked Nobby. The question startled Bill and the almost cheerful look on Nobby's face worried him,

"Did you understand what I just told you, Nobby?" asked Bill
"Yep!"
"Doesn't it worry or bother you to find out that mankind is doomed?"
"Nope," said Nobby "I can't say I ever really cared for the rest of humanity anyway"
"Oh!" was all Bill could say to this.
"So what are you then?" asked Nobby again,
"Sorry?" said Bill much bemused
"What are you then" repeated Nobby "If you're not human, that is?"
"Oh, er ... I suppose the nearest example you would have on your planet is a dolphin"
"Oh, that's bloody brilliant that is!" exclaimed Nobby sourly
"What is?" asked Bill
"Humans die out and the fish take over the world"
"Dolphins aren't fish, they're mammals." corrected Bill
"Are they?" mused Nobby with surprise, and after a moment said, "Well, I suppose that alright then!"
"Yes" continued Bill "it was really a reversal of what originally happened"
"What was?" questioned Nobby, feeling that he had somehow missed an important fact somewhere along the line
"Dolphins venturing back onto the land"
"Excuse me, but are we both talking about the same dolphins, because the only ones I know of live in the sea. And as far as I know, they always have..." Nobby didn't get to finish, Bill held up one of his two thumbed hands as a signal for Nobby to stop talking. Nobby shut up, Bill

closed his eyes for a second and bowed his head slightly in Nobby's direction,
"I'm sorry," he said "I forgot that you are not familiar with our history and as a scientist who mainly socialises amongst fellow scientists I often take for granted that what I know is common knowledge. Part of that knowledge being that our race were once land animals long before they were sea animals"
"Really?" said Nobby not sure how to take his alien companions new revelation, "I didn't know that"
"No, I don't suppose you would," said Bill "But you live and learn!"
"Yeah, don't I just know it" quipped Nobby with a chuckle, he was starting to relax and Bill could sense the ease of tension between them and that was good.
"So what were you before you were dolphins if you see what I mean?" enquired Nobby.
"Some kind of ungulate"
"Whoops lost me there for a minute, I can only speak English and on occasion even that baffles me," said Nobby, he was feeling a lot better now, more relaxed and it had been a long time since anyone had ever spared the time to talk to him. He was now beginning to realise just how much he actually enjoyed company, no matter how strange.
"Right, an ungulate is a kind of grazing animal, such as a cow" clarified Bill
"This just gets better and better" laughed Nobby who was having visions of cows in water wings.
"Why are you laughing?" asked a perplexed Bill, taking silent note of the human's behaviour

"I'm sorry "said Nobby between giggles "But I find it amusing, please carry on and just ignore me"
"I see, very well" began Bill "these ungulates lived at the beginning of what you call the prehistoric period, at a time when dinosaurs were abundant. They were one of the earliest mammals and they grazed peacefully among the rich and varied foliage of the time. They were small compared with the dominant reptiles of the era and many fell victim to hungry carnivores. Many of the ungulates lived by the coast lines of the continents and would flee into the water to escape attack by predators. Gradually they began to spend more and more time in the waters refuge, being just as at home in the water as they were on the land, quite similar to the hippopotamuses that you have at present only much smaller. As the population of carnivorous dinosaurs increased, the less time the ungulates spent on land. A result of this was that over a multitude of millennia their limbs began to flatten out and shorten into what were to become fins. Eventually the ungulates stayed in the water completely, and so the dolphin evolved."
"What happened next, I mean why did you return to the land?" Nobby asked, his initial mirth had given way to genuine interest.
"Well the dolphins remain in the sea virtually unchanged for approximately seventy five to eighty million years or so. Now no one knows exactly why they ventured back on to the land, but legend has it that the dolphins noticed the absence of man. Naturally being inquisitive creatures they started to gather around the coasts of the planet, looking and watching, occasionally wriggling on to the shore for a better look, before quickly returning to the

sea. Eventually a reversal of what had happened many millions of years earlier occurred. Their fins became limbs as each successive generation spent more and more time on the land and within around ten to fifteen million years they were completely land animals again. After a further fifteen million years, give or take a few million, they evolved into what you see before you now"
Nobby was awestruck to say the least, as a child and even as an adult he had often dreamt of swimming with dolphins. It was only in his wildest nightmares that he could ever have imagined being sat in a room talking to one. But somehow he felt easy about it, and listening to Bill recount a history that, as far as Nobby was concerned, hadn’t even happened yet. Even the dreadful news of the imminent demise of the human race seemed strangely distant and unrelated to him, it bothered him as much as a someone wearing a sandwich board with the words "the end is nigh" would.
"It's incredible" Nobby spoke in awe "it really is"
"No, not really" replied Bill "just over a million or so years ago, your ancestors were still swinging around in trees and munching bananas"
"Oh, I thought we had been around much longer than that," said Nobby "it's not a long time really, compared with the length of time your race has been around"
"No, you’re confusing the facts Nobby," Bill said
"Am I?"
"Yes, you see Dolphoids have..." started Bill
"Dolphoids??" questioned Nobby
"We, as a race refer to ourselves as Dolphoids, in much the same way as you call yourselves Humans."
"Oh right, now I know what you are" smiled Nobby.

"As I was saying, Dolphoids have only been around for roughly two million years, and it's only in the last hundred thousand years or so that we have become the dominant race we are now, you see, evolution gradually turns us from one species to another. We would no more consider the dolphins of this planet as close relatives, as you would a monkey."
"Oh, I don't know, I have my doubts about my uncle Norris" said Nobby with a smile
"No but seriously" continued Bill" our relationship with the Earths dolphins is only one of curiosity, we feel no kinship towards them, our evolutionary connection to them is really no greater than my evolutionary connection with you. After all we are all related at a very basic level"
"We are?" questioned Nobby
"Of course, at one time our planets contained no life at all although the seas were brimming with proteins and amino acids, which separately amount to very little but join them together with a couple of other basic elements under the right conditions and you have life. Granted it's only a single celled creature, but none the less life. From this simple unicellular life form and the effects of billions of years of evolution sprang all life that our planets contain. So looking at the situation from the broadest possible angle, like it or not, we are distant cousins"
"Fuck!!" exclaimed Nobby who was having trouble accepting that his great, great, great, great Grandad several billion times removed was nothing more than an amoeba bobbing about in the sea or that his Aunty and

Uncle could have given rise to Flipper. "I suppose when you look at it that way, we must be related"
"Well not really, time and evolution has destroyed any real common ancestor that we may have had, but logically as a scientist it is easy to say that all animal life began from that first single celled creature. I suppose what I'm really trying to say is that we are neither more important nor less important than the humble Earthworm, as far as the right to exist is concerned. We may be more advanced and intelligent, but when it comes down to who owns the planet we must not place ourselves higher than any other creature that lives and breathes upon It." preached Bill. Nobby felt like he was going to be lectured on the merits of remaining at one with nature or declaring your love for the world by hugging trees. He decided to change the subject,
"Right, so how long have you been here?"
"About a month," Bill had been a little taken back by the suddenness of Nobby's question. He had been trying to work out if he should feel guilty or not about once treading on a worm as a child. He composed himself before resuming the conversation. "Although we have had a team of probes monitoring and mapping your planet for the past seven months. Truth is we only discovered your planet by sheer accident."
"Really, how come?"
"Well, we are scientists and explorers and our task is to visit other worlds and solar systems, collecting information and data as we go and on occasion, where necessary, make contact with other races. Unfortunately, to the sheer vastness of space, we are limited to the amount of time we can spend in each system, so as a rule

what we do in an attempt to save time is send a team of probes ahead of us to next system we intend to explore. This way while we are finishing off amassing data from one system, the probes are beginning to collect data from the next. So when we get to the next system we simply download whatever information they have already gathered and send them on their way to the next solar system. Thing is, while they were passing through this system ..."
"Hang on" interrupted Nobby "are you saying that you weren't going to explore this system?"
"Exactly!" exclaimed Bill
"Why not?" retorted Nobby indignantly?
"Because, Nobby there are roughly something like twenty-two billion solar systems in this part of the universe alone, so it would be impossible to even consider visiting each one, therefore we select systems at random and hope for the best. Occasionally the probes will find something they consider significant whilst passing through systems and dutifully report it back, and if we feel it necessary we investigate further.
That is what happened here, our probes were on their way to a neighbouring system when they detected sounds that they recognised and as programmed traced the source of the sounds before reporting their finding on to us"
"Blimey!, what exactly did they hear?" asked Nobby
"Dolphin calls" replied Bill
"Dolphin calls" Nobby repeated quite unnecessarily
"Yes"

"You mean that your probes heard dolphins talking to each other, all the way from God knows where in space?"
"No, not exactly" explained Bill "As they were passing they automatically monitor for radio waves and broadcast signals. It was amongst all these transmissions that the probes singled out the dolphin calls, obviously, once we were informed of the findings we cancelled our expedition to the other system and after receiving permission to change the mission parameters we proceeded straight here. As you can imagine we were all very excited"
"No not really," said Nobby "a short while ago you said that you felt no kinship towards dolphins, now you're saying that it's exciting."
"Nobby, do you feel any bond between yourself and, let’s say, a dinosaur?"
"No, not really" answered Nobby
"So, would you or would you not feel excited if you discovered a lost island that was chock full of them?" asked Bill
"Ok, yeah you’re right, I'm sorry " apologised Nobby, " I can imagine it was very exciting"
"Ah, but that is not the best bit," said Bill, he rose from his chair and purposefully strode across to a blank wall to his left. Nobby was relieved to see that Bill had two legs that ended in a pair of boots, and not wheels. Bill touched the wall and almost instantly it magically spread open to reveal a display screen. Down the left-hand side of the screen was a series of symbols which Nobby didn't recognise, Bill studied the symbols for a moment before touching one. Again the screen changed, this time it

displayed two apparently identical rows of planets, one above the other. Bill turned back to face Nobby, he pointed at the screen,
"Do you know what these are?" He asked. Nobby regarded the images for a while before stating the obvious,
"Er. Planets!" he said. Bill rolled his eyes slightly, but his facial expression never altered,
"Yes Nobby, but which planets?" Bill folded his arms and waited for Nobby to answer. Nobby again studied the display, they did look vaguely familiar,
"They're the solar system," he said like the good little pupil he was.
"Very good," said Bill before turning back to face the display, "but only half right" he added.
"Oh!" was all Nobby could say
"Don't be disappointed Nobby, it was a bit of a trick question really," Bill said, he beckoned to Nobby.
"Come closer and then you will see what I mean."
Nobby pushed himself from his chair, which he had found quite comfortable considering how uninviting it looked, and walked over to Bill. He stood himself by the side of the alien and facing the screen. Nobby was struck by two things about Bill that he hadn't noticed before, the first being that the Dolphoid was a good foot shorter than he was although a damned sight stockier and secondly was those deadly looking razor like teeth. Nobby reasoned to himself that Bill surely wouldn't go to the trouble of educating him, if all he was to become was dinner.
"The thing is.." began Bill "these are in fact two different solar systems, the top one is mine, the bottom one is

yours" he turned to face Nobby and gave what Nobby hoped was a smile, it more resembled the poster for JAWS. Nobby smiled back, Bill winced visibly.
"Er.. right..Ok" said Bill, slightly shaken after witnessing, at close proximity, the torturous effort which was Nobby's smile. "Take notice of these two planets" he pointed at the third planet in each row, he touched a symbol by the side of the screen and all other planets disappeared. "This one is Muck," Bill said pointing to the left image" and this is Earth" he indicated the remaining planet. Each planet had increased in size and each now filled one half of the screen.
"As you can see," said Bill "the land masses of either planet differ significantly"
Nobby viewed the images and nodded in agreement
"Now watch this" Bill touched another symbol and the planets began to change.
Nobby watched the screen closely as the land masses of each planet began to move, the ones on Muck away from each other, the ones on Earth towards each other. Half way through the transition Nobby gasped as the realisation of what he was witnessing dawned on him. By the time the display had completed its programme he was confronted by the planet Muck looking exactly like the planet Earth and vice versa.
Nobby pulled his eyes away from the screen and turned to Bill. The aliens gaze was still transfixed to the display as though hypnotised by the view. Nobby returned his attention to the screen; many small blue arrows had appeared pointing at various areas on each planet. Each arrow was accompanied by a multitude of symbols that

Nobby correctly guessed as being the Dolphoids written language. Bill leaned forward to read the wording,
"This is more amazing than we first thought," he said abstractly
"What is?" put in Nobby still watching more and more arrows fill the screen
"All of it" Bill gestured towards the display "each arrow represents a feature common to both planets, mountains and rivers, volcanos, that sort of thing...Umm, now that is interesting" Bills attention was back on the screen, several flashing red arrows had appeared.
"What's interesting?"
"These red lights, each one represents where both planets have cities or major industrial centres in common. As you can see, although the land masses may have moved in relation to each other, the densest populated areas appear to be almost identical on either planet" answered Bill, " Do you know what this means?"
"Er. No" stated Nobby honestly,
"No, neither do I, but it is probably quite important. Anyhow it's a strange coincidence whatever the reasons" Bill said turning from the screen and returning to his desk.
"Spooky I'd call it" muttered Nobby as he turned to face Bill. The Dolphoid was reseated at his desk staring intently at his computer screen, occasionally punching in data via the key pad. Nobby returned to his own seat opposite Bill and sat and watched in silence. Bill continued to work at his computer, his hands moving with practised ease over the key board, his eyes never leaving the monitor. Nobby’s eyes on the other hand never left the keyboard. It certainly didn't resemble any

other keyboard he'd ever seen, for a start it wasn't so much a keyboard more a key orb. It was about the size of a melon, only grey, and totally covered in fingertip sized circles each embossed with a single symbol, Nobby surmised that they were most likely letters of the Dolphoids alphabet. Bills fingers moved frantically around the Orb, almost a constant movement broken only by the need to wait for further data to appear on the screen. His hands practically encased the sphere, and Nobby could see where having two pairs of thumbs would come in handy.

Bill's hands dropped from the globe of the key pad and in one swift movement, it descended into the desk, disappearing with a faint popping sound. Bill looked up at Nobby,
"You're not going to believe this," he said
"Twenty four hours ago I would have probably agreed with you, but at present, I'm game for anything" answered Nobby
"Well, when we first realised the similarities between our planets our computers hypothesized the theory of a string of solar systems, each one containing the exact same characteristics, stretching from the universal centre all the way to the furthest reaches of space. So using Earth as a starting point, a pair of probes were sent in a straight line towards the universal centre in the hope that yet another system would be found and if it was, would it be at an earlier developmental stage than Earth. Anyhow we have just had the first confirmation from the probes and on initial data received it would appear that the computers hypothesis was correct"

"So what are you trying to say?" queried Nobby
"Guess what the probes have found Nobby?" asked Bill
"Another identical solar system?" replied Nobby
"Oh, you guessed"
"Yeah, well I'm a regular genius sometimes"
"Anyway," continued Bill "when the computers first formulated the theory of more twin systems we informed our government, and after much serious debate, it was decided to also launch probes from Muck to explore in the opposite direction. It is hoped that yet another system, perhaps one in a later stage of development, will be found. So far there has been no information back from those probes, but results are expected within the next day or so. If they find one do you realise the implications of it?" said Bill
"No" answered Nobby simply. Bill frowned at Nobby and sighed,
"Ok, so far we have three solar systems, all at various stages of development, all seemingly identical in respect to their shape and sizes, which in itself is pretty unique. The fact that all three systems sit in a direct line to each other in relation to the universe centre, that is beyond all probability. Now, using the information we have gathered up to present and apply the same theory to a neighbouring system by tracing the line of travel to and from the universal centre and the same results are found as were found here.." Bill paused to take a breath "..well basically the whole concept of the universe being an unorderly and chaotic place will have to be seriously rethought. What we are looking at is the possibility of the existence of some sort of universal production line, churning out stars and planetary building materials at

regular intervals, each one a replica of the one before it" by this time Bill was leant forwards at his desk, palms flat down on its surface. His entire body was tingling with excitement, in his eyes the agitated look of someone who had just won the lottery but didn't know how to tell their significant other to pack their bags and piss off.
"If that is the case," asked Nobby "wouldn't every planet in the universe be the same as ours?"
"No no, you misunderstand" protested Bill waving his hands about for extra emphasis
"Really... I am surprised" said Nobby sarcastically
"What I am trying to say is that the universe's centre is not unlike a gigantic factory, which is in the sense that it may produce many millions of different star types, but like a car factory that produces different model cars, only one type of car is made on each particular production line. We believe that only one type of star, complete with planetary building materials, is produced and ejected into space from one particular area of the universal centre. Therefore giving a string of identical systems that can be followed back to their source." Bill looked at Nobby hopefully, he really didn't want to go into any greater detail at the moment, and it would only confuse Nobby even more. Nobby slowly nodded his head in understanding, Bill felt as though a large weight had been lifted from him and he felt the need to smile.
"Ok," said Nobby finally "If your theory is correct and the universe is full of mass produced planets and stars etc, and not the messy jumble previously thought, what does it all add up to and what difference does it make?" Bills smile faltered at Nobby's statement

" Er... truth is, in general, it won't make any difference at all. At least not as far as everyday life is concerned" Bill admitted
"So why all the fuss and bother then?"
"I don't really know to be frankly honest, call it scientific curiosity if you like. It's just a basic need to know kind of thing" Bill slumped back into his chair, folded his arms and let out a sigh. Nobby noticed the sunken look in Bills eyes and felt a little sorry for the alien, he was a bit surprised to find that he actually felt comfortable talking to Bill. Nobby decided to change the subject,
"Talking of need to know', I need to know why I'm here and exactly where here is." Bills body jerked at the sound of Nobby's voice, he had quickly become wrapped up in his own thoughts regarding the validity of the new discovery that he had for a moment forgot Nobby was there.
"Oh yes, right" Bill stood up "I appear to be forgetting my duties" he held out his hand to Nobby, who gawped at it for a moment before realising that he was expected to shake it. Nobby gripped Bills hand and Bill nodded, cleared his throat and spoke,
"Welcome, on behalf of myself, the crew and complement of this vessel, The Traveller. We wish your stay to be as pleasant as possible and please feel free to use any of the on board facilities at your disposal. At present we are cruising at 1.5 times the speed of light and will shortly be leaving this solar system. We also..." Nobby jerked his hand away from Bills as though struck by an electric shock, he staggered backwards until his legs hit the edge of the chair. His body flopped into it,

his jaw began flapping and several moments passed
before he found his voice,
"I'M WHERE?" was all he could say.

CHAPTER FIVE

Bill sat on his desk, an unmistakable perplexed expression on his dolphin like features; he wasn't sure what to make of the situation. One minute he was shaking Nobby's hand and going through his welcome aboard speech, the next Nobby was slumped in the chair gibbering. Bill was a little shocked at the sudden transformation, he and Nobby seemed to be getting along quite well, given the circumstances and he knew it wasn't easy to suddenly come face to face with an extra-terrestrial. But after his initial shock, Nobby appeared to accept the situation fairly quickly, with the exception of one or two minor misunderstandings. Yet now Nobby was anything but at ease, he was no longer sat down, at present, he was stomping up and down the length of the room and muttering away to himself stopping only occasionally to kick walls that dared get in his way.
Bill had tried several times to talk to Nobby, but each attempt resulted in Nobby shouting things like:
"Kidnapping, that's what it is" or "Invasion of civil fucking liberties, mate!"
Bill was becoming increasingly worried about Nobby, he really did care for the human. On the other hand, Nobby, at this point couldn't give a monkeys arse about Bill, he was too busy feeling sorry for himself and at this particular moment in time was deeply engrossed in conversation with no one in particular.
"Kidnapped! Me kidnapped, held against my will, tortured and mutilated. Kidnapped! Was it by the I.R.A?

nope! Islamic fundamentalists? Nope! Or perhaps the well-known evil militia wing of Mothercare?. Oh no, not me, no such luck! Fucking Flipper and his mates got me. Can't even get kidnapped properly. Anyway, who the frig do they think they are travelling half way across the universe just to pick on me? Well they can shite, 'cos next time I go to a zoo I'm going to piss in the dolphinarium, that's what I'll do, and I'll eat as much tuna as humanly possible. Let the Japanese net the bastards, that'll show 'em, turn the twats into sushi, fucking overgrown smart arsed smiley fish carting me off into space and then telling me that mankind's going to pop its clog's a week next Thursday, cheeky bastards! Give me a harpoon and I'll show you who's going to become friggin' extinct" Nobby paused for a moment as he came up against a wall, he gave it a sound kick before doing an about turn and resuming his stomping and ranting. "Kidnapped! Me, kidnapped, and who would believe me if I told them? I can see the headlines now" I was kidnapped by alien space fish" the Sunday rags would have a field day with that one, not that anyone would really give a toss. I'd probably end up in a padded cell somewhere, and all the while the dolphins will be swimming about in the sea, looking cute and laughing their bollocks off. Well
I hope they all get eaten by sharks, the smarmy grey bastards, that's the last time I cut up the plastic rings from my beer cans, I can tell you that for nothing pal!"
As Nobby continued his pacing and ravings, Bill called out to him a number of times, but to no avail. Bill was by no means an expert on humans, Nobby was the first live one he'd ever met, but he recognised the onset of a

possible nervous breakdown. The gentle approach wasn't working and Bill knew that more extreme measures were called for before it was too late. He knew what he needed to do, but that didn't necessarily mean that he wanted to do it, but he felt that there was no other option, the time had come for action. Reluctantly Bill stood up and watched Nobby for a while as he rambled back and forth, grumbling as he went. He really didn't want to have to do this, but if he didn't Nobby's mental health could be in for a big fall. Bill focussed his attention solely on Nobby, his body trembled nervously, and he inhaled three times deeply and after the third released with all his energy, an ear piercing high pitched shriek. Nobby's head suddenly felt as though it was about to explode, he could feel his brain vibrating within his skull and his spine threatened to shatter. Automatically his hands clamped tight over his ears, attempting in vain to shut out the horrific noise and he collapsed to the floor, drawing up his knees in a protective foetal position. Nobby was unable to distinguish the source of the noise, it sounded as though it filled the whole world, but it felt as though it came from within him, vibrating every atom in his body. He was beginning to shake violently, when as suddenly as it started, it stopped. He remained on the floor panting and sweating, his hands still clasped over his ears. His body was trembling visibly, his vision blurred from tears, his ears buzzing with a resounding echo. Nobby felt weak and physically sick, it was several minutes before he regained enough control of his body to be able to speak,

"Jesus .. What the hell was that?" he shouted over the ringing in his ears, Bill was knelt at his side his hand laid gently on Nobby's shoulder
"I'm sorry Nobby" Bill apologised" but, it was me."Christ... why?"
"You were becoming hysterical, you needed to be calmed down. I'm afraid a shock to the system was my only option"
"Fuck," said Nobby struggling to his feet "why didn't you just slap me?"
"I'm sorry, violence is not in my nature" Bill helped Nobby up and guided him to his chair. Nobby slumped into it gratefully, his limbs still shaking. He removed his hands from his ears, but the ringing seemed to increase so he put them back.
"If that wasn't violence, then I don't know what is!"
"Not physical violence," said Bill "that would be against everything I believe in, this was just a necessary shock, no actual physical harm but just as effective. The nausea will soon pass"
"How soon, I can't hear a damn ..." Nobby's words trailed off, confusion flitted across his face. He took his hands away from his ears and held them in front of him. He looked them over before clapping them together. He stared at Bill and opened his mouth to speak, then closed it again without saying anything. Nobby clicked his fingers directly in front of his ears and then clapped them together again in front of his face.
"What's going on Bill?" demanded Nobby
"I don't understand what you mean" replied Bill truthfully, he felt as confused as
Nobby looked.

"Okay, then I will make it as clear as I can" said Nobby purposefully "How come my ears are buzzing that badly that I can hardly hear myself clapping my hands in front of my face, yet moments earlier I had both ears covered by my hands but I could hear every word you said perfectly. Now, do you understand?" Nobby's voice had taken on a slightly menacing tone

"Ah!.. yes, that will be the Universal matrix wavelength decoding cyphenator" Bill answered matter of factly.

"The what?"

"The ..er.. universal matrix wavelength decoding cyphenator" this time Bills tone was less matter of fact and more whoops, what have I said'.

"And exactly what the jiggery buggery is one of them?" asked Nobby

"Well it's nothing really, just a small device which enables people or even different species to speak to each other without going to the trouble of having to learn each other's language" Bill answered carefully not wanting to commit himself to a more detailed explanation

"It's a translator then?" said Nobby looking about the room whilst rubbing his ears gently "Where is it then?"

"Ah!" said Bill

"Ah!?, what do you mean Ah!, I don't like it when people say Ah! like that. It usually means that I'm not going to enjoy the answer. Ah! is not a nice thing to say to anyone, it normally has a nasty sting in its tail, and believe me I am not in the mood for any more surprises, so think very carefully before you answer" threatened Nobby, although he was in no state to contemplate anything more physical than breathing.

Bill opened his mouth to answer but quickly closed it again when he saw the menacing look in Nobby's eyes, so he stayed quiet and stared at Nobby's bald head instead.

They had been staring at each other, in silence, for around three or four minutes before Nobby realised exactly where Bills gaze was directed.
"Oh no, no way, you've got to be joking" Nobby raised his hands protectively to his shiny head "peaceful creatures my arse, I don't call experimentation and vivisection very peaceful"
"We are peaceful, we have done nothing to harm you" pleaded Bill
"Piss off Nazi fish" shouted Nobby "opening up people's heads and poking their brains about for fun is not what normal peace loving people do!"
"Please Nobby, we haven't.."
"Listen Frankenfish, why don't you and your fishy sadistic pals find someone else to pick on and leave me alone, I'm quite capable of having a shite and miserable existence without your help thank you very much!!" at this Nobby crossed his arms and lowered his head to his chest whilst simultaneously sticking out his bottom lip. And considering the proportions of his upper teeth, it wasn't an easy task.

Bill stood before Nobby and slowly shook his head, he just couldn't fathom out this human. In his capacity as ships alien initial contact specialist and prominent, respected anthropologist he had been the first on numerous occasions to welcome aboard intelligent alien life forms. Many, after the first meeting, had been quite happy to remain aboard and help the Dolphoids with their studies, in fact, several had opted to remain aboard and now are active members of the crew. Although on occasion Bill had come across alien races who, either from religious dogmas or xenophobia, had point blank refused to co operate in any way what so ever. In these cases, the alien were promptly returned back to their home planet unharmed, albeit minus a small gap in their memory. Bill's job was normally straight forward, welcome the alien aboard, explain the situation and ask if they would be willing or not to assist them in their studies by answering questions and submitting hair and skin samples for genetic cataloguing. The answers were either yes or no, simple, no pressure, no forced cooperation, nothing is done without consent. Yet Nobby was posing a bit of a problem, one minute he was calm and apparently relaxed with the situation, the next, he was shouting and throwing accusations all over the place. Bill had to make him understand that the Dolphoids were truly a peaceful race and meant him no harm what so ever.

Nobby calling him Nazi had hurt, although he didn't have the faintest clue what Frankenfish meant, over the past month Bill had done a lot of research into human history by down loading information directly from the planets satellite network and the internet. He had been particularly appalled by the treatment of fellow humans by these Nazi's, simply because of having a different life style or set of beliefs. He was saddened that Nobby thought of him in this way, Bill was determined to make Nobby listen whether he liked it or not.

Bill returned to his desk, sat down, and began to speak to Nobby slowly and calmly.
"Okay Nobby, let's presume for a moment that we are in fact the evil and barbaric race you think we are, what would we achieve by telling you about our discovery of the twin solar systems?" Nobby didn't respond, he continued his super sulk.
"Also you keep accusing us of experimenting on you and opening you up. Well answer me this, are you in pain, do you feel any symptoms of being operated on, can you detect any sign of scar tissue or healing wounds"
"Why did you shave my head then?" spat Nobby venomously
"We didn't.." started Bill
"I suppose it fell out on its own then, did it?" interrupted Nobby, he was sat upright again and peering maliciously at Bill
"No, the transferral beam removed it by accident" stated the Dolphoid
"What..?"
"When you were beamed aboard by the transferal beam, your body was automatically scanned for disease or toxic substances. Unfortunately, the hair gel that you were wearing came into one of these categories, although I'm not sure which, either way, it was deemed dangerous and removed. Unfortunately again there was so much of it the scanner couldn't distinguish between the gel and your hair, so removed both as a precaution" enlightened Bill.
"No wonder it was only twenty pence for a litre tub," said Nobby abstractly.
"Also while you were being transported aboard" continued Bill "all dental decay in your teeth was

removed, your acne was eradicated and the warts on your penis were filtered out." Nobby was stunned by the latter part of Bills statement

"Excuse me a moment," he said as he stood up and moved behind the chair. Once out of direct view of the Dolphoid he cautiously lifted the front of the gown he was wearing. Bill watched in some amusement Nobby's actions, from where he was sat Bill could only see the Humans head and shoulders above the back of the chair, but it was plainly obvious what was happening out of sight. Nobby studied his rejuvenated genitalia for a moment or two before commenting,

"So the knobbly bits weren't supposed to be there then?" he said over the back of the chair to Bill

"No" the alien answered

"I didn't know that!" replied Nobby after a short but thoughtful pause. Bill gestured for Nobby to return to his seat and he complied with out argument, he was still marvelling over his wartless whacker. Bill waited in silence until his companion was seated.

"Where are your glasses Nobby," he said finally. Nobby automatically felt for them at the bridge of his nose, where they were normally perched.

" I.. er ...well it's ... erm..!!" stumbled Nobby, gesticulating frantically in a poor attempt at explaining.

"You don't need them anymore, do you?" asked Bill with a dangerously toothy grin.

"Er... No" said Nobby quietly like a naughty little boy who had just chastised by an adult.

"No you don't, and that also is a result of the transferal beam. It re aligned the lenses of your eyes as a matter of course. Now truthfully Nobby do you still believe that a

group of maniacal torturers would go to all this trouble if all they wanted to do was dissect you?" asked Bill.
Nobby lowered his head in shame, he could see the logic in the Dolphoids words,
"No, I suppose not," he said
"Also," said Bill " I would be grateful if you could stop saying that we kidnapped you"
"Well, you did!" said Nobby grumpily
"No we didn't" replied Bill "We only did what you wanted"
"No you bloody well didn't!!" blurted Nobby incredulously "I can't remember anyone, let alone a friggin' dolphin, asking me if I minded being whipped into space!"
"What was the last thing you remember before waking up here?" asked Bill leaning forwards on his desk, staring intently at Nobby.
"I was walking my dog," Nobby searched his memory "and then he vanished!"
"And just before that happened what were you thinking?" probed Bill. Nobby mentally retraced his steps in his mind. He could see himself in the park, dragging Rambo reluctantly around the grassed area in the rain. Both looked thoroughly despondent, Nobby's face a dark mask of utter misery; an air of foreboding surrounded him. Suddenly the memory of what he was thinking at the time came to him
"Oh!" he said in surprise
"Exactly," said Bill "you were wishing to be somewhere else, anywhere but where you were. You were hoping for that some miracle would happen and you could escape it all. Well, Nobby we are that miracle, and we

helped you escape." Nobby was amazed, to say the least, he did remember thinking those exact thoughts but never in a million years did he believe that it would happen.
" I.. I don't know what to say," stuttered Nobby " I just thought ...well, truth is I don't really know what I thought, I mean this sort of thing doesn't happen to me every day. But when I woke up bald and wearing this" Nobby tugged at his gown for added effect" Well I just jumped to conclusions, I guess!"
"Do you still think us evil or are you willing to trust me?" asked Bill, he held his arms open in a gesture of goodwill to Nobby.
"I'm sorry," said Nobby "I was getting a bit stressed out, I didn't really mean the things I said, I was just scared and confused!"
"I understand" replied Bill pleasantly "Can we be friends and put all this behind us, start again so to speak?"
"Yeah sure, okay. But there are still a couple of things that need to be cleared up first"
"Certainly, I will endeavour to put your mind at ease" answered Bill
"This translator device?" said Nobby.
"Ah!"
"Look there you go again with the Ah! business. Why do you keep doing that, what are you, Jewish?. You know I don't like it when you say Ah! like that, it worries me"
"Sorry," said Bill "I will explain. When we first brought you aboard we had a choice to make, either keep you for several months and attempt to teach you our language, although I don't think your vocal cords would have coped, or fit a decoder. We decided that the decoder option would be both quicker and less stressful"

"So you did operate on me?" said Nobby sharply
"No we didn't, look" Bill reached into the drawer of the desk and removed a small disc like object. He handed it to Nobby, "This is a universal matrix wavelength decoding cyphenator." Nobby regarded the object in his hand; it was roughly the same size as a penny although much thinner and slightly concaved. It was made of the same dull grey material as everything else, but on closer inspection, he could see a vast amount of minute circuitry incorporated into its design.
"As you can see" continued Bill "it is very small and weighs practically nothing and if you feel just behind each ear you will notice the slightest of bumps. They are the translators"
"Two?"
"Yes they work as a pair, each one is placed under the skin behind the ear and before you start shouting they were put there by a transferral beam, not by an operation. They can be removed at any time if you wish, the procedure is instant and painless"
"Are you sure it's painless?" asked Nobby sceptically.
Bill smiled at Nobby and pressed a button on his desk
"What are you doing?" said Nobby, Bill opened his mouth to speak but all that came out was a string of high pitched squeals and squeaks. After several seconds Bill stopped the noises, once again he smiled at Nobby and pressed the button on his desk
"Did you understand what I just said?" asked Bill still smiling
"Er.. when?" replied Nobby
"Just then, the high pitched sounds" clarified Bill
"No I didn't, what was it?"

"Well, that is what you would be hearing now if it wasn't for the decoders. You see, at present I am speaking in my native language, but the decoders are stopping the real sounds I make from entering your ears and at the same time translating what I said into sounds you understand. That is why earlier you could hear me clearly even though you had your hands over your ears, the words you are hearing are not actually entering your ears, but being transmitted directly into your ear drums by the decoder"
"Oh, I see" answered Nobby
"Did you feel any pain in the last couple of minutes?" asked Bill
"Er.. no, I can't say that I have"
"Well, when I pressed this button here" Bill indicated the button on his desk "both your decoders were removed, that is why you couldn't understand me!" Nobby was speechless, he hadn't felt a thing. He rubbed the area behind his ears, the small bumps were still there,
"How do I know that you really removed them and not just switched them off for a few seconds?" argued Nobby. Bill leaned forwards and pressed the button on his desk once more. Beneath his fingertips Nobby felt the bumps suddenly disappear, an unnerving sensation at the very least, Bill only smiled at Nobby's surprised expression, he depressed the button once more and watched Nobby's eyes widen in amazement as the decoders returned.
"WOW!! " managed Nobby "that was weird, with a capital W!" he pronounced the W as a wuh rather than the usual double u. He continued feeling at the lumps behind his ears.

"Are you in discomfort?" asked Bill, a hint of concern in his voice
"No, why?"
"I am concerned about the way you are massaging your ears, are they causing any distress or agitation?" Bill questioned
"No, none at all. It was just a spooky feeling that's all, no pain, not so much as an itch." smiled Nobby, Bill flinched slightly at Nobby's smile, he was having difficulty becoming accustomed to it.
"Are you sure?" said Bill still looking at the straining smile on Nobby's face.
"Positive" returned Nobby through saliva covered lips.
"Okay then, now that everything seems to be sorted out," said Bill "perhaps you would like a tour of the ship, get to know the place, so to speak"
"Yeah, sure, but how long are you planning to keep me here?" asked Nobby
"Well that is entirely up to you, of course, we would like to ask you some questions and possibly, with your permission, take some genetic samples from you. But if you wish to go home then you are free to do so, no one will try and stop you" Bill stood and moved around the table and sat on its edge facing Nobby. "Would you like to go home?"
"I thought we were leaving the solar system?"
"We are, but only to pick up some supplies, we will be back again in roughly sixteen to eighteen hours. So we can drop you off then if you wish to leave" Bill answered.
Nobby considered his options, if he went home he would just be his usual boring self, in his usual boring life with

no friends or close family that gave two slaps about him and the highlight of his week was the opening credits of Baywatch. If he chose to stay, well, who knows what, but it had to be better than masturbating over Baywatch and waiting for his giro to arrive.

"If I decide to stick around, what would I do?" asked Nobby "I mean, I couldn't just expect to live here for free"

"No, that's right," said Bill "If you opt to stay aboard you could become a member of the crew. You would be assigned quarters, given a duty to perform in the day to day running and upkeep of the ship and on top of it all, you will be paid. As we tour the ship you will notice that there are many different life forms serving as crew, all of which were, at one time, in the same position as you are now. Six years ago when this ship first left Muck, the crew consisted solely of Dolphoids, now there are forty three different species serving aboard. Each one has stayed of their own free will and are free to leave whenever they wish." Bills expression deepened, a slight frown furrowed his brow "Now I have to ask you again, do you wish to stay or do you wish to go home?" His gaze fixed firmly on Nobby.

"Well, I would really like to stay, but.." began Nobby "I have this dog who.."

"You mean Rambo?" interrupted Bill

"Er.. yeah, how did you know?"

"He also is on board," answered Bill with a smile. Nobby thought about this for a moment, leaving Rambo behind was the only thing that would have prevented him from staying with the Dolphoid,

"I that case I choose to stay if that's alright with you!" he said finally, he rose and stood before Bill and held out his hand. Bill grasped it firmly and shook it.
"Thank you, Nobby, you are welcome to stay as long as you wish"
"Smashing, now about this duty that you said I would be given!"
"All in good time Nobby," said Bill "for the time being you are officially a guest aboard this ship and as such you are not expected to work. For the next week or so all that you need do is answer some questions relating to yourself and your planet and submit some hair, nail and skin samples for our records. So, for now, relax and enjoy your stay. Are you hungry?"
"Starving!" exclaimed Nobby; his belly began to rumble in anticipation.
"Good, perhaps we should start our tour at the mess hall"
"Great, but I'm not exactly dressed for it," said Nobby turning round to show his exposed behind. Bill regarded the bare arse for the fleetest of moments before moving to a wall and touching it, as before with the other walls a large section of it disappeared revealing a long rack of silvery grey all in one boiler suits identical to the one worn by Bill
"Help yourself," he said gesturing towards the garments. Nobby moved to the rack and began looking through the suits.
"Er.. there's no sizes on them"
"It doesn't matter, they will automatically adjust to fit you"
"Oh, neat!" said Nobby, he took a suit from the rack and held it to his body. It was far too big for him, but never

the less he removed his gown, unfastened the front of the suit, stepped into it and pulled it on. It was too big, he looked like Stan Laurel in Oliver Hardy's clothes. Nobby was just about to complain to Bill when the suit began to shrink around him. It was quite an unnerving experience for Nobby and he uttered an eek of surprise. The suit only took a couple of seconds to adjust, but it seemed longer and at one point he thought it wasn't going to stop and subsequently squeeze the life out of him instead. Bill handed him a pair of boots which Nobby eyed suspiciously, they resembled size fifteen N.C.B wellies.
"I suppose these adjust as well?" asked Nobby. Bill nodded so Nobby reluctantly pulled each one on in turn. He looked down at them and to begin with they were enormous, but like the suit soon adjusted to fit. Nobby now had a smart looking pair of slim line boots, opposed to the stupendously huge pair of dock workers hobnailed clodhoppers that he began with.
"How do I look?" asked Nobby, suspecting that he resembled a left over from Gary Glitter's backing band. Bill stepped in front of Nobby and pushed the remaining suits to one side revealing a full length mirror,
"See for yourself," he said moving out of the way.
Nobby studied his reflection, his eyes scanning up and down the image, the silver suit made him feel very like an oven ready turkey at Christmas, his bald head somehow adding to the illusion. Nobby twisted his body from left to right in an attempt to see the rear of the suit. After several tries at possibly inducing a slipped disc and contorting his body into grotesque forms, he smiled
"Not bad these suits really," said Nobby still viewing his reflection out of the corner of his eye

"Standard issue I'm afraid," said Bill "not very fashionable, but functional none the less"
"Right," said Nobby rubbing his hands together "what's for dinner, I could eat a scabby monkey!"
"I'm not sure we have any" replied Bill thoughtfully "But I will certainly enquire for you."
"No, no," said Nobby hastily "It's just a figure of speech, it means that I am very hungry"
"I see, in that case, we shall go to the food hall and you can see what you would like. Have you any preferences?"
"Oh, I'm not too fussy, anything really" answered Nobby, "except scabby monkeys that is!" he added quickly.

Rambo trotted happily behind the probe, although waddled would be a more apt description considering the vast amount of steak he had consumed in the last couple of hours,
" So, where are we going?" asked Rambo, not that he was really interested, just he didn't want to walk too far as all that steak was working its way through his digestive system and right now he really needed to drop a bomb, so to speak.
"To meet someone" intoned the probe grumpily, it was in a foul mood because it wanted to go out and play with its friends, but instead it was walking a smelly flea bitten domesticated canine mammal around the ship.

"Oh," said the smelly flea bitten domesticated canine mammal "is it far then?"
"We shall arrive there presently" snapped the probe
"Oh, right." said Rambo "sorry to bother you and all that but, well thing is I had quite a lot to eat and I, er, well I need to.."
"We are here" announced the probe with a hint of relief. Rambo regarded the three blank walls that surrounded him and his stomach rumbled menacingly.
"Ok, well there's no one here, maybe we could come back later" Rambo turned and began to head back the way he had come.
"This way please" informed the probe. Rambo turned back to face the probe and sat down heavily,
"Why it's a dead end, there's nothing here only ... oh, look at that!" remarked Rambo as a section of wall before him began to disappear to form a door way.
"Ah, there you are," said a soft voice from within the newly appeared room, Instinctively Rambo cowered down.
"Look, I never touched the wall" Rambo pleaded "I was over here, never went near it and if you don't believe me ask this floaty thing up there" He indicated the probe with his nose whilst simultaneously wagging his tail hopefully.
"It's ok Rambo no one is blaming you, it's supposed to do that" reassured the voice
"Ok, right then," said Rambo getting up "it's just that normally when things like that happen, I usually end up getting kicked in the arse and locked in the shed" he explained as he ventured forwards towards the door way.

"Rest assured that no one is going to kick you in the, er, anywhere here" soothed the voice. Rambo stood just with in the doorway, he studied the darkness with in the adjoining room. His sensitive nose located the owner of the voice and even though he couldn't see it, he knew exactly where it was. He also knew that its scent reminded him of fish.
"It's a bit dark in here" stated Rambo
"Would you like the room illuminated?" asked the voice
"I don't know about that, but some lights wouldn't go amiss!" answered Rambo honestly
"Er, right, but don't be frightened by what you see, prepare yourself for a shock" warned the voice. Rambo was about to ask why when the room suddenly lit up. By reflex action he crouched low into a defensive position, poised for attack. His eyes quickly scanned the whole room, he focussed for a second on the creature sat behind the desk and then resumed his visual sweep of the room. Once he was certain that there was nothing lurking in the corners or behind any furniture he returned his attention to the creature.
"What exactly am I waiting for?" asked Rambo. The owner of the voice seemed a little taken back by his question.
"What do you mean?" it replied
"Well, you said be prepared for a shock," Rambo said, " so what's the big surprise?"
"Oh, er, well, I.." the creature flustered "well it's me!"
"What's you?"
"Er, the shock" replied the creature somewhat pathetically
"Really, why?" asked Rambo

“Well, it's ... er, because I am different to you, much different" it tried to explain.
“So are birds, but I'm not scared of them either" countered Rambo
"Oh, right, so my appearance doesn't bother you then"
"Why? should it?" enquired Rambo simply.
"Er, well no, I suppose!" admitted the creature
"So why all the fuss and bother then?"
"I don't know," reflected the alien "Truth is I didn't know what to expect. Maybe it would be best if we put this behind us and start again"
"Fine by me" agreed Rambo
"Good, Look come in and make yourself comfortable," said the alien indicating the chair which stood before the desk, but seeing as Rambo wasn't allowed on the furniture he chose a comfy looking piece of the floor instead.
"Carry on, don't let me stop you," Rambo said sitting down .
"Right, my name is er, well, you can call me Jill , yes I think that would be best, certainly a lot easier, anyway I digress, I suppose you are wanting to know ... er, why you er, ... sorry Rambo, but what are you doing?" asked Jill, Rambo looked up from his squatting position on the floor,
"I'm having a shit" he replied, "you said I was to make myself comfortable and I've been desperate to drop this one for ages"
"RAMBO,!" shouted Jill in disgust "you can't just go around defecating on the floor when you feel like it. It's obvious that you know nothing of hygiene or social behaviour"

"It's obvious that you know nothing about dogs" answered Rambo, he stood up and turned round to view his creation "Anyway I've finished now, would you like a sniff?"
Jill stared open mouthed in shock at what she was witnessing, it took her several seconds to compose herself enough to say anything, “I just can’t.., you are nothing but a filthy animal" she shouted. Rambo cocked his head to one side and wagged his tail,
"Yep, that's me!"

CHAPTER SIX

"So, what exactly did you say this was again?" asked Nobby, he was prodding with his fork at the purplish gluttonous blob on his plate, which he could have sworn was still alive.
"It's called Gelckik, it's very nice, bit of a delicacy really, had to have it imported from home" enthused Bill whilst tucking into his portion with vigour.
"Gelckik" repeated Nobby who was squinting at his helping dubiously, "So, what's it made from then because it looks like a cross between foam rubber and lard?"
"It comes from the Sharkbird" answered Bill between mouthfuls
"A sharkbird, um ... well I must admit I'm no expert when it comes to either poultry or game, but judging by the look of this it must have been an extremely sick bird" said Nobby stabbing his dinner with a knife and watching with unease as purple slime oozed from it.
"The sharkbird isn't really a bird" pointed out Bill
"So, what is it then?" Nobby was determined to get to the bottom of this.
"It's a shark," said Bill after swallowing what looked, to Nobby, like a particularly unnecessary large fork full.
"Oh well, that makes all the difference then" replied Nobby pushing his plate away.
"Don't you like it?" enquired Bill on observing Nobby's actions

"Truth is Bill, I'm not usually a fussy eater, but saying that I've never been asked to sample something that resembles an overgrown tumour before," said Nobby "anyway, if it's not a bird why is it called a sharkbird?"
"Well basically, to condense history, shortly after the dolphin left the sea, the sharks decided that it would be a good idea to do the same. Only sharks are notoriously stupid, so instead of doing something useful and advantageous like growing legs and learning to stand upright, they grew wings with bright red feathers and tried to fly"
Nobby eyed the Dolphoid suspiciously
"You're taking the piss," he said
"No, I am not" insisted Bill "you can check for yourself on the ships data files, everything about Mucks history is in there"
"Jebus, flying sharks. I bet they were dangerous, swooping down and attacking people ... er, sorry, Dolphoids" corrected Nobby
"They were dangerous, but not for that reason. You see sharks have very poor eyesight and even though their bodies had evolved and changed over many years, their vision didn't for some reason. So as a consequence of this they had a tendency to collide with each other or trees whilst flying and crashing down on top of innocent passersby. Then after several millennia of being mocked and ridiculed by other species, regarding their ineptitude at navigating around trees and mountains, they quietly slunk back to the sea and tried to pretend that the whole episode in history never happened" explained Bill, pausing only briefly to devour more of the purple mush

"So that's why you still call them sharkbirds?" asked Nobby who had become quite fascinated in his companions tales of future history.
“Yes and no," said Bill "It was all such a long time ago, officially they are referred to as just sharks, but we call them sharkbirds as an insult to remind them of how stupid they are" added Bill with a large smile on his face.
"So, Gelckik is part of a sharkbird then?" ensued Nobby, wondering exactly what transformations the sharks must have gone through to end up looking like the slimy quivering pulp on his plate.
"Well, not exactly" continued Bill " on Its return to the sea the sharkbird more or less returned to its original form, but for some reason remained bright red. Now being a predator this was something of a disadvantage, it is practically impossible to sneak up on anything when you're fourteen foot long and bright red. So as a result of not being able to eat other animals, unless one accidentally swam into its mouth, the sharkbirds diet is now on the whole vegetarian, and in particular a certain type of sea grass. Again unfortunately for the sharkbirds, this sea grass only grows around a specific type of seaweed, which the sharkbird cannot digest. So, whilst the sharkbird is feeding on the sea grass, it inadvertently ends up eating some of the seaweed, and as it cannot be digested it remains in the stomach being constantly churned and all the while fermenting. Over a period of time the sharkbirds stomach fills with the mulched seaweed, thus preventing it from eating, so obviously it needs to be rid of the seaweed otherwise it starves to death. So approximately about once a month the sharkbird will regurgitate the fermented seaweed, and

that my friend is Gelckik!" exclaimed Bill shovelling yet another foul looking blob of goo into his mouth with obvious relish. On the other hand, Nobby stared in disgust, first at Bill, then at his rejected food.
"Fish vomit!!" Nobby stated incredulously "and that's what you call a delicacy is it shark sick? Lovely" he mocked "I can't wait for dessert, what is it, let me guess .. er, how about giraffe shit in a monkey spunk sauce?"
"I don't believe so, but I can check," said Bill rising from his chair.
"Whoaa, no, no, I was kidding Bill, sit down it was just a joke," said Nobby panicking over the thought of being served a huge dish of steaming hot southern fried turds and boil in the bag baboon jism.
"I see," Bill said as he returned to his seat, "I take it you are not fond of Gelckik then?"
"Er, no, not really, more of an egg and chips man myself, not one for all this, er, fancy food"
"Would you prefer some egg and chips' perhaps?" offered Bill
"Yes, if you can" replied Nobby thankfully
"I'm sure we can" answered Bill cheerfully "Any preference to which type of egg, we have various kinds in our kitchens"
"Oh, er do you have chicken eggs" opted Nobby not wanting to have to munch his way through strange looking blue ones or have his fingers bitten off by some mutant reptilian embryo who's taken offence to him cracking open its home.
"Yes we have, would you like them boiled, poached, fried or scrambled?"

"Fried will be champion" answered Nobby with a sigh a relief. Bill rose once again from the table,
"I shall not be long," he said as he picked up the plates that they had already used.
"Ok," said Nobby, at this Bill left and Nobby watched him walk the length of the mess hall and enter a doorway at the far end, presumably into the kitchen. Nobby leant back in his seat and took the opportunity to take in the sights of the dining hall. As with every other part of the ship he had seen so far the dining hall was no exception when it came to decor. The tables, chairs, floor, walls and ceiling were all grey and seemingly made from the same material. The tables, as Nobby had observed earlier in Bills office, appeared to sprout directly from the floor. They were arranged in three long rows stretching from one end of the hall to the other, very much like the way Nobby had seen them set out in numerous films that were set in prisons. He reflected on this thought for a moment, in a way this was a prison, sure Bill had said that he was free to leave whenever he wanted, but it wasn't exactly true. For one thing he couldn't just get up and leave now, even if had wanted to, where would he go, according to Bill they were travelling faster than the speed of light, so it wasn't like he could get off and walk home, it was more like a prison than it seemed, the only difference being that he had requested to be here. Truth was Nobby liked it here despite the prison like overtones and accordingly decided not to worry about it. He leaned forwards placing his elbows on the table, interlocking his fingers and then resting his almost non-existent chin on them. Nobby viewed up and down the long room, estimating that there were probably thirty or so other

diners sat around the room, some in groups some alone. The majority of them were Dolphoids, but dispersed about them was roughly a dozen aliens that Nobby couldn't even begin to guess their origins. Sat alone in a far corner was a creature that had a head which was the same shape as a motorbike's petrol tank, it also had two extra pairs of arms which it seemed to be employing quite deftly. One pair was holding what looked like a newspaper, another was being used to cut up food on a plate before delivering it to its mouth and the third pair were rummaging through its pockets. Further along, the room was a group of six or seven Dolphoids all sat eating and chatting together. Amongst them sat another strange non-human creature, Nobby found it difficult to make out any features on this alien as its skin was transparent. As it moved and spoke Nobby could clearly see its muscles, arteries and bone structure beneath the see through skin.

Nobby found the alien both interesting and scary at the same time, interesting in the way you could see its muscles flexing and undulating as it talked, and scary as it reminded Nobby of too many gore filled zombie films. An unpleasant chill ran down his spine as he suddenly realised that the alien was staring back at him, Nobby smiled feebly and then pretended to have found something interesting to look at on the floor in an attempt to avoid further eye contact. After a short while of fiddling unnecessarily with his boots Nobby glanced quickly towards the translucent being, he was glad to find that it had returned its attention to the group of Dolphoids. Nobby sighed with relief and sat upright

again, this time being extra careful as to where he looked.
"I'll never get used to this," he said softly to himself,
"Yes you will given time" came a reply, Nobby let out a small yelp of surprise on almost fell off his chair. He hadn't seen Bill return to his side.
"Jesus Christ Bill, don't do that." gasped Nobby over his pounding heart beat
"Do what?"
"Sneak up on me like that" answered Nobby clutching his chest with shaky fingers
"I didn't sneak, I walked. Anyhow it would be difficult to sneak anywhere with this" replied Bill indicating the huge covered tray he held before him. He placed it down in front of Nobby and lifted the lid.
"What the fu..!!!" exclaimed Nobby loudly in disbelief, what was on the tray was unmistakably egg and chips, the only problem was that the eggs must have been two foot in diameter and the chips were all about four inches thick and eighteen inches long. Nobby looked up at Bill, opened his mouth, closed it again and returned his gaze to the eggs and chips. Bill sensed that something was amiss,
"Is er, something wrong Nobby?" he asked. Nobby didn't look up, instead he grabbed Bills arm and physically pulled him down into the opposing chair. Bill looked around frantically, everyone in the room had stopped what they were doing and were now staring this way.
"What's the problem Nobby?" said Bill as calmly as possible, "you asked for egg and chips and that is what I have brought you"

"I asked for chicken eggs" growled Nobby still not looking up
"They are chicken eggs, freshly laid this morning at that" answered Bill honestly
"Do you actually know what a chicken is Bill?" said Nobby Menacingly
"Of course I do, they're farm birds that peck at the ground and strut around going cluck, cluck' and laying eggs," said Bill indignantly
"And they must be about six foot tall to lay these fucking eggs!" snorted Nobby sarcastically
"Yes, that's right," said Bill
"And as for these chips, I don't know where ..." Nobby stopped talking suddenly and stared directly at his Dolphoid companion, "What did you just say?"
"When?"
"Just then when I said that chickens must be six foot tall to lay these eggs" elaborated Nobby
"Oh, er, that's right," said Bill hoping that was the right answer. Nobby exhaled heavily and sat back in his chair, "Bill, chickens are only about a foot tall, not six. An ostrich is six foot tall, but not chickens. A chicken would have probably exploded before laying an egg this size; in fact, I don't think an ostrich would be able to sit down after parting with these"
"I assure you Nobby, these eggs were indeed laid by a chicken, in fact, I will show them to you and then perhaps you will believe me," said Bill standing up
"This I have to see" replied Nobby standing also. Bill turned and headed back towards the kitchen; Nobby stuffed his hands in his pockets and plodded along behind him.

Rambo sat in the large leather chair opposite Jill, he had sat there in silence for quite some while, he didn't even say anything when the service droids had come in and completely disinfected the whole floor. The room still reeked of disinfectant and air freshener. Jill looked directly at Rambo, a hint of distaste in her eyes. Rambo thought about licking his balls but decided against it.
"Perhaps we should start again" spoke Jill rather sharply
"What, you want me to have another shit?" asked Rambo
"NO!!" Jill practically screamed, "I meant let’s forget what has happened and begin where we left off"
"Oh, right"
"So, I suppose you are wondering why you are here?" she asked.
“Nope!" said Rambo
"What!"
"I said nope!"
"Aren't you interested as to why we brought you here?"
"Not really, as long as you carry on feeding me I couldn't give a damn" replied Rambo honestly. Jill leant forwards and studied the dog more closely, she had never seen a dog before, well, not one from this stage of evolution. The dogs from her planet were much more advanced and civilised, many breeds had been walking upright for several millennia and were extremely good at law enforcement. Rambo was something completely different; he was rough, uncouth, unmotivated and unpleasant.

"Don't you have any goals in life?" she asked
"Of course I do," said Rambo
"Such as?" Jill coaxed
"Sex" answered Rambo wagging his tail.
"Sex!!" repeated Jill unnecessarily
"Yeah, the truth is I've never done it before, never had the chance really. Have you?"
"That's none of your business," Jill said sternly, Rambo ignored the tone of her voice.
"I bet you have, what's it like?" he asked " I don't suppose you have any bitches around here, do you? I mean, you can only lick your own dick for so long. Know what I mean?" Rambo winked at Jill. Jill shuddered at the thought of anything wanting to have sex with this creature, no matter how primitive they may be.
"Maybe we should engage in another subject" suggested the Dolphoid
"Why? Frigid are you?" teased Rambo
"Certainly not, not that it has anything to do with you !" snapped Jill rising to the bait.
"Enjoy a good bonking then do you babe?"
"W, w, what!!" spluttered Jill
"Perhaps we could get together again later and you could show me a thing or two?" said Rambo panting. Jill blew her top.

Fifteen minutes later Rambo was back in his room and licking his genitals vigorously. He sighed deeply. Rambo was in love.

"I don't believe this" stated Nobby, and he wasn't kidding, he really couldn't believe his eyes. Bill had led him through the kitchens and into what could only be described as a vast cargo area, equivalent in size to perhaps a dozen or so football pitches arranged into a square. Nobby followed Bill past several enclosures built into the cargo area, some of which held strange and alien animals. Nobby wanted to stop and look at them but Bill carried on walking, so reluctantly he followed, resolving to have a good look on his way back.
"Where are we going?" Nobby had asked, catching up with Bill
"To see some Chickens" replied the Dolphoid casually
"Oh, great!" lied Nobby. They had traversed roughly half the length of the cargo area when Bill took a sharp left, almost leaving Nobby behind. Bill stopped before a large enclosure and pointed into its interior.
"There you are, chickens," Bill said. Nobby's eyes followed the direction of Bills out stretched finger,
"Christ on a bike!" uttered Nobby as he stood only a few feet away from the biggest most dangerous looking clutch of chickens he had ever seen. Each chicken was indeed between five and six foot tall and apart from the sheer size of them, they were identical to the breed of poultry that Nobby was more familiar with.
"This is incredible," Nobby said in awe, "I've never seen anything like it in my life, well, I have, just not this bloody huge." He moved closer to the enclosure and leant on the small perimeter fence, resting his chin on the top slat. He reached out and tried to touch the nearest one.

"I wouldn't do that if I was you" warned Bill, coming up beside him. Nobby withdrew his hand quickly,
"Why do they bite?" he asked nervously
"The hens don't but the cockerel doesn't always take kindly to strangers" explained Bill.
"Where is it?" asked Nobby, his eyes searching up and down the enclosure
"Most probably having a snooze in the main coop over there," said Bill indicating the large structure at the far end of the enclosure.
"Oh, right," said Nobby, not averting his gaze from the four or five hens that were in the open, "Why have you bred them so large?"
"We haven't, up until now I presumed that they have always been this size. During the month or so we have been studying Earth we have really only had chance to examine things that we considered important, and chickens were not one of them. So the size difference was over looked, which would explain the difficulty we had with the potatoes"
"Huh!!" Nobby gave Bill a puzzled glance, "what potatoes?"
“The ones that you had with your eggs" Bill said, Nobby continued to look quizzically at him.
"Do you mean the chips?" asked Nobby
"Yes, the chips. You see, when you asked for chips and eggs I didn't actually know what a chip was, but I thought that the cook would. But he didn't, so we searched through the Earth data files that we have for a picture and recipe for egg and chips. When we found one we then couldn't find any potatoes large enough to make the chips from, not realising that the picture we had of

chips and eggs were not to scale with the eggs that we had. We ended up having to use the food processor to reproduce chips that were to scale with the eggs that we had and presumably under the circumstances much larger than you expected." said Bill with an apologetic shrug of his shoulders. Nobby was still enthralled with the giant chickens and hardly heard Bills words, it was only when he noticed the silence did he turn his attention back to his companion.

"I wonder why they grew so bloody big" mused Nobby

"Well, there could be many factors involved," said Bill, parking his bum on a large wooden pallet that had been left near to the gate of the enclosure.

"Such as?" asked Nobby taking position next to the Dolphoid.

"Well, for example, the chicken has more or less always been a domesticated bird, so perhaps the fact that it was domesticated kept it small. Farmers often kept them in small areas and fed them the bare minimum to live and at the same time produce eggs, even so called free range hens that found their own food had to share the ground that supplied them with worms and other insects with many other hens. But when your lot died off.." Bill instantly regretted his choice of words, he turned to apologise to Nobby. "I'm sorry Nobby; I didn't mean to be so insensitive."

"About what?" he asked

"The, er, end of mankind"

" Oh that, well the way I look at it, all that stuff about the human race dying out hasn't happened yet, at least not as far as my planet's concerned, so I can see no point in dwelling on something that may or may not happen in

several hundred years' time. All that you are doing is talking about your own planets particular history, and I can no more apologise for my planets history than you could your own" Nobby smiled at Bill, and every muscle in Bills body tensed for a second. The Dolphoid feared he would never get used to Nobby's smile.
"Thank you," said Bill after regaining his composure, "I feel more at ease speaking about the subject now that I know your feelings regarding it"
"No problems mate," said Nobby placing his hand on Bill's shoulder and giving it a bit of a squeeze, "Anyway, you were telling me about the chickens."
"Was I?, Oh that's right I was," Bill muttered, slightly at a loss for words for the moment. Nobby's simple act of placing his hand on Bill's shoulder had meant so much to the alien, it was a sign of trust and more importantly to Bill, friendship.
"Where did I get up to?" he asked.
"Mankind has snuffed it and hordes of wild chickens rule the Earth" joked Nobby
"Well, that is more or less what occurred, although they never ruled the planet. With the death of mankind, many things began to happen which one way or another affected the growth of the chickens. Now you have to remember that what I am telling you is only my personal theory of why the chickens have grown to their present size and there for must not be taken as gospel, do you understand?" Nobby nodded agreement. Bill carried on, "Okay, with man out of the way, the chickens gain freedom and as man isn't around to spray fields with insecticides and pesticides the insect population flourishes. Which is good news for the chickens as it

also means a greater supply of food for them. Now as a result of the food increase the chickens can eat more and one side effect of eating more is that you get slightly larger, in fact I would say that probably each generation of chickens were slightly, although not visibly, larger than the previous one. So, if each generation was only a hundredth of a millimetre larger than their parents, after a thousand years or so the resulting offspring of further generations would be several inches taller than their fore fathers. Now times that equation by twenty five million years, give or take natural periods of non-growth, and then you have what you see before you." Bill indicated the enclosure to his side. Nobby pondered the theory for a moment, as far as he knew it was as good an explanation as any, he personally couldn't think of any other theory that would sound more plausible. Bills potted history may not have been based on solid fact, but it would do as far Nobby was concerned.
"Have all animals grown in size?" asked Nobby
"Some have, but not many. Some have completely changed size and shape, so much so that you wouldn't recognise them if you saw them."
"Like yourself?" said Nobby. Bill considered the statement for a while before answering,
"Yes, I suppose that from your perspective I am an example of how many species have evolved and changed."
"I would really like to see some of the other animals that you have on board." said
Nobby remembering the enclosures that he had passed on his way here.

"You will, all in good time. But first let's sort out your dinner," replied Bill standing up and dusting the seat of his uniform with his hands. He held out a hand for Nobby to pull himself up with, Nobby didn't hesitate in taking it. Bill smiled, the lack of hesitation in Nobby's actions showed that he didn't in any way fear or distrust him. For a while, Bill had feared that he wouldn't be able to gain Nobby's trust, and as a result, would be forced to erase his memory before sending him back home. As it was things had worked out and hopefully Nobby would be able to help them.
Together they made their way back through the cargo hold, towards the dining area.

A short while later Nobby had managed to force down two chips and approximately 20% of the egg, and surprisingly despite their comical size, they were quite delicious. The belt around the middle of the boiler suit he wore automatically readjusted to the swell of Nobby's now bloated gut. He leaned back in his chair and let out a contented sigh, Bill was sat opposite, he had ordered himself another dish of Gelckik and had walloped it down as though it was going out of fashion.
"Ah," said Bill "There is nothing like a good meal."
Nobby regarded Bill empty purple stained dish,
"And that looked nothing like a good meal" he replied
"You really should try some" insisted Bill
"No thanks" answered Nobby waving his hand before him, "Eating something that has already gone the rounds of someone else's digestive system is not in any way appealing to me!"

"Not to worry," said Bill with a smile "It means there will be more for me" Nobby laughed along with Bill for a moment before his thought turned to more serious matters,
"Earlier on you said that if I stayed aboard after you had finished your tests and questions with me, I would become part of the crew and given a job," said Nobby
"Yes that is true"
"Exactly what kind of job?"
"Well, what are you good at?" asked Bill. Nobby pondered the question for a short while and was disappointed with his only answer,
"Er, nothing really, I'm not very dexterous, I lack creativity, I possess little if any motivation and I have a limited knowledge of anything more strenuous than getting out of bed first thing in the afternoon."
"I must say that you seem to have a very low opinion of yourself," said Bill
"I've had twenty odd years to think about it" grunted Nobby despondently
"Surely there is something that you are good at" prompted Bill not wanting his new friend to feel inadequate.
"Not unless you count wanking," said Nobby "I would be Olympic standard if they were to make it into a competitive sport. Gold medals all round, 10 out of 10 for performance and technique."
"Do you like animals?" asked Bill trying to change the subject
"I prefer women or at least I think I would, not had much experience with either so I couldn't really be certain"

"I actually meant do you enjoy looking after animals, that sort of thing?" explained Bill quickly
"Oh, I see, sorry" apologised Nobby, "thought you were just being a bit kinky, sorry. what type of animals?"
"We have many different types aboard, the majority of which are in the kitchens supply area, that's the place that you visited earlier."
"You mean like the big chickens?" asked Nobby with a hint of enthusiasm.
"Yes, and others like them. They all need feeding and watering, the enclosures need cleaning on a regular basis, so perhaps we could give you a job working there if you like."
"Are there any dangerous ones?" queried Nobby not wishing to meet his end after being ravaged by a twenty foot tall vampire bunny rabbit.
"Not really, most of the animals in that area are domesticated, but if you prefer dangerous animals we have some that are kept in the science section of the ship!" explained Bill
"I think I'll stick to the chickens if that's okay with you" opted Nobby
"Right, that's that sorted out, when the time comes you will be designated a job in the kitchen supply area," said Bill rubbing his hands together, "Is there anything else bothering you that I can help with?"
"Well, these tests that you want to do, what exactly do they entail?"
"Just simple routine tests, nothing harmful. Things such as weighing and measuring, studying your nervous system, circulatory system, bone structure, muscle

structure, brain functions and bodily organ functions." outlined Bill
"Sounds extremely harmful if you want my opinion" exclaimed Nobby dubiously.
"I promise that you will not be harmed in any way what so ever. Everything will be done with surgical scanners that are able to see inside your body, all that you will be required to do is lay still while the scanners pass over you."
"Are you sure, I mean there's not going to be any strange side effects like my skin turning black and dropping off?"
"None at all I promise." assured Bill, "If at any time during the tests you feel nervous or anxious just say so and we will stop immediately, okay?" Nobby nodded silent agreement, and for some inexplicable reason he trusted Bill not to lie to him, despite the fact that he was from another planet, his ancestors were dolphins and they had only met a short while ago under some extremely strange and unpredictable circumstances.
"So, what happens now?" he asked Bill
"Maybe going to bed would be a good idea." was the reply
“Why? What time is it?" said Nobby looking at his wrist, only to find that it didn't have a watch on it. Bill dug into one of his pockets and fished out a gadget similar in design to a mobile phone. He popped open its casing and pressed at the buttons that were revealed,
"By Earths time system it is approximately two thirty a.m." informed Bill
"Right then, in that case, I suppose bed would be a good idea, but there is one small problem."

"Oh!" Bill said raising an eyebrow inquisitively
"The thing is, I haven't the slightest clue as to where my room is let alone the bed, I could wander around these corridors for years," said Nobby sheepishly. Bill smiled and rose from his chair,
"Follow me," he said
"I'm glad you said that."

CHAPTER SEVEN

Nobby stood beneath the shower, letting the powerful jets of water bombard his skin, washing away any remnants of his night's sleep that tried to linger on. He had surprisingly slept soundly for eleven hours and would have probably slept longer if the intercom hadn't woken him with a message from Bill saying that he roughly half an hour to get up and dressed before the Dolphoid arrived to take him to meet some of the ships other scientists. Nobby had acknowledged the message with a grunt as he dragged his body off the mattress and plodded wearily towards the far wall of his room. He placed his hand on the wall like Bill had shown him the previous night, and dutifully the wall opened up to reveal a small but none the less functional bathroom.
He had slept in the nude, apparently futuristic space dolphins don't wear pyjamas, so he stepped straight into the shower area, which started automatically, and began to wash. After roughly ten minutes of soaping and rinsing, he stepped from the shower and stood beneath a large circular hole in the ceiling which began to blast warm air at him, drying his scrawny body in just a few seconds. Once dry he moved back into the main area of the bedroom to dress, he found his uniform boiler suit that he had worn yesterday at the end of the bed. He stared for a moment at the large yolk stain on the breast of the suit, "shit" he thought to himself before remembering that Bill had also shown him where the closet was, explaining that clean suits were put there on a weekly basis, one for each day of the week. Nobby

dropped the dirty suit back on the bed and moved over to one of the rooms side walls and placed his hand against it, the wall retracted swiftly and he stepped into the opening. It came as a great surprise to Nobby to find himself bollock naked in the middle of a rather busy corridor.
Fortunately, many of the corridor's occupants paid little notice of Nobby, the majority of them being various types of aliens that were as far from being humanoid as could be possible, his nakedness obviously meant little if nothing to them. Several Dolphoids regarded him briefly as they passed, nodding polite acknowledgement as they went by, and rather than offend them Nobby smiled like an idiot in return. A floating probe whizzed past him only to return again seconds later. It floated before him for several seconds making quiet clicking noises, as though taking photos to show its friends later on. It then circled him slowly moving up and down as it went, Nobby stood stock still as it floated about him silently, straining his eyes to the left and right trying to follow its course without moving his head. Suddenly the probe swung in front of him, about two feet away but staying at his eye level.
"Identify yourself" demanded the probe, Nobby flinched at the suddenness of its question, he was feeling pretty inferior stood there in the nude whilst being interrogated by a potentially lethal probe.
"I'm sorry!!" blurted out Nobby, after his last run in with one of these things he was in no way tempted to upset it.
"Crew member Soree," said the probe "you are in breach of clause four, paragraph seven of the ship's code of conduct manual, which clearly states that all individuals

must dress in accordance with their position whilst anywhere other than their private living quarters. Although sub section twelve does allow for modifications to standard issue clothing, to accommodate for religious or medical purposes, I can find nothing in the code of conduct manual that would allow for total nudity in a public place. Please give your reasons for violating section four, paragraph seven of the code of conduct manual."

Nobby squirmed under the gaze of the probe. To make matters worse a small crowd had begun to gather around them and it was getting larger by the minute.

"Well, the thing is.." began Nobby, "I was looking for my closet and I .."

"Does crew member Soree realise that closets are not located in public access ways such as this corridor" interrupted the probe sharply.

"Yes," sighed Nobby, the crowd had increased to around forty or fifty individuals stood in a rough semi circle around him, each one as alien as the next. Many were talking amongst themselves but at the same time keeping a watch on the proceedings before them.

"I know it only too well" he added looking at the growing audience.

"Then please explain why are you here in the corridor completely naked?" the probe asked sharply.

"Truth is I don't really know," replied Nobby

"Are you implying that you suffer from some kind of mental illness and that you are not able to remember or control your actions?" said the probe loud enough for everyone to hear. Increased conversation broke out amongst the assembled; Nobby could see several

individuals making looping actions with their fingers against their heads.
"No, not at all, I simply meant that I am here due to an unfortunate mistake." pleaded Nobby. There was a moment of silence before the probe spoke, "I'm sure we'd love to hear your unfortunate mistake story." There were several mumbled words of agreement from the crowd to accompany the mass head nodding.
"Well, I was in this room here," said Nobby indicating the wall behind him where the door had been. "But I seem to have stumbled out of it by mistake while trying to find the closet," he explained to everyone in ear shot.
"Those quarters are allocated to Visitor Nobby." announced the probe, still loud enough for everyone to hear. A subdued murmur ran through the crowd and all eyes, and antennae, turned to Nobby.
"Yes, that's right" stated Nobby "and that's where I was until I accidentally walked through the wrong door way." At this the murmur in the crowd reached fever pitch, many of the aliens were having discussions amongst themselves, some were pointing to him and explaining what was going on to latecomers. The probe moved closer to
Nobby, he took a step back and bumped into the wall.
"Crew member Sorry, I am placing you under arrest for violating the codes of conduct manual and trespassing in the quarters of Visitor Nobby." announced the probe, the crowd began to applaud the probes decision.
Nobby stared in opened mouthed bewilderment, "how the hell do I get myself into these situations" he thought. He waited until the clapping had diminished before speaking,

“I am Visitor Nobby” he snapped at the probe, a sudden gasp of surprise escaped the amassed horde
“Impersonating a visitor will also be added to your charges” replied the probe. The crowd went wild, clapping and cheering the probe. The probe turned to the crowd and bobbed up and down in the air as a bowing gesture.
“WHAT!!” Shouted Nobby over the crowd, the probe turned and bore down upon him. “Look,” said Nobby "if you don't believe me then ask Bill!"
“Bill who?” asked the probe, the crowd had fallen silent in anticipation of Nobby answer.
“Er, well,” stumbled Nobby "Er, just Bill.” A low murmur echoed through the crowd.
“I can find no reference to any individual named Bill aboard this vessel” replied the probe smugly, the crowd let out a mass tut.
“Ah, well the thing is, Bill is not his real name"
“So what is his real name?” asked the probe
“Er, I don't actually know!” said Nobby sheepishly, the crowd tutted again, the probe moved closer to Nobby, swishing through the air dramatically.
“So, exactly how do you know this Bill' "
“He's my friend and..” started Nobby, he was interrupted by the probe.
“An accomplice?” it said accusingly, more to the crowd than Nobby. The crowd reacted accordingly with various noises of surprise and astonishment. Nobby, on the other hand, let out a deep sigh and shook his head slowly, things were getting ridiculous and he'd had enough, if things carried on any longer he would probably end up being charged with treason, blasphemy and unsolicited

donkey buggery. Nobby turned on the spot to face the wall; he reached out to touch it.
"HALT!" boomed the probe from behind him, "step away from the wall". The probe voice was accompanied by a high pitched whine that Nobby was all too familiar with. A cold sweat appeared on his skin and his legs felt weak, slowly he stepped back from the wall and turned to face the probe. As he had imagined the small but lethal ray gun thing was protruding from the probes head and it was trained directly on him.
Not only had the crowd fallen silent, they had fallen back a couple of steps.
"Any further escape attempts will be dealt with severely" proclaimed the probe, Nobby felt no reason to doubt it.
"Security has been informed and will arrive shortly to escort you to the brig," said the probe. Nobby looked helplessly at the crowd, who in turn looked back accusingly at him. Just when things seemed hopeless, suddenly Nobby spotted a face that he recognised in the crowd.
"Rambo!" shouted Nobby
"What did you say?" demanded the probe swooping in front of him. Nobby pointed past the probe,
"There in the crowd, that's my dog, Rambo"
"Where?" said the probe moving over to the crowd.
"There, the small furry one" replied Nobby pointing frantically. The probe stopped in front of Rambo, Rambo sniffed the probe.
"Please identify yourself!" the probe demanded.
"He can't answer you, he's a dog." interrupted Nobby
"Silence crew member Sorry!" ordered the probe, Nobby shut up and smiled smugly.

“Identify yourself!” repeated the probe to Rambo.
“My name's Rambo,” said Rambo
“WHAT!!!” blurted Nobby uncontrollably
“Silence!” Bellowed the probe
“But...” began Nobby, the probe darted to within an inch of his nose, its Disruptor glowing angrily.
“One more sound from you and I will take it as an act of aggression!” stated the probe. Nobby remained silent but kept his eyes firmly on Rambo. The probe returned slowly back to the dog, keeping its weapon targeted on Nobby as it moved.
“Visitor Rambo,” said the probe, “according to the ship computer system you are well acquainted with Visitor Nobby are you not"
“Er, yes, why?” asked Rambo
“This individual claims that he is Visitor Nobby, Could you please help us to clarify the matter as to his real identity. Do you know this individual?” asked the probe. Rambo looked at Nobby’s pathetic form for a moment before returning his attention back to the probe, a wicked smile playing on his lips,
“No, I have never seen this individual before in my life,” he said. Nobby’s smile faded abruptly.

“Ah, there you are!” said Bill through the bars of the cell door, Nobby jerked upright from his reclined position on the narrow hard bed.
“Where the hell have you been!!” snapped Nobby, he pulled the thin bed sheet around his naked form.
“Looking for you if you must know.” smiled Bill, "you're not an easy person to find."
“Very funny, how about getting me out of here?”

“No problem, that's why I'm here,” said Bill cheerfully, he tapped the key pad on the wall beside the door. The key pad beeped and the door slid open, Nobby was out of the cell before it had fully opened.
“Right, where's Rambo?” demanded Nobby while storming out of the main gaol area into the adjoining corridor.
“Er, I'm not sure, why?” asked Bill trying to keep pace
“I'm going to kill the scabby bastard, that's why!"
“Oh dear,” said Bill “Is that necessary, I mean I'm sure he was only having a little joke with you” he added in an attempt to pacify his blanket clad companion.
“Well let’s see the little shite laugh after I've kicked his teeth through his arse.” seethed Nobby.
“Oh dear,” said Bill again, "I'm afraid that I cannot allow you to do that"
“And who's going to stop me?"
“Er, they are!” said Bill, indicating over his shoulder with one of his thumbs at the two burly security Dolphoids that were following them. Nobby stopped to look at them both, in turn, they also stopped.
“Are they following us?” Nobby whispered to Bill.
“Not us, just you,” replied Bill
“Why?”
“Well,” said Bill "after I explained the mix up to the security council they agreed to release you on the condition that you were to be closely monitored for the foreseeable future, just to make sure that you are not dangerous."
“Dangerous!! I'm not dangerous” snorted Nobby indignantly

“Personally I agree with you,” said Bill "but the security council had to take into account the probes report and sixty or so independent eye witnesses who all claim that they saw you attack Rambo without any provocation and would have caused him serious physical harm if it wasn't for the intervention of a group of security officers who promptly arrested you."
“What about me!!” protested Nobby, "I'm the one who was flattened to the ground by Torvill and Dean there,” Nobby indicated the two large Dolphoids, "It was me who was handcuffed and forcefully marched bollock naked half way around the ship before being roughly pushed into a cell, and why? All because I forgot where the friggin' wardrobe was. I mean, what the hell did I do to deserve all this?"
“Well the problem began when the probe asked you to identify yourself” explained Bill, "the thing is when you replied I'm sorry the probe mistook you for one of the crew members, whose name happens to be Soree.”
“And that gives the probe the right to threaten to disintegrate me, does it?” ranted Nobby, readjusting the thin blanket around him.
“Well, yes and no,” answered Bill
“What's that meant to mean, yes and no?” demanded Nobby
“Well it's like this, if you had identified yourself as Nobby, the probe would only have not raised its Disruptor. But seeing as you identified yourself as Soree the probe had no choice but to arm its Disruptor,” explained Bill
“Why is this Soree bloke a wanted criminal?” asked Nobby

“No, nothing like that, it's just that Soree is a Megoloid!"
“A Megoloid?” repeated Nobby
“Yes, a Megoloid.” Bill noticed the confused look on Nobby’s face. "Perhaps it would be better if I showed you.” Nobby nodded vaguely. Bill took his arm and led him back up the corridor towards the prison area.
“Whoa,” said Nobby breaking free from Bills grip, “why are we going back there,” he said pointing at the jail entrance. The two security Dolphoids had quickly moved in and were at present flanking Nobby, ready to make a move if necessary. Bill waved them away.
“I need a computer to show you a Megoloid, and the closest one is just in there, trust me,” Bill said calmly.
“Right, okay.” replied Nobby, “I knew that,” he added, Bill retook his arm and walked him to the jail. On entering the main prison area several of the guards stood up and saluted Bill. Bill saluted back quickly and led Nobby into a small office; he closed the door behind him, allowing him and Nobby some privacy.
“Sit down Nobby,” said Bill indicating one of the room’s two chairs, Nobby gathered his blanket around himself before sitting. "Remind me to get you some clothes before we leave.”
“Oh, I don't know,” mocked Nobby, “I'm getting used to the Gandhi look.” Bill sat at the room’s desk, opposite Nobby. He pressed the desk top and the keyorb rose swiftly from it, his hands encircled it and he quickly tapped in the relevant instructions. After only a few seconds Bill turned the computer screen towards Nobby, “There you are, a Megoloid,” Bill announced. Nobby squinted at the screen, more out of habit than need. On the screen was a 3 D rotating image of the afore

mentioned Megoloid, it resembled a short, fat, upright rhinoceros that hadn't shaved. Nobby regarded the picture for a moment before returning his attention back to Bill.

“You’re taking this piss, aren't you” Nobby half laughed.

“Er, no. Why?” replied Bill

“Well, surely you’re not suggesting that I resemble that bloody thing there!” snorted Nobby, pointing at the computer image.

“I never suggested any such thing,” said Bill indignantly

“Yes, you did, you said that the probe mistook me for one of those!"

“Ah, yes I did, but you're confusing the matter of identification” explained Bill, he cleared his throat before continuing, "when you accidentally identified yourself as Soree the probe simply checked against the ships data files to establish if there was indeed an individual aboard named Soree. The probe would not have received any visual information about Soree, only the fact that he was a Megoloid and if he refused to cooperate the probe was instructed to fire upon him at full power with its disruptor."

“Jesus, that's a bit drastic isn't it!” said Nobby, “I thought you were a peaceful race."

“We are, but the thing is the Megoloids are possibly the single most toughest race of creatures that we have ever encountered and a full power blast of a Disruptor is probably just enough to stun one, and that is the reason why the probe armed its Disruptor while dealing with you earlier."

“What would a full powered blast of the Disruptor do to me?” asked Nobby nervously.

“It would turn you into little more than a puff of steam,” answered Bill honestly
“Christ, and it only stuns these bastards,” said Nobby tapping the image on the screen with his finger, “How come you've got something so bleeding dangerous roaming the ship?"
“The Megoloids aren't dangerous, in fact, they are possibly the most placid and peaceful race this side of the known universe. It's just that they are so strong that the slightest show of anger from one of them would be enough to destroy part of the ship,” Bill saw the look of panic on Nobby’s face. “Don't worry Nobby, the Megoloids come from a planet called Haven, and their recorded history goes back over thirty thousand years and in all that time there has never been a war. The only conflict that ever seems to have occurred on their planet was a dispute between two separate clans over land ownership."
“Hang on, I thought you just said that there was never a war on their planet?” interrupted Nobby
“There hasn't"
“Well what about that conflict between the two clans, surely the word conflict means war?” stated Nobby
“Normally yes, but the Megoloids way of settling disputes like that one was to have both opposing clans face each other in a field and blow raspberries at each other until one side gets fed up and goes home.” Bill sat back in his chair and swung his feet up on to the table, "So in terms of being dangerous the Megoloids rank just below cheese."
“I once blistered my lips on some cheese on toast!” grumbled Nobby in a vain attempt to try and prove that

cheese can be a vicious enemy. Bill eyed Nobby's sorry form and slowly shook his head in despair, Nobby noticed Bills actions,
"What, don't you believe me, here then look at this" protested Nobby whilst pulling at his top lip, "I'll probably be scarred for life because of it!"
"Yes very nice, now put it away." said Bill to Nobby's proffered lip, "I was not shaking my head at your statement as regards to its factual content, only at the fact that you seem to be an eternal pessimist always looking for the bad in every situation, trying to find an evil motive behind every action."
"No, I don't." proclaimed Nobby
"Ok then, what was your first reaction to your bald head?" asked Bill
"Ah, well that's.."
"Or your reaction to being told that you were no longer on Earth?" continued Bill
"Well yes, but the..." spluttered Nobby
"Or perhaps you could remind me of the way you responded to finding out about your translator?" interrupted Bill again, "In fact, while you're at it I would like you to remind me of anything at all that you have responded positively to!" Nobby opened his mouth to protest but quickly shut it again when nothing sprang, or even dragged itself feebly, to mind. He averted his gaze from Bill and stared in silence at his hands clasped in his lap, Bill was right and Nobby knew it. Since he had been here he had been shown nothing but kindness and understanding by the Dolphoid, yet he still insisted on jumping to unfounded conclusions and making damning accusations. It was lucky for him that the Dolphoids

were a peaceful race otherwise he may well have ended up being kicked out into space by any less tolerant race. He dwelled on his treatment of Bill, feeling ashamed and undeserving of the chance he has been given, to live and work on an actual alien space ship. He was better off here than what he could ever remember being back on Earth, yet almost everything he has said since arriving puts his stay here in jeopardy. Several minutes had passed since either one of them had spoken, Nobby was wrapped up in his thoughts while Bill studied Nobby's reactions, his own thoughts revolving around his human friend. It was little wonder to Bill that the human race died out so quickly if Nobby's suspicious, wary, doom and gloom outlook on life was anything to go by. Bill found it hard to believe that the human race had lasted as long as it had, how could any kind of structured society flourish when so much loathing, distrust and scepticism bubbles only a fraction below the surface.

Nobby finally raised his head and looked into Bills eyes, he saw no contempt or mistrust in them, only curiosity and patience. Nobby felt small and petty, despite all his ranting's the Dolphoid had refused to give up on him, no matter how wild an accusation Nobby had thrown at him. Nobby couldn't see himself being so understanding if the roles had been reversed.
"I don't mean to do it," Nobby said quietly, "It's just a defence mechanism I suppose."
"Defence against what?" asked Bill equally as quiet.
"Life I suppose"
"In what way?" Bill question gently, he needed to find the basis of Nobby suspicions, the cause of his distrust.

Only when the problems were uncovered would he be truly able to help Nobby.
“I don't really know,” sighed Nobby heavily, “It's just that life has a way of dealing me a bad hand. If something can go wrong, then it will wait till I'm doing it."
“So, you think that nature is deliberately picking on you?"
“I know it sounds ridiculous, but yeah. I mean just look at me, my teeth stick out, my ears aren't aligned, until recently I couldn't see without glasses and I have all the social graces of a gorilla with colossal throbbing haemorrhoids. I have spent the majority of my life being the object of ridicule for anybody and everybody. I can't remember the last time anyone actually spoke to me other than out of necessity."
“Surely you have family?"
“Oh yes, I have family alright, not that any them would know if I'm alive or not. I make one little mistake and all of a sudden I'm an outcast.” reminisced Nobby humourlessly
“Why, what happened?” Bill felt that the answer to Nobby’s guardedness was close at hand, he asked his questions in the same way that a psychiatrist would gently and carefully probe for more answers without exerting any additional pressure.
“Well, it was such a long time ago at my granny’s funeral. That was back in 1976, she had died in a bizarre accident, I'm not exactly sure of the circumstances but it involved a skateboard, a three hour police car chase, and a combine harvester. There was talk at the time of her doctor accidentally prescribing steroids instead of her

usual water tablets, but I couldn't be sure." Nobby blew his nose on the blanket before continuing, "Anyway for one reason or another the coffin lid had to be kept shut due to the severity of her accident, you know what I mean?" Bill nodded his head in understanding, although he didn't really understand, but at the same time didn't want to side track Nobby.
"Well," continued Nobby, "on the day of the funeral we, that's all the family, gathered at my parents' house. Grannies coffin was in the front room waiting to take the final journey down the road to the cemetery. My father, his two brothers and three close friends volunteered to carry the coffin on their shoulders the short distance to the church. So as they moved the coffin outside I snook upstairs to change my shoes." Bill raised his eyebrows at this odd statement, Nobby smiled and elaborated, "The thing is my Mam had bought me a pair of black sensible shoes, especially for the funeral, only I didn't want to wear them, I wanted to wear my brand new Bay City Roller six and a quarter inch platform heeled boots, which at the time I thought were the coolest things in the whole world. So, while my Mam and dad were getting things moving outside I took the opportunity to put them on. By the time I had put them on and gone outside the funeral cortege was already on its way down the road, so I had to run to catch up. Now this was the first time I had ever worn these new boots and believe me wearing stilts would have been easier, I was wobbling all over the place trying my hardest not to sprain my ankles. I didn't actually make it into a run, the best I could manage was an erratic hobble, which with a lot of effort allowed me to catch up with the rest of the procession. Only I was

using my entire concentration on staying upright and watching my footing that I completely failed to notice that the cortege had stopped outside the local pub where granny had spent the majority of her time since granddad died several years earlier. Unaware of the unscheduled stop I careened straight in to the last person in the procession, who in turn fell into the person in front of them, who then repeated the action to the person in front of them and so on and so forth all the way to the front of the line until it reached the coffin bearers, who were skittled by my extremely over weight Aunty Betty. At this time I remember looking up from the back of the fallen queue and seeing grannies coffin sailing gracefully and unaided through the air and heading towards the pub's gates, which led down into the landlord private yard. The momentum or the coffin hitting the gates forced them open; the coffin itself fell into the gateway and began to bounce down the sloping drive way, breaking open as it went. At the bottom of the drive, it crashed into the garage doors cracking the coffin in half, spilling several thousands of pieces of my granny in every direction and attracting the attention of the three great Danes that the landlord of the pub kept as guard dogs. Any way to cut a long story short, by the time the dogs could be beaten back by the landlord and my dad and uncles, there wasn't much left to bury." Tears had formed in Nobby's eyes and he used the blanket to wipe them away, He also blew his nose for good measure. Bill, who had remained silent up till now leaned forward onto the desk, his heart went out to his friend, the pain behind the human's eyes was unmistakable, but Bill felt

that there was more to be told. He spoke to Nobby softly and with true sympathy,
“What happened after that?"
“Well, my mother had a nervous breakdown and spent several weeks in hospital. My father had to be restrained by other relatives from killing me there and then, once the cause of the er, accident, was established. I was sent to live with my Aunty Mavis for the next five months until I had finished school for good, and then I had to find my own place to live. Since then I have had practically no contact what so ever with my family, except for the odd Christmas card from my cousin Sharon, that's one of my Aunty Mavis' daughters. But then again I haven't heard anything from her since Aunty Mavis' funeral, which for me was yet another disaster in the field of family relationships.” Nobby looked drained and tired, the earlier anger he had was now completely forgotten, he was dredging up memories and emotions that he had kept hidden within himself for many years, yet somehow, he felt better for doing so. He couldn't actually tell why he felt better; maybe it was just the act of sharing his secrets and unburdening his guilt that seemed to remove a heavy weight from his soul. “What happened at Aunty Mavis' funeral?” probed Bill. Nobby spent the next two hours or so relating the unfortunate tale of his ill-timed giggles and other dark chapters of his life to Bill.

“What are we going to do with you, Rambo?” asked Jill from her position from behind the desk. Rambo had

opted to stretch out on the offices couch, in what he hoped was a provocative manner.
“Lock me in a room full of red hot bitches,” replied Rambo with a hopeful wag of his tail. Jill frowned deeply,
“This is a serious question,” she said
“It was a serious answer,” answered Rambo. Jill slapped her hand down on the desk causing Rambo to jump slightly,
“Look dog, this isn't a time for flippancy, you could be in a lot of trouble."
“Why, what have I done wrong?” asked Rambo
“You knowingly caused an innocent person to be falsely arrested and incarcerated."
“Who?” quizzed Rambo
“Nobby!” Jill almost shouted
“Oh, him."
“Yes, him. Because of you, he has been humiliated and treated like a common criminal.” the anger she felt spilt into her words, the tone she was using was harsh and uncommon to her, but there was something about this wretched dog that brought the worse out in her.
“Yeah, I know,” Rambo said, "But you should have seen his face, it was a picture.”
Jill inhaled deeply and counted to ten before continuing.
“Listen Rambo, what you have done is in direct violation to everything the crew of this ship stands for. The codes of conduct manual have very strict guidelines relating to behaviour such as you displayed earlier."
“Look I was only having a joke with him, nothing serious.” defended the dog

"Section eight, paragraph two of the manual quite clearly states that deliberate derision of amusement at another individual expense, causing that individual stress, embarrassment and/or unnecessary related consequences, will not be tolerated. The punishment for such actions could result in the instigator being exiled from the ship on to the nearest inhabitable planet. Now, do you understand the severity of your situation?" Jill stood before Rambo with her hands on her hips.
"No, you used too many big words that I didn't understand." Rambo stretched his neck forward and tried to sniff Jill's genital area. Jill quickly stepped out of reach.
"You're disgusting." she snarled venomously, as she returned to her seat at the other side of the table. "I can't believe that I'm wasting my time trying to communicate with you, you're nothing but a poor excuse of unnecessary evolution, a pathetic and insignificant species that doesn't deserve to share the benefits that civilised society can offer. You're a parasitic creature living on the handouts of other better and more deserving species, which out of kindness and pity allow your kind to live amongst them. Personally, I despise you and if it was up to me, I would have you thrown off the ship at the earliest available opportunity." Jill practically spat each word out, accentuating every one with numerous and varied hand movements. Rambo had sat and listened to Jill's personal tirade on his character in silence, unblinking and unmoved by the onslaught. He sat in silence for a few seconds longer.
"Have you finished?" he asked calmly and deliberately

“I have nothing further to say to you!” puffed Jill with an air of finality. With surprisingly rapid movements Rambo pounced from the couch and on to the desk in front of Jill, placing himself in a position which prevented her from pressing any type of alarm button without him being able to stop her.
“Right, in that case you can shut up and listen to me you pompous bit of fluff” growled Rambo only inches from her face, “I have spent my entire life living with somebody who has had little if nothing to say to me. I have not had any kind of education or lessons in social behaviour, I have had scant experience with the world outside the house in which I lived. Until the day before yesterday I had never in my life held a conversation with anyone, the majority of words I have heard in that short time were unknown. I am trying my best to cope with and understand many things that are said to me. I only live on the kindness of others because I have never been taught to fend for myself, also I didn't choose to live the way I do, the choice was made for me, and since then I have been little more than a prisoner forced to make do and accept the life I have. As for being a poor excuse of evolution may I remind you that long ago my ancestors were fierce, yet proud hunters who survived on their wits and intelligence. The way I look today is not the way we would have naturally evolved, but again the forced product of a stronger more dominant species that took away our proud heritage, for no other purpose than that it suited them. Perhaps if I had belonged to a privileged race like yours then maybe I would be a better animal than I am today, but I haven't had your chances, your education, your civilised society to hide behind, your

good fortune to be a dominant species, your freedom to grow and learn, your ability to explore more than the places that you are imprisoned. Yes, I may be insignificant to your standards, but that is not my choosing, yes I may seem parasitic, but it's the only way I know how to survive. Do you really think that given the choice I would opt for the life that I am leading?" Jill shook her head quickly, Rambo's snarling jaws were dangerously close to her face, her body was slick with sweat, and never before had she felt so belittled and afraid. For years she had worked with species which she classed below herself and never before had she felt any need to understand the personal histories of any of her subjects. Yet now, here in her office she was faced with, what until a few moments ago, she had regarded as a stupid and worthless creature, not only was what Rambo saying making her reevaluate her opinion of him, but also for the first time in her life did she realise just how lucky she has been in the stakes of life.

"And another thing," said Rambo, "Nobby has practically held me prisoner for the past few years, so I can't see any harm in him having a bit of the same, ok!" Jill nodded agreement, she could see his point.

"Good, we'll say no more about it then!" At this Rambo hopped down from the desk and headed back to his room. Jill sat silently as Rambo walked casually from her office, she no longer saw him as a flea bitten bag of fur, to her eyes he had suddenly become a tortured individual who needed help. In her mind, she swore to give him all the help he needed.

CHAPTER EIGHT

Nobby sat patiently waiting for the questioning to begin; he and Bill arrived in the conference room a short while ago. The room consisted of little more than a long table capable of seating twenty individuals, but only eight of the seats were occupied when they both arrived. The council, as Bill had called them, sat at one side of the table, he and Bill seated themselves opposite to them. The council was made up entirely of Dolphoids, Bill had explained to him on their way there that the members of the council were all scientists of different aspects of research. Biologists, zoologists, archaeologists, anthropologists and even a psychologist. Nobby had been sat facing them for ten minutes or so and as yet none of them had spoken to him, although they were whispering and exchanging notes between themselves. He looked at Bill with questioning eyes; Bill nodded slightly and gestured with his hand for Nobby to remain patient just a while longer. Nobby sighed and relaxed back into his chair, he took the opportunity to study the council members. Although each were dressed in identical uniforms, they differed significantly in appearance. The Dolphoid to the left of the group as Nobby looked at them was obviously very old; his hair was quite sparse and silvery white, his complexion pale and wrinkled. Next to him sat a Dolphoid whose skin colour was very much darker than that of Bill or any of the other council members, Nobby wondered if like Humans, the Dolphoid species also contained various

coloured races, he would have to ask Bill later. The next two looked almost identical to Bill, except for minor facial features. The Dolphoid that was sat directly opposite Nobby was what can only be described as being extremely fat, his face was not sleek or tapered like the other Dolphoids, but bloated and round. He mopped his sweaty brow with his chubby fingers; his uniform seemed to be stretched to its limit.
In comparison, his neighbour was painfully thin, more weasel like than Dolphoid, his eyes were nothing more than narrow slits that seemed to be scrutinising and holding in suspicion everything they saw. The next council member came as the biggest surprise to Nobby; this Dolphoid quite obviously had a large pair of breasts encased beneath its uniform. This was the first female Dolphoid that Nobby had encountered since arriving; in fact, the thought of female Dolphoids hadn't occurred to him. He found that his gaze kept returning to her involuntary, not that he found her attractive or anything, her being an alien and all that, but she did have a huge set of knockers.
The last member was again similar to Bill apart from obvious features around the face.

Nobby had returned his attention back to the silver clad fleshy love mounds that were the female's mammary glands when the fat Dolphoid spoke.
"Firstly," he said, "I would like to welcome you aboard and thank you for agreeing to answer our questions."
Nobby tore his eyes away from the female's boobs when he realised that the question was aimed at him,

"What, oh! yes, er, no problem" He stuttered, blushing slightly.
"And I trust you have had a pleasant stay" Asked the fat Dolphoid, Bill shot a glance at Nobby.
"Yes, thank you, I have" replied Nobby with a smile, Bill let out a silent sigh of relief.
"Good," said fatty, " Allow me to introduce the council to you, to my far right is Dick," he indicated the old one, "next to him is Mick" the coloured one, "and then Nick and Vic," the two plain ones, "I am Andy, this is Randy," he pointed to the thin one beside him, "further along is Mandy," the female one, "and last but not least Rasputin."
Nobby almost laughed out loud as the last Dolphoid was introduced. He struggled desperately to suppress a giggle and would have failed if Bill hadn't kicked him below the table.
"As you may have guessed these are not our real names," said Andy "but as my colleague, er, Bill here will have no doubt explained our real names would be unpronounceable to you. If you have any difficulty with any of the names we have chosen, please feel at liberty to say so, we would like to make things as uncomplicated as possible."
"No, the names are fine, and I appreciate the efforts that you have made on my behalf," replied Nobby as diplomatically as possible. At this, the council members all nodded and uttered some form of gratitude in Nobby's direction.
"Thank you, I presume Bill has explained the nature of this meeting to you?" asked Andy.

"Yes, he has, and may I just say that Bill has gone far out of his way to make my stay here so far as easy and comfortable as possible." Bill squirmed in his seat at Nobby's praise.
"I am very glad to hear it, and I will personally make a note of it in the ships records. Now if we may carry on with the meeting, if everyone is ready?" the rest of the council members nodded, Andy looked at Nobby, Nobby nodded.
"Right then, we will be asking you a series of questions; some may seem mundane and irrelevant but as far as we are concerned each one is significant. If there are any questions to which you do not know the answer just say so and we shall move on. If at any time you wish to answer no further questions and leave the room, please feel free to, you are under no obligation, and no pressure will be exerted to make you feel that you need do otherwise. Do you have anything to ask in relation to these conditions before we begin?"
"No, that's fine." said Nobby.
"What is the name of your Planet?" asked weasel face
"er..Earth, I thought you knew that." answered Nobby
"Yes, we do, please just answer the questions; there is a method to the questions we ask. Who owns your planet?" weasel again
"Er, nobody actually owns it as far as I know although judging by the internet you would be forgiven for thinking it was a coalition between teenaged boys who swear to have had your mother and kittens falling over."
"So the planet belongs to no one?" asked Vic ignoring most of what Nobby said

"Well, I'm not sure, but the meek are set to inherit it, so I suppose it will belong to them one day, probably," said Nobby
"If no one owns it now, who is going to give it to the meek?" Weasel asked, eyeing Nobby dubiously.
"I honestly don't know, it just says so in the Bible."
"The Bible?" asked the old boy
"Er, basically it is a small book that vicars threaten you with when they can't think of anything else to say."
"I see, and do these vicars have some sort of authority over how the ownership of your planet is divided or appointed?" Mandy with her voluptuous appendages asked,
"er, no not really, they're just religious men that wear dresses and hang around choir boys, according to the Sunday papers!" There was a murmur of discussion among the council members.
"Let me get this straight," said Andy "the people who have the power to grant possession of the planet are some sort of transvestites with a penchant for paedophilia?"
"Well not precisely, vicars are not transvestites, well maybe some are, I don't really know any personally, it's just that the robes of office that are their uniforms look indeed like dresses, as for the liking of children all I can say is that many over the years have been found guilty of such things, although I wouldn't think it was part of their job description. I also doubt that they have the power to grant the Earth to anyone. They are more likely to try and sell you a place in heaven, that's the whole purpose of religion."
"What is the purpose of religion?" asked Mick

"Again, I can't be 100% sure; there are so many different types, although I believe that the aim of each one is similar. Convince yourself you are being nice whilst actually being a bit of a twat really. Many quite terrible things have been done in the name of different religions."
"Who is responsible for the regulation of these religions?" the dark Dolphoid asked
"God I suppose, although I don't think he shows up at any meeting they have, more a sort of silent partner."
"Do you believe in the existence of God?" Mandy again
"Erm, well that's a difficult one to answer," replied Nobby
"Why?" asked weasel
"Um, well the thing is I don't know if God really exists, but there again I can't prove one way or the other that he doesn't exist either, but even if he did, I doubt he wants to be seen, not as a person anyway. He's sort of everywhere at once and nowhere to be seen at the same time if you see what I mean!"
"No," said weasel, "If this god isn't around who controls religion?"
"It all depends on which religion you believe in. In my country there are.."
"What is your country?" questioned Rasputin
"It's called England, or Great Britain or the United Kingdom depending on where you live and how you view yourself really."
"Carry on," Rasputin said
"In my country, there are many different religions, but the two main ones are Catholicism and Protestantism, now don't ask me what differentiates them because I

don't know. If you are a Catholic your leader, as such, is the Pope, if you are a Protestant, then your leader would be the Queen."
"What is the pope?" the old one wheezed.
"He's an old man from Buenos Aires called Jorge, who changed his name to Francis and moved to Italy to sit on a gold chair and wear a frock."
"Really?" Vic asked
"Yes, but they do things strangely in other countries," said Nobby
"Your country is ruled by another country?" Weasel said
"No, my country is ruled by the Queen, the Argentinian bloke just over sees some of the morality."
"Does this Queen own your country?" queried Mandy
"I think she would like to, but no. Although she does own a lot of it."
"So, this Queen only rules the country?" asked Andy
"Not really, that's the government's job; they make the decisions."
"Do they own the Queen?" weasel features asked
"No, they work for the Queen."
"The Queen gave them the task of running the country?" Rasputin said
"No, we did" replied Nobby simply
"We? Who are we?" Mick chipped in
"The citizens of England."
"So, you are a citizen?" old boy asked
"Yes, er, well no. Or rather yes and no!"
"Surely it has to be one or the other." pointed out Andy
"I wish it was that simple." sighed Nobby.
"Why?" weasel asked sharply

"Well, because we have a Queen, that makes our country a sovereignty and therefore anyone who lives in that country is a royal subject. But at the same time we have a democratically elected government, so we are also citizens, confusing isn't it?" added
Nobby after seeing the puzzled looks on the council's faces.
"Very." said Andy, "So if you gave the government the job of running the country, who gave the Queen her job?"
"No one."
"No one?" blurted Weasel face
"She was destined to become Queen since she was born."
"She was chosen at random as a baby to be the ruler of your country?" said Nick incredulously
"No, she was to become Queen because her father was King."
"What is a King?" asked Rasputin
"Same as a Queen, only male."
"So, who or what made him the King?" the old Dolphoid asked
"His brother I think."
"How?" said Mandy, Nobby was forcing his eyes not to wander to her chest as he answered.
"Well, his brother was King first, but he fancied this American slapper, so he went to live with her instead, and in his spare time he sold state secrets to the Nazi's or something like that. Anyway, the Queens dad then had to become King, see!"
"No.," said Dick, the oldie, "Who gives permission for them to be King or Queen?"

"Themselves, you see when one dies the next relative steps forward and the arch bishop of Canterbury plonks a crown on their head and Bobs your uncle, a new King or Queen!"
"So, the arch bishop of Canterbury makes them King or Queen?" asked Nick.
"No, not really. They're already King or Queen; it's just his job to make it official."
"So, who employs the arch bishop of Canterbury?" Mandy asked
"The church."
"Who owns the church?" asked weasel face
"The Queen."
"How strange!" exclaimed Andy
"Exactly," replied Nobby. "I live there, and I don't understand it?"
"Let me get this straight," Andy said slowly, looking at his notes for guidance, "The
Queen, who is the leader of the church in your country, employs the person whose job it is to make her Queen in the first place."
"More or less, yes!" replied Nobby
"So that would imply the arch bishop of Canterbury is effectively employed to make his boss the Queen otherwise she could simply sack him and find a replacement who will do the job." queried weasel face.
"Never thought of it that way, but yeah that about sums it up!" stated Nobby with a shrug of his shoulders.
"Well I'm sorry, but this is totally unbelievable." ranted weasel face, "I have studied well over three hundred civilised and structured societies on numerous alien planets, and as yet I have never heard anything so

preposterous in my entire life. Are you sure this is correct or are you not just making this up?"
"Oh shut up." bellowed Andy, before Nobby had a chance to protest, "Every time you come to a council meeting all you ever do is moan and whine on about how everyone we interview is telling lies!"
"No I don't." said weasel features defensively
"Yes, you do." Mick intervened, "You nearly started a full scale interstellar war when you told the Grand Chief of the Yanork warriors that you thought he was nothing more than a common imbecile sent by the Yanork government to try a lull us into a false sense of security."
"I did not," grunted weasel, "I merely stated that I found it hard to believe that a two foot tall, one legged midget was the most fearsome and highly respected warrior chieftain on the Yanork's planet that is all."
"No you didn't." said Dick, with a heavy wheeze, "you called him, and I quote from the records, A lying little bastard who was obviously too stupid to be anything more than a village idiot'"
"Well nothing came of the incident!" protested weasel face
"Only because we had the good sense to erase any memory of the meeting from his mind as he transferred back down to his planet." pointed out Andy.
"So I make one mistake and all of a sudden everyone turns on me?" said weasel slamming his fist on the desk top.
"One! I can name quite a few." answered Andy, "how about the time we were in negotiations with the prime minister of the Murlugian planetary system and you told him that it was inconceivable that anything so hideously

blubber like and mentally backwards could hold a single thought, never mind a position of office. We were lucky to get out of that one."
"So, what exactly are you trying to say?" demanded Weasel face
"That you are an irritating pain in the arse who has caused this council nothing but problems since you wormed your way into it!" roared Andy only inches away from his neighbour's face. Weasel face was stunned into silence by his colleague's outburst. Bill took this opportunity to make a suggestion to the council.
"Gentlemen!" he said loudly over the growing hubbub, "And lady," he added bowing ever so slightly in Mandy's direction. "Perhaps it would be best if we continued this meeting at some other time. I'm sure our guest here has no desire to get involved in personal council er, business."
"Yes," said Andy eyeing Randy with evil contempt. “Perhaps that would be a good idea." At this Bill escorted Nobby out of the conference room and into the adjoining corridor. No sooner had the door closed behind them did Bill burst into gales of laughter, Nobby stood and stared at his friend, tears of merriment rolled down the Dolphoids face. Bill leant against the nearest wall and tried to regain his composure, taking in great lung full of breath between whoops of laughter. His face was starting to turn an alarming purple hue, Nobby stepped forwards and patted him roughly on the back. Bill gestured for Nobby to stop with a wave of his hand; his laughter was beginning to subside to mere giggles, accentuated with sharp intakes of breath. Nobby decided

to wait it out and leaned against the wall opposite Bill, who by now was wiping the tears from his eyes and blowing his nose on a hanky,
"Sorry about that," said Bill straightening himself up and smoothing his hair back.
"Care to share the joke?" asked Nobby
"Yes, but I'm afraid you may not understand."
"Try me, you could be surprised." returned Nobby
"Okay, I'll tell you about it as we walk back to dining hall, I'm starving," said Bill,
Nobby nodded and fell in beside Bill as they walked.
"Several years ago before this ship had been built, there was a sister ship in service called the Searcher, Its mission was exactly the same as this one, to find new planets and study the inhabitants. Only the Searcher was out in space for two years, and in that time it had failed to make the slightest study of any of the planets it had come across."
"Why's that?" asked Nobby
"It was all down to the chief of security aboard the Searcher." recounted Bill, "He was, let's say, a bit over cautious. Every time the captain of the Searcher tried to stop and orbit a planet for observations, the security chief over rode the order stating that to do so would seriously compromise the safety of the ship and crew."
"Can the security chief do that, I mean cancel the captain's orders?" asked Nobby.
"Oh yes," replied Bill nodding his head, "he has the power to counter command any order if he believes that there is an immediate danger to the lives of the crew, in fact, the captain of the Searcher gave the order to observe various planets on one hundred and six separate

occasions. The security chief cancelled every single one."
"Blimey, that's a bit drastic."
"That is exactly what the government thought when the Searcher returned after two years without a single piece of new data. The security chief was duly dismissed from his post despite his plea that anything that is alien, is potentially a danger to the integrity of the safety of the ship."
"Okay," said Nobby, "that's a nice story, but it doesn't explain the reason for your sudden outburst of hilarity."
"Ah well, the funny part is still to come. The head of the Searcher's science and research team was posted to this ship to carry out the work he had been unable to do on the previous mission. At the same time the ex-security chief, by way of punishment, was also transferred aboard the Traveller, as the head of Research's assistant. Now as you can probably imagine they don't get along very well, and just to show his new assistant that he bears no grudges about wasting two years in space, he insists that the ex-security chief meets and actively gets involved with every alien race that is brought aboard." explained Bill. Suddenly the penny dropped for Nobby; he stopped in his tracks.
"You're talking about fatty and weasel feat.., er, I mean Andy and Randy aren't you?" Bill smiled at Nobby's astute, if not somewhat derogatory, description of his two colleagues.
"Correct, Andy was the head of research on the Searcher and Randy was the security chief, and just to make things a little more uneasy between them, Randy

somehow managed to get himself voted onto the committee of the research council."
"How?" asked Nobby.
"I'm not really sure, but he can be quite persuasive. He probably talked the others into voting him on to the council. Whatever the reason since he's been on the council he has tried, in vain, to prevent any contact with alien races."
"I wonder why?" mused Nobby.
"I don't know," said Bill, "but I do know one thing for certain.."
"What's that?"
"I'm hungry, fancy something to eat?" smiled Bill
"Sounds good to me." replied Nobby, "as long as it's not that purple goo!" he added.
"You have no taste for the finer things in life." joked Bill
"Lucky me."

"Sorry about earlier." said Andy, "I hope it hasn't changed your mind about answering our questions?"
Nobby and Bill had returned to the conference room after they had eaten. Nobby hadn't been at all surprised to find that weasel features was no longer present. At the same time, he was glad to see that Mandy and her pendulous paps were still there.
"No problem," said Nobby, "I have no objections to carrying on."
"Splendid, splendid," puffed Andy rubbing his sweaty palms together. "There is just one or two things that we would like to clarify from earlier if that's alright?"
"Sure, I will try my best to help." charmed Nobby under Mandy's watchful gaze.

"Okay, you mentioned a book called the er, bible, which you claimed stated that the ownership of the planet would eventually be handed to a particular group of people, the er, Meeks. Now I don't wish to cast aspersions on the validity of your answers, but we can find no mention of a race of people on your planet called the Meeks. We have found references to a race of people known as the Greeks and also a variety of vegetation named Leeks. Is it possible that you either misheard or confused the name of one of these as the Meeks?" asked Andy diplomatically, not wanting his words to be misconstrued as an accusation.
"Well for a start there is, as far as I know, no race called the Meeks on the Earth," Nobby noticed a few raised eyebrows at this, including Bills. "The meek that the Bible refers to are not a specific race of people. They could be any one, to be meek means to be mild mannered, peaceful and kind to others. I think what the Bible is trying to say is that when the time comes, only these kind of people, will be looked upon with favour in the eyes of God."
"I see, so what the Bible is telling its readers is be good or else!" said Andy
"Well, yes I suppose so, that is the basic message of all religions," answered Nobby.
"In that case," said Mandy, "why is the history of your planet littered with wars which were supposedly in the name of religion, if religion is meant to be about being nice to each other?"
"Excellent point," Gushed Nobby, "I only wish I knew the answer. The basis of religion is indeed to live in peace with your fellow man, but at the same time, there

are so many different religions. Each religion has its own set of beliefs, its own way of doing things. Unfortunately, each individual religion believes that theirs is the only right one, henceforth many arguments, and wars, have been fought between two different religions trying to prove that they are right and everyone else is wrong. Somehow the true point of religion seems to get swept under the carpet."

"So, who is right?" asked Dick the old Dolphoid.

"Nobody knows, that's why they fight. If there was an answer and one, in particular, was found to be the true religion, the others would probably dispute it and fight over it anyway."

"So, what you are actually saying is that there is no proof to substantiate any religion at all?" asked Vic

"Not as far as I know, although each faith has its own kind of bible, and each one says different things, But at the same time each religion claims that their bible is the true words of God. So either there are numerous different Gods all writing their own best seller bibles, or somebody a long, long time ago made them up just for a laugh with his mates, they probably got drunk one day and had a competition to see who could come up with the most outrageous religion or something. But whatever the reason, the fact is no one can prove it."

"Well that clears that point up, I think!" said Andy, "the other thing was about this

Queen that you have, when we searched our data files, we came up with a rather strange piece of information. The computer said that a Queen is a man that dresses like a woman and tends to have er, homosexual tendencies. The thing is, earlier you mentioned something about your Queen being the leader of one particular religion, and you also mentioned that with in that religion were men who wore dresses and harboured secret desires for choir boys, I believe you called them vicars. We were wondering if by any chance that the two meanings of the word Queen are somehow related because of this religious connection?" Andy asked. Nobby stifled a laugh and was forced to bite the inside of his cheeks to prevent him from grinning.

"Well," began Nobby after a moment, "I've never thought of it like that, it could be, but I very much doubt it. Anyway, all vicars don't lust over young boys; it is just that some of the more unsavoury of tabloids would like you to think that. Many vicars are happily married men who are strictly heterosexual."

"I see," noted Andy, "so your Queen is not a man in a dress?"

"Well I've never personally seen her in the nude, but she has given birth to four children, so I very much doubt it." replied Nobby.

"Thank you, does anyone else have any questions regarding our earlier session?" asked Andy to the rest of the council. The members shook their heads. "Good, then let us resume the questioning."

"Do you consider yourself a superior species in relation to the other creatures that share your planet?" asked Mick without looking up.

"Er, I've never really thought about it, I suppose that as Humans we are more technologically advanced than other species. But at the same time many other creatures are better developed for the way they live than we are."

"In what way?" asked Mandy

"Well for example if you were to strip us of our technology and place us on a desert island to fend for ourselves, we would most likely not fair very well. But do the same to, say, a dog, it would probably manage a lot better, in fact, I suppose the same would apply to the majority of animals. So in truth, I don't really think I'm more superior to any other species in that respect."
"Is it not true that you keep a dog as a pet?" Mick said
"Er, yes," admitted Nobby.
"Doesn't keeping an animal for your own amusement signify your superiority over it?" said Mick again coldly
"Ah, well that is different altogether." defended Nobby.
"Why is it?" joined in Rasputin.
"Er, well firstly, Rambo, that's my dog's name, was an unwanted puppy. The person who owns his mother couldn't afford to keep him, and if they couldn't find him a home, they were going to put him in a sack, along with all the other puppies, and throw them in the canal."
"That's terrible!" said Mandy, obviously shocked.
"Exactly, and that is why I rescued Rambo from this gruesome fate and gave him a home. If it wasn't for me he would have been dead years ago," said Nobby playing the good Samaritan for all he was worth.
"Is it not true that you keep him imprisoned in your home, depriving him of his freedom?" Mick said with an air of distaste.
"Well, yes" started Nobby, one or two of the council members tutted, "But not because I'm cruel or twisted and enjoy locking innocent animals up. The truth is that where I come from thousands of dogs, like Rambo, go missing or end up dead as a result of their owners allowing them to roam freely."

"Why?" asked Dick
"Unfortunately, the world I live in is not always a kind place, some people enjoy seeing dogs fight each other and will often cruise the streets looking for stray animals, which they can take and use. The fate for these helpless strays is to end up in a makeshift arena fighting for their lives against larger and highly trained specially bred fighting dogs. As you can imagine this would be a horrible way to die. Another reason that many dogs meet their end is by being run over on busy roads. It is extremely difficult to teach a dog how to cross roads safely, as they don't always recognise the danger. Many thousands, maybe even millions of dogs are killed this way each year. So yes, I do keep Rambo locked in my house, but not because I hate him, because I care about him and I don't wish to see him dead."
"So, are you implying that you keep your dog for totally unselfish reasons?" asked Vic.
"Not entirely, no," replied Nobby honestly. "I have always led a lonely life, and I saw Rambo as a companion, something to break the tedium of everyday life. I have fed him, housed him, cared for him in any way I was able and all I wanted in return was company."
"Do you believe that Rambo benefits from living with you?" asked Mandy leaning forwards causing her breast to rest on the table top. Nobby's heart skipped a beat at the sight.
"Er, well I'm not really sure, all I can say is that I try my best. It may not be the perfect life for him, but he is fed regularly, has a warm place to sleep, regular visits to the vets to make sure he is healthy, and if I go anywhere, I always endeavour to take him with me. As I said it may

not be a perfect life but it is a life, which is more than he would have had without me."
"Who is the most powerful person on your planet?" Andy asked, the sudden change of questioning threw Nobby for a moment.
"Eh, what?" he mumbled
"Who is the most powerful person on your planet?" repeated Andy.
"Oh, er, powerful in what way. Are we talking powerful as in physical strength, or powerful as in who has the most technology and resources?" asked Nobby.
"The latter please." clarified Andy.
"Well, in that case, I would probably think that the President of the U.S.A was the most powerful, but that's just my opinion," Nobby said
"What is a U.S.A?" asked Dick
"It's the United States of America, which is a large country on Earth, just before you ask." replied Nobby with a smile, each member of the Council flinched visibly.
"Thank you," said Andy who was still slightly shaken at Nobby's smile. Bill who was sat to Nobby's left covered his mouth with his hand to hide a smirk caused by the council's reaction to his friend's smile.
"What is a President?" asked Rasputin, a minute tremor was audible in his voice, Bill coughed loudly to stifle a laugh, all eyes turned to him as he coughed several times more to stop himself giggling.
"Are you alright Bill? do you want me to call for a medic?" asked Andy with some concern after seeing Bills strained and slightly purple face.

"No, no" spluttered Bill, " Just, ahem, something caught in my throat, I'll be fine in a second, sorry."
Nobby regarded Bill suspiciously; he had caught sight of the broad grin Bill was trying to hide.
"Are you sure?" asked Andy.
"Yes, absolutely, I'm fine. Please carry on," replied Bill forcing a straight face.
"What is a President?" repeated Rasputin quickly. Nobby returned his attention back to the council members.
"A President is the ruler of a country."
"I thought a Queen was a ruler of a country?" Questioned Mick
"It all depends on which country you are in. Some countries call their rulers Queens or kings, some call them Presidents or Prime ministers, some countries use titles like
Emperor, Shah or Chief, but they more or less amount to the same thing."
"So, this President of the U.S.A is Earths most powerful person?" asked Nick
"Well, he is one of them. Each countries leader pretends to be more powerful than the next, but I think the President has the edge on them all."
"Who else is powerful?" Asked Mick
"I'm not totally sure anymore. At one time the Russians were quite powerful, but I think that they have fallen back in the power stakes."
"Are these Russians from another one of your planets countries?" Dick asked.
Nobby nodded agreement.
"How many countries does your planet have?" asked Mandy.

"Hundreds, and before you ask no I can't name them all," Nobby said
"What do you know of the history of your planet?" questioned Vic.
"Only what I can remember from school, which isn't a great deal."
"Perhaps you can tell us what you remember?" said Andy
"Right, which part of history are you particularly interested in?" asked Nobby.
"All of it." replied Mick.
"What!, all of it, as in from the beginning of time, Dinosaurs and all that?" remarked Nobby hoping that he had misheard the question.
"Yes, all of it," repeated Mick. Nobby looked at the other council members who were nodding in agreement.
"Shit." He said with a sigh, "That will take ages."
"We have plenty of time that is unless you have anything more important to do," said Mick in a sadistic manner.
"No, not really," said Nobby in despair.
"Good, please begin when you are ready." prompted Mick. With a deep sigh, Nobby made himself comfortable in his chair and began.

Three and a half hours later Nobby finally finished giving his history lecture to a group of aliens that probably knew more about it than he did. He had covered everything he could remember from the dinosaurs to the present day. He endeavoured to describe the great civilisations of the past, the Romans, the

Greeks, the Egyptians and the Incas. He told of the mighty wars that the world had endured, the Mongol tirades, the Napoleonic wars, the first and second world wars. He touched on the subject of the great explorers, Amundsen, Scott, Livingstone, Columbus, Gagarin. He delved into the pioneering scientists, Pasteur, Curie, Newton, Copernicus, Galileo. He covered them all, politics, religion, races, cultures and people, all with an accuracy level which he felt was at least 50% correct . Nobby sat back in his chair while the council members talked quietly amongst themselves, making notes as they did. They had remained on the whole quiet during Nobby's oration, only interrupting on a couple of occasions to have certain things clarified. Nobby felt relieved that it was over for now, but at the same time, he felt a kind of warm glow all over his body, a type of proud satisfaction that comes with the knowledge of a job well done. To be honest, he was surprised to find out that he actually knew so much, he would have been even more surprised to find that actually his 50% self-assessed accuracy level was a tad of and in fact 70% of what he had said was wholly inaccurate and bore little resemblance to the truth.

"Perhaps we should end the meeting here." suggested Andy, "We certainly seem to have plenty of data to keep us busy for a day or two, wouldn't you say?" the other council members nodded agreement. Andy went on "Good, good. Thank you for your time Nobby, you have been of great assistance to us, would it be imposing too much to ask if you could rejoin us again at a later date for further talks?"

"Not at all." said Nobby, "It would be a pleasure," he added
"Good, good. Well till we meet again may I extend the hospitality of the ship and hope that your stay is a pleasant one." Andy stood and extended his hand to Nobby,
Nobby stood and took the offered hand and shook it vigorously. Before he had the chance to sit back down each member of the council had stood and were waiting in line to shake his hand. Nobby took them one at a time, shaking each one as vigorously as the last, except for Mandy's, which he shook gently; just enough to make her breasts wobble without being obscene.

Finally, the council filed out of the room leaving Nobby and Bill alone.
"There that wasn't so bad was it?" asked Bill
"Well, not as bad as I thought it would be."
"I'm proud of you, you did very well." praised Bill while patting Nobby gently on the back.
"There's just one thing that bothers me though, Bill." said Nobby turning in his chair to face the Dolphoid.
"Oh yes, and what is that?" queried Bill
"Why were the council so interested in who actually owned the Earth?" a worried frown played across Nobby's brow, the questions had bothered him from the beginning, but he had decided not to raise the issue with the council, he had waited patiently to ask someone he trusted like Bill.
"Ah, well, the reasons for trying to establish the owner ship of the Earth is not a sinister one, I assure you. It's

due more to diplomatic matters than anything else. In the past we have made contact with the leaders of some of the planets we have studied, asking permission to land and carry out further studies. Maybe even establish trade links or cultural exchanges with their scientists, swopping information and that kind of thing. Only on one particular planet, we had begun diplomatic relations with the world's leader, and a formal landing party had been invited down for initial contact meetings. Now everything was going smoothly, and a cross world data exchange system was being put into operation, when all of a sudden from nowhere thousands and thousands of war ships appeared in orbit, completely surrounding our vessel and the planet. We were given very strict orders via a radio message that stated that the planet on which we were trespassing belonged to some great Emperor from some far off distant planet and we had ten minutes to recall our men and leave, or else they would open fire. They were also kind enough to transmit a list of nearly two thousand other planets that belong to the Emperor and which we were forbidden to contact. So since then, we have always tried to establish the ownership of planets before we attempt any formal contact."
"Christ, I'm not surprised. I bet you felt like kicking that planets leader for not mentioning it and putting you in danger like that," said Nobby
"Not really, the truth is, the leader that we made contact with was totally unaware of his planet being owned by someone else, and he had personally never heard of the Emperor who claimed it was his!"
"Eh, how come?" Nobby asked.

"Well apparently this so called Emperor, who comes from a large technologically advanced planet, just decided one day that all these smaller under developed planets, which were no match for his huge powerful armies, were part of his empire. Although he never got round to mentioning it to the inhabitants of the newly acquired editions to his empire that they belonged to him. Until we arrived the planets occupants were unaware that they belonged to some intergalactic empire, and believe me Nobby, they were more surprised at the news than we were." recounted Bill.
"I don't think I'll ever really understand the complexities of space, but it sounds one hell of a crazy place." said Nobby ending the sentence with a yawn.
"Tired?" asked Bill
"That's funny, so am I." Joked Nobby, "It's been a long day."
"Undoubtedly," replied Bill rising from his seat "Come on, I will walk you back to your quarters."
"Cheers," said Nobby, he got up and followed Bill into the corridor. They walked together in silence down the mostly deserted passageways until they reached the lift which took them down to Nobby's floor. They entered the lift and the doors closed silently behind them.
"Deck four," said Bill to the lifts control panel. The lift began its smooth descent.
"How are you finding your quarters, comfortable enough?"
"Fine, very nice indeed, er, only I was wondering, er, if it is possible to have a television that is if it's no trouble." stammered Nobby bashfully.
"Television." repeated Bill, "I don't think we have any."

"Oh, right." said Nobby despondently "It doesn't matter."
"But," added Bill, "If you tell the computer in your room that you wish to monitor Earths television broadcasts, it will display the images on its screen. Will that suffice?"
"Spot on, cheers." said a much happier Nobby. The lift doors opened, and they both stepped out into the corridor that had caused Nobby so many problems earlier. They turned left and walked a further fifty yards until they reached Nobby room.
"Here we are then." said Bill.
"Thank you; I'm sure I would get lost in these bloody corridors. How do you tell them apart?"
"I don't know, I just do!" answered Bill honestly,
"Anyway, I have work to do so I will leave you in peace to watch television."
"Right then, er, have we got anything planned for tomorrow?" asked Nobby
"No, nothing, you are free to do as you like. Ask the computer and it will tell you everything that you need to know about the ship and location of the on board amenities. If you need to contact me just ask the computer." Bill explained. "Oh, right, okay. Er, just one more thing, Bill."
"Yes!" asked Bill.
"Where is the computer in my room?" Nobby asked sheepishly
"It is to the right of the doorway as you look at it from the inside."
"Thanks, well I'll see you around then." said Nobby placing his hand on the wall to open his door, it opened quickly and silently.

"I may call you tomorrow if the council wishes to see you or not. Otherwise, enjoy your television and have a pleasant night's sleep." Bill turned and began his way back down the corridor.
"Yeah, see you later," Nobby called after him. He watched Bill down the corridor and into the lift before he entered his quarters. The wall closed up behind him and he turned to look for the computer. He placed his hand on the wall a few feet to the right of the door way, and the computer revealed itself as the wall around it disappeared. He sat on his bed and stared at its blank screen; nothing was happening.
Bill had said to ask the computer, so Nobby asked.
"Computer, I wish to monitor Earths television broadcasts," he said to the blank screen. Moments later the screen began to glow an eerie green.
"Please state from which country you would prefer the broadcast to come" intoned the computer.
"Oh, er England." said Nobby, "or America." he added as an afterthought.
"There are currently three hundred and sixteen channels at your disposal." said the computer. A small rectangular hole appeared below the screen. "Please take the handset provided; it will allow you to change between channels at your leisure."
"Oh cheers," replied Nobby getting off the bed to retrieve the offered handset.
"Will there be anything else?" the computer asked.
"Er, no, I don't think so." answered Nobby sitting back down on the bed.
"In that case, I will bid you good night. Please don't hesitate to call if you need my

assistance." at that the voice of the computer ceased.
Nobby began flicking through the channels quickly, seeing what was on offer, suddenly he stopped and went back a channel or two.
"Ace, Baywatch !" he said gleefully as he began to undo his boiler suit.

CHAPTER NINE

The council met again the following day, Dick, Mick, Nick, Vic, Andy, Mandy and Rasputin sat in the same places they had occupied the previous day. Randy's seat was empty. Across the table from the council, sat in the seats that had been used Nobby and Bill, were Rambo and Jill. Rambo was wearing a silver jacket in the same material as everyone else's uniforms, he didn't want to wear it, but Jill had said that it was ships policy and that the council would not be very pleased if he were to show up naked, so to speak. So reluctantly he had allowed Jill to dress him in the ridiculous looking thing. Hc wasn't used to wearing anything and the jacket was making him hot and sweaty, he was fighting a losing battle against the urge to scratch himself vigorously. He and Jill had been sat there around fifteen minutes, and as yet no one had spoken to them, Rambo was in two minds to get up and go back to his room, but a stern look from Jill convinced him to stay.

Finally, Andy cleared his throat and spoke to Rambo, "Firstly I would like to welcome you aboard and thank you for agreeing to answer our questions."

"What questions?" queried Rambo, "Nobody said anything about questions." Jill shot Rambo a stunned glance.

"You mean no one told you why you were brought here?" asked Andy whilst eyeing Jill with obvious displeasure.

"Look," said Rambo "All I know is that I had to come here because you wanted to talk to me and I have to wear this stupid coat because you don't like nudist dogs."
"Er, Jill.." said Andy slowly, "Can you explain to the council as to why our guest here has not been briefed in regards to the nature of this meeting, considering that he has spent the last three days in your care, the purpose of which was to prepare him for this and other meetings!"
Jills eyes worked frantically in their sockets, her temples began to pound furiously, and her mouth had gone dry. In the past three days, she had spent the majority of the time thinking of Rambo as an inferior, worthless life form who didn't deserve any attention. She had spent the time that she should have used to brief him, on trying to show off her superiority towards him. A superiority that this simple creature had shown her was not an inherent right, but a remarkable privilege that could be taken away by other species, whom in turn are more superior. She had wasted the time trying to inflate her own ego at Rambo's expense. She had completely failed in her duties, and there was no way of denying it. The council stared at her from the opposite side of the table, accusations playing in their eyes. She could offer them no explanation that would excuse her actions. She felt her career slipping away from her, and she had no one to blame but herself. She would tell the truth and accept the consequences. Jill steeled herself in her chair and cleared her throat to speak. At that moment Rambo stood up on his chair and placed his fore paws on the table,
"Er, sorry, " said Rambo to the council, "But I don't think Jill is to blame." The council's attention turned to Rambo.

"You don't?" asked Andy after a moment.
"No, I don't." Stated Rambo. Everyone was staring at him now, including Jill who had a puzzled but thankful expression on her face.
"Would you care to elaborate?" asked Andy
"Er, I'm not sure whether I would or not," replied Rambo, there was a slight ripple of hushed conversation amongst the council. Jill continued to look at Rambo in bewilderment.
"Why are you unsure as to whether or not to elaborate?" asked Mick
"Well, for one thing, I have no idea what elaborate means," answered Rambo.
“I see." said Andy, "Let me rephrase the question, would you please explain why you don't think Jill is to blame?"
"Oh right, I think I understand now." said Rambo wagging his tail, "Thing is, in the last couple of days Jill has indeed said quite a lot of things to me, yapped quite lot really, hardly stopped" Jill flinched in her seat, "But thing is, the bulk of what she said I didn't understand."
"Did she not explain things clearly?" asked Mandy
"I don't really know, half of what she said I didn’t understand one way or the other and the rest of the time I wasn’t really listening because I had lost the trail of the conversation."
"Obviously not!" said Mandy looking on Jill scornfully
"Well that is the problem," said Rambo
"What is?" asked Dick the old Dolphoid
"I can't tell if Jill explained things clearly or not." replied Rambo, "using words and a language as a whole is a relatively new experience to me. I have only been exposed to a limited supply of words during my life

time, so many of the words that Jill has spoke to me over the past couple of days held little meaning to me."
"I see," said Andy, "Did Jill not offer to explain the words that you failed to understand?"
"I never asked her. I felt a bit daft, she sounds dead clever and stuff, so I just kept nodding my head as she talked." lied Rambo.
"Did Jill not ask you at any time whether you understood what she was telling you?" asked Mandy
"Yes, quite a few times really, but I didn't want to look stupid, so I always said that I had understood, sorry!" Rambo gave his tail a short wag and lowered his ears as he apologised.
"So, what you are saying is that Jill may well have explained the purpose of this meeting, but unfortunately you didn't understand and were too embarrassed to say so?" asked Mick suspiciously.
"Yes. I am not the cleverest of dogs at best" said Rambo simply
"Is this true Jill?" asked Andy. Jill opened her mouth to answer, she looked at Andy and then back at Rambo. Why had this simple creature gone out of its way to protect her after what she had done? Rambo stared at her with a menacing glint in his eye.
"Yes." she eventually spluttered out, "But I take full responsibility for the situation, I failed to take into account for Rambo's limited scope of understanding and overestimated his grasp on vocabulary, I wrongfully presumed that he understood everything. I wish to apologise to Rambo and the council over any confusion my actions have caused." The council members seemed appeased by Jill's quick acceptance of her failure and

subsequent apology. Andy took note of the rest of the council's reactions,
"Your apology is accepted and duly noted by the council, and no further actions will be taken over the matter. Er, that is if Rambo has no objections of course?" said Andy in an official manner.
"No, I'm ok," Rambo said returning back to his seat.
"Thank you," said Andy, "perhaps we can now continue with this meeting." Rambo nodded agreement. "Good, the purpose of this meeting is for us to ask you some questions about where you come from. If at any time you don't fully understand a question, please don't be afraid to ask, no one here will think any less of you for it. We are all fully aware of the difficulty of learning new words or phrases, so we will try and keep the questions as simple as possible. You are not under any pressure to answer the questions, and you are totally free to leave whenever you wish. Do you understand these conditions?" asked Andy
"Yes, I do," replied Rambo
"Do you really?"
"Oh yes. I mean it this time."
"Good, are you ready?"
"Yes, fire away," Rambo said whilst settling down into the chair.
"Who owns your planet?" asked Rasputin
"What planet?" Rambo asked back
"Er, the Earth," said Rasputin
"Never heard of it," replied Rambo
"You don't know where you live?" asked Mick dubiously
"Of course I know where I live," said Rambo indignantly
"Well, who owns where you live?" asked Rasputin

"Nobby!" said Rambo
"Are you trying to suggest that Nobby owns the Earth?" queried Mick
"Do I live in the Earth?" asked Rambo sheepishly
"Well yes, you live on the Earth." clarified Mandy
"In that case, all I can say is that Nobby owns where I live, so he must own the Earth then." There was much hushed conversation amongst the council members.
"Who is the Queen?" asked Vic when the hubbub had abated.
"I don't know" replied Rambo "who is the Queen?" he added
"Er, the Queen is the ruler of where you are from." enlightened Vic "do you understand what a ruler is?
"yes, it is what Nobby smacks my arse with occasionally when I have supposedly done something wrong, which I haven't, it is all coincidence that the plant pots fell over while I was next to them," said Rambo.
"Er, no, not that sort of ruler. A ruler is another word for someone who makes all the decisions, gives all the orders that you have to follow, someone who tells you what to do and when to do it." Said Vic
"Oh, well, in that case, Nobby is the Queen."
"Do you think Nobby rules the Planet?" asked Dick
"Er, well he rules where I come from, er, Earth I think you said it was called," answered Rambo. More muffled conversations between the council.
"Let us get a few things straight;" said Andy after a minute or two, "You live on the planet Earth, yes?" Rambo nodded in reply, "and Nobby is, as far as you are aware, the owner and ruler there?"
Rambo nodded again.

"Are you sure?" asked Mandy
"I am not sure of anything but I think so, I've never seen anybody else give orders or claim to own where I live. So, as far as I know, Nobby is the ruler and owner of Earth," replied Rambo. Once again the council talked privately among themselves, Rambo and Jill sat in silence waiting for them to finish. After several minutes of discussion, the council members stopped, and Andy cleared his throat,
"Er, due to the information that Rambo has given us, we feel that the meeting should be adjourned until further notice while several facts can be checked. I am sure you understand. Thank you for your assistance and enjoy your stay." Andy had hardly finished speaking as he got up with the rest of the council and left the room.
"What was that all about?" asked Rambo when they had all gone, Jill shrugged her shoulders,
"I have no idea."

The glow of the computer screen was the only illumination in Nobby's room. Columbo was half way through a particularly vexing murder case which involved a deaf chess player who had decided to kill off his greatest rival. Despite Columbo's efforts to add an air of mystery and suspense to his show, they were totally wasted on the likes of Nobby. He was currently asleep on the bed with his boiler suit around his ankles; he had been like this since about half way through Baywatch several hours earlier. In his dreams he was lying on a sun swept Californian beach surrounded by a bevvy of buxom big breasted bronzed beach babes, all vying for his favour. They had rubbed his body sensually with gentle yet probing hands, covering him from head to toe with sun lotion. They had brought him drinks and fed him exotic foods. They had laughed with him as he recounted amusing adages in an Oscar Wilde manner. They had frolicked like playful children at the water's edge as the tide lapped gently around their feet. The sun stayed high in the bright azure sky; filling the sea with a million diamond like sparkles as the waves swelled and ebbed smoothly against the golden sand of the beach. Everything was perfect, or at least it would be if that infernal beeping noise would stop.

Nobby forced open one eye and squinted at the computer screen; it was flashing on and off with an incoming message display which was accompanied by the audible beeping signal. Nobby opened his other eye and sat upright on the bed, he noticed his half-mast boiler suit and pulled it up quickly to hide to splatter marks on his lower abdomen, he made a mental note to have a shower before going anywhere. The computer screen continued to blink and beep,
"Who the hell could it be at this time?" he grumbled to himself, he looked at his watch for the time and realised that he didn't have a watch. "Er, computer display message please." the incoming message display disappeared and was instantly replaced by Bill's fishy face.
"Sorry Nobby, did I wake you?" he asked
"No, no I've been up for seconds. What time is it?" said Nobby rubbing his eyes tiredly.

"Er, ten past two in the afternoon in your time," replied Bill
"As early as that!" said Nobby with mock shock. "I just can't get any peace what so ever."
"Nobby, listen to me, I think there is a problem." interrupted Bill, his face wore a worried frown.
"A problem with what?" asked Nobby, he didn't like the expression on his friends face.
"I'm not sure, but the council have called an emergency meeting, which is not a good sign," said Bill
"What's it about?"
"Again I'm not sure, but they have requested that both you and I attend, so I will be round to collect you in about twenty minutes ok."
"Er, yeah, sure, see you later then," replied Nobby, he hadn't liked the way Bill had emphasised the word requested. The image of Bill vanished from the screen and was instantly replaced with an unflattering close up of Columbo, Which startled Nobby for a moment. He took a deep breath and ordered the computer to discontinue with the broadcasts, the screen fell silent, and Nobby retreated to the bathroom.

Fifteen minutes later he was washed and dressed in clean clothes, he sat on the bed waiting for Bill to arrive. Several thoughts played across his mind, why had the council called an emergency meeting, why had the council requested their company and why had Bill looked so worried. He couldn't find an answer for any of the questions, he would just have to wait and see. He looked at the blank computer screen and toyed with the idea of watching a bit of t.v. until Bill got there. A sudden disturbing thought occurred to him, what if they, the council that is, were monitoring him by means of hidden security cameras. Bill had mentioned that the Security Council had recommended that he be watched closely for a while, and as far as he could remember he hadn't seen Pinky and Perky the burly security guards last night after the meeting when he and Bill had walked back to his room through the mostly deserted corridors. Maybe the Security Council had opted for a more discreet method of observation; lull him into a false sense of security, so to speak. But as far as he was aware he hadn't done anything wrong, he had only watched some telly, and he had asked Bills permission first. Nobby's train of thought came to an abrupt halt, a cold shiver ran the length of his spine.

"Oh my God," he thought to himself, "what if masturbation is considered an abominable affront to the moral integrity of the Dolphoid culture." Nobby began to sweat profusely at the sudden knowledge that someone, perhaps the whole complement of the ship, had probably watched him having a crafty shifty at his Mr. wobbly. That's just what he needed, a member of every intelligent alien race in the galaxy going home and telling their friends and families that the human race are a bunch of wankers. The beeping of the door chime brought him out of his thoughts; he stood up and straightened out his uniform as he walked over to the door. The wall opened at his touch revealing Bill. Nobby was just about to speak when he noticed the presence of the two guards, one stood at either side of the door way.

"What have you brought these two for?" said Nobby indicating the guards. Bill looked briefly at the two security men and then back at Nobby,
"I didn't they were already here when I arrived," Bill turned to the security men to the left of the doorway,
"Why are you here?" The guard stiffen and saluted Bill,
"Sir, we have orders to escort visitor Nobby directly to the conference rooms, sir," he said sharply.
"And who gave you this order?" demanded Bill. The big Dolphoid made a high pitched series of squeaks and then added the word "sir" to the end of it. Bills face looked puzzled for a moment.
"It appears that they were sent by Andy himself and with the full backing of the rest of the council."
"Oh, is that good?" asked Nobby hopefully.
"On the contrary, it's quite a bad sign. Andy doesn't normally give these sort of orders unless it is a matter of ships security, and even then the order has to be sanctioned by the security chief." replied Bill, "So, for some reason, you are being considered as a potential threat or danger to the ship."
"Oh God!" Nobby's complexion suddenly turned very pale. He placed his hand over his mouth and shook his head slowly.
"Are you ok, Nobby. You look as though you've seen a ghost," said Bill stepping forwards and placing his arm supportively around Nobby's shoulder.
"I, I.. I think I know why they want to see me." stuttered Nobby quietly, Bill could feel the trembling of Nobby's body against his own.
"Do you want to talk about it before we go?" asked Bill gently, Nobby nodded. Bill turned him around and

headed back into his quarters. The two security men began to follow, Bill turned on them sharply,
"And just where do you think you are going?" he practically barked.
"Sir, our orders are.." began one of the guards,
"You will wait outside," ordered Bill cutting off the guards words
"Sir, but.." the other guard started.
"Outside, now!!" Bellowed Bill directly into the face of the closest guard. The guard lowered his head,
"Sir, yes sir!" he replied quickly as he spun about and exited the room with his companion closely on his heels. After the door had closed behind them, Bill guided Nobby to the bed and sat him down, he then positioned himself next to Nobby.
"What's on your mind?" Bill asked softly. Nobby looked Bill directly in the eyes,
"We're friends aren't we Bill?"
"Yes, I would like to think so, why?" asked Bill.
"And you would understand if I was to make a terrible mistake?" Nobby's eyes pleaded to Bill
"Of course, I and indeed everyone aboard this ship would be understanding at any genuine error. Have you done something that we should know about?" Bill continued to speak slowly and calmly.
"Well, I'm new here, and I don't pretend to understand all about your culture, shit I've lived all my life on Earth, and I still don't understand that. But some things are considered quite commonplace back on Earth, and we do them without much thought, well you do think about it but, not in a serious way. Do you understand what I

mean?" asked Nobby. Bill regarded his friend for a moment.
"No, not really." he replied honestly.
"What I mean is that there are some things that one culture may consider normal or usual, yet the same things could be held in disgust or considered a vile sin by another culture. Do you see what I mean?"
"Yes, I do. But I can't see what that has to do with our being called by the council!" exclaimed Bill, his concerned expression turning to one of bewilderment.
"Well, the thing is I think I may have done something last night that may be unforgivable." Bill noticed seriousness in Nobby's eyes and realised his breathing had deepened. Nobby's chest rose and fell at the strain of holding back his emotions. Bill placed one hand on each of Nobbys shoulders and gently turned him so that they were face to face.
"Nobby, what is it that you have done?" Bill spoke slowly but firmly, he saw a single tear roll down Nobby cheek as he fought to make his confession to Bill.
"I..I..., I'm sorry, but I masturbated last night." Nobby collapsed into Bills arms and began to sob loudly. Bill held Nobby, although he wasn't sure why. He waited for Nobbys sobs to die down slightly before speaking.
"And what happened after that?" he asked gently pushing Nobby away from his chest so that he could see his face, Nobby wiped his nose on his sleeve,
"W, w, what?" stuttered Nobby while rubbing his eyes with the sleeve on which he had just wiped his nose.
"What happened after you er.. masturbated?" repeated Bill
"I don't know what you mean." sniffed Nobby

"Well, er did your masturbating cause some sort of accident?"
"Er, no. Why?" asked Nobby, this wasn't what he had expected the outcome of his confession to be.
"So, why are you telling me then?" said Bill, his tone not as soft as previously
"Er, well I, er, I just thought, er, that maybe.." Nobby stumbled over almost every word, Bill saw the pained expression on Nobbys face and he had heard the embarrassment in his voice.
"Oh," said Bill simply as the penny finally dropped, "Now I understand."
"You do?" said Nobby through a snotty nose.
"Yes, I do," said Bill, "I believe that you thought that we Dolphoids would take great offence at your masturbating while aboard the ship, am I right?" Nobby nodded weakly.
"Well, let me put your mind at rest," said Bill, a hint of amusement in his voice, "As far as we are concerned you are quite welcome to masturbate whenever you like, providing that it is done in the privacy of your own quarters. In fact between you and me, I have had cause to er, well you know, it has been a long journey so far" Nobby smiled and nodded.
"I feel a right daft sod now, but I am glad that it's not what I thought it was," said Nobby. Bill forced a semi smile, but it didn't last long,
"But it still leaves the mystery as to why we have been summoned." the Dolphoid said.
"Any ideas?" asked Nobby whilst distractedly wiping the silvery trails of snot from his sleeve onto the beds blanket.

"None at all, but they did interview Rambo this morning, and I have heard that for some unexplained reason they cut the meeting short," replied Bill. Nobby stopped what he was doing as soon as Bill had mentioned Rambo's name.
"Rambo, they interviewed Rambo?" babbled Nobby, Bill nodded, "Why? I mean he's just a stupid dog, what could he possibly tell them. Mind you knowing Rambo he's probably told them that I am a raving beastiliac or something."
"You're not are you?" asked Bill nervously
"WHAT!!," yelled Nobby jumping from the bed, "you of all people. I don't know how you could even suggest such things. I may enjoy twanging my jism muscle, but I have never, ever in my entire life entertained the idea of prodding the hairy arse end of an animal, let alone Rambo." Nobby's face had taken on a strange purple tint.
"I didn't intend to insult you, I merely wished to make sure that bestiality was not an accepted Earth custom." answered Bill calmly.
"Yeah, I bet you did, anyway if that friggin' mongrel has said something to the council just to get me into trouble, I swear Bill, I'm really going to kill him." Nobby flopped tiredly onto the bed beside Bill.
"Well, there is only one way to find out," Bill said noting the exasperation in Nobby's movements.
"I suppose you're right." Nobby punctuated the sentence with a deep sigh, "I'll just have a quick wash first ok?" Bill nodded, as Nobby got off the bed and headed for the bathroom.

Twenty minutes later they were once again sat before the council. All the members were there, including weasel features, and the atmosphere within the room seemed darker than it had been the previous day and somewhat foreboding. When Bill and Nobby entered the room, the council members had fallen silent and had remained so until they were both seated.
Andy quickly brought the meeting to order with his usual throat clearance,
"Thank you for coming on such short notice," he said, "but we needed to determine the validity of some recently acquired information. Do you have any objection to answering some more questions Nobby?"
"May I ask why this was classified as an emergency meeting?" interrupted Bill before
Nobby could answer.
"It was classified as an emergency because we have reason to believe that our guest may have purposefully tried to deceive us by plying us with false and untrue information." answered Randy with a sneer.
"Whoa," said Nobby rising to his feet, "look, yesterday I was asked numerous questions about different subjects, which I answered freely. Now I am not perfect, and I may have made some mistakes in my answers, but I never purposely tried to deceive you."
"I am sure that is the case," said Andy indicating with his hand for Nobby to re seat himself, "and I am also sure that we can resolve this matter quickly with your cooperation."
"Is Nobby to be considered a threat to the security of the ship?" asked Bill.

"That is yet to be determined," said Randy
"So, as yet, he is not considered a threat to the safety of the ship." returned Bill.
"Er, no. Nothing has been determined as yet," replied Andy.
"In that case, I request that the word emergency be struck from the records of this meeting and also that the security presence that escorted Nobby from his quarters be cancelled until a decision has been reached," demanded Bill. The council members conferred amongst themselves for a moment.
"Agreed." said Andy on behalf of the council.
"And one more thing," said Bill, " If our guest is found not to be in any way connected to any allegations that have been made against him, that he will receive a full public apology from the Council?"
"No allegations have been made against our guest." said Andy defensively.
"I believe that council member Randy only a few moments ago stated that the council believed that Nobby had deliberately lied and deceived them. Is that not an allegation against our guest?" Bill stared directly at Andy, Andy, in turn, stared menacingly at Randy. Andy cleared his throat again and mopped the sweat off his brow.
"Perhaps certain words may have been said in haste, and I would like to make it known for the record that the council do not believe that our guest, Nobby, has in anyway purposefully and wittingly supplied us with false or misleading information.
We would also like to take this opportunity to apologise to Nobby for any misunderstanding caused by any

misleading statement given by this council. Is this acceptable?" Andy directed the question to Bill rather than Nobby.
"We find that quite acceptable." replied Bill on Nobbys behalf, Nobby just grinned and nodded.
"Excellent, perhaps we can continue then?" said Andy, "As before we will ask you a series of questions and we would appreciate your cooperation in answering them. You are under no obligation and may end the session whenever you wish. Do you understand these conditions?"
"Yes I do, and I have no objections." said Nobby, Andy and the other council members nodded thanks.
"Who are you?" asked weasel features straight away.
"What?" Nobby was a little taken back by the first question.
"Who are you?" repeated Randy, "you do know who you are, don't you?"
"Of course I know who I am, I'm Nobby."
"What is your job?" asked Mick the dark skinned Dolphoid.
"Er, well I'm unemployed at the minute, so I haven't got a job."
"Wouldn't you consider ruling the Earth a job," asked Randy
"Er, yes I suppose that would be a job," replied Nobby.
"So, I ask you again, what is your job?" repeated Mick.
"I haven't got a job, I just told you."
"What about ruling the Earth?" said Randy
"What about it?" parried Nobby.
“Is that your job?" replied Randy.

"Is what my job?" Nobby was becoming very confused, "look you're not making sense, what exactly is it that you want to know?"
"How long have you ruled the Earth?" asked Mick
"Wha.., hang on, Time out a minute," Nobby made a T shape with his hands, "What's all this nonsense about me ruling the Earth?"
"We have reason to believe that you are the ruler of the planet Earth," said Andy meekly. Nobby sat in stunned silence for a few seconds.
"How the hell did you come to that conclusion?" demanded Nobby.
"One of your subjects told us." said Randy with a small evil smile.
"What subject, I haven't got any subj...." Nobbys brow furrowed deeply in thought,
"Rambo, you're talking about Rambo aren't you, what the hell has he been saying?"
"He stated that to the best of his knowledge, that you are the Queen and you rule and own the Earth." clarified Andy. Nobby stared open mouthed in shock. He turned to Bill, who in turn looked as surprised as Nobby.
"Well, are you the owner of your planet or not?" demanded Randy.
"No I'm bloody not, I can't believe that you could even consider such thing, I don't even own my own home, that belongs to the council."
"Are you implying that we own the Earth?" asked Mick.
"What, oh, no I didn't mean this council, but the local council back home on Earth." replied Nobby.
"So you claim that your home is owned by a council?" Mandy enquired

"Yes, that's right."
"Do the council own everything?" said Dick the decrepit Dolphoid.
"They own lots of things, But I would seriously doubt that they own the whole Earth if that's what you are trying to say." said Nobby.
"So you are denying that you personally own the Earth?" asked Andy.
"May I interrupt a moment?" said Bill interrupting anyway.
"Of course." replied Andy in a tone that suggested otherwise.
"Thank you," nodded Bill, "It seems that a lot of energy is being exerted into not directly accusing our guest that he is, in fact, the owner of the planet, So I was wondering if anyone has actually gone to the trouble of doing a data search in the Earths computer systems to verify the validity of Rambo's claims?"
"Yeah, that's what I was going to say." lied Nobby.
"After the meeting with Rambo, especially considering the accusations made, obviously we undertook every measure available to substantiate the information that we had. Every data link we have with the Earth was used to discover the identity of the owner of the planet," answered Andy.
"And did you find any evidence to back up Rambo's allegations?" asked Bill.
"Well, no we didn't.." began Andy, he was interrupted by Randy,
"But none was found to prove that Nobby isn't the owner either."

"And while you were searching did you happen to spot your own name?" Bill asked the question directly at Randy
"No, why?" said Randy with a puzzled expression.
"You didn't? well, in that case, you must be the owner of the planet as well, congratulations." Bill spoke as sarcastically as he knew how this whole meeting was becoming a farce. Randy's face had become hard and menacing, his eyes were little more than slits,
"Are you trying to make a fool of me?" he almost spat at Bill, in return Bill remain calm and showed indifference to Randy's obvious displeasure,
"It is not my intention to deprive you of the job that you do so well on your own," replied Bill with a slight smirk, Nobby choked back his laugh at the insult. Randy exploded with rage, he slammed both his fists on the table and jumped to his feet sending his chair toppling backwards,
"Mister Chairman, I must protest against these uncalled for insults!" he shouted at Andy. The fat Dolphoid looked Weasel features up and down with evident distaste.
"Oh shut up and sit down," Andy said eventually
"But I..." began Randy.
"I said sit down," repeated Andy, "it's your own entire fault anyway!"
"How is it my fault?" demanded weasel face.
“I am not prepared to discuss it while you are hovering over me, now sit down," warned Andy sternly. Randy sat down on the chair that wasn't there and hit the floor with a resounding thud. This time Nobby couldn't hold back

his laughter. Tears streamed down his cheeks as he bent double with hilarity.

Several minutes had passed before Nobby could control himself, his vision was blurred with tears, and his ribs ached. Even when Randy, who had re seated himself in the meantime, stared venomously and directly at Nobby with hateful and loathsome dark eyes, Nobby found it difficult to suppress a snigger.

"Er, are we quite finished?" Andy asked Nobby hopefully. Nobby didn't answer verbally but chose to nod and give the thumbs up instead; he feared that opening his mouth would let forth another bout of giggles.

"Good, good," said Andy acknowledging Nobby's gestures, "Now where were we?"

"We were blaming that shark there," said Dick pointing a knobbly wrinkled finger at Randy. There was a burst of snickering, not from Nobby, but the other council members at the old Dolphoids insult. Randy was not at the least amused,

"How dare you call me that, I can retrace my family history for over a hundred generations and I take being called a shark as a slur on my family name?"

"Shark! " said Dick again. Once more Randy jumped to his feet,

"If you were any younger, I would challenge you to a match of unarmed combat for your insults." ranted weasel features. At this Dick also jumped, well more struggled, to his feet,

"Just try it sonny, and I'll show you a thing or two!" he shouted whilst waving his fist and almost teetering over at the same time. Andy stood up and used his large bulk to come between them,
"Gentlemen please, control yourselves. Is this the way to act in front of a visitor," said Andy in a raised but controlled voice. Both Randy and Dick stood silent, glaring at one another.
"Now both of you sit down," ordered Andy firmly. With a final glare at each other, they reluctantly sat back down. Dick lowered himself slowly and stiffly into his seat, using the huge table for support. Randy made sure he had a chair to sit on before doing anything. Nobby sat in relative silence during the incident, his giggles forgot for the moment as the drama unfolded before him.
"Before things get out of hand can I ask on what actual evidence was this so called emergency meeting assembled because so far none has been presented?" asked Bill wanting to resolve the matter before a full scale war broke out.
"Yes, good question," said Andy, "and I will let Randy explain as to why he used his influence with the head of security to insist that we have this meeting, without consulting with the rest of the council first." All eyes fell on weasel features. He shifted uncomfortably in his chair,
"Ah, well I had my suspicions at the first meeting with the Human, that we were not being told the truth, and this morning as I listened to the computers report of the meeting with the dog my suspicions were confirmed." He said matter of factly.

"And on what evidence are these suspicions based, other than what Rambo said this morning?" asked Bill leaning forwards and resting on the desk.
"Like I have already said, I believed from the beginning that we were being lied to." stated Randy.
"And what is your proof?" questioned the old Dolphoid
"What the dog said," remarked Randy. The room fell silent for a moment and the only sound that could be heard, apart from Dick's wheezing, was the sound of Andy drumming his fingers on the desk top impatiently.
"You alerted the whole of the ship's security," Andy spoke slowly and deliberately to Randy, "Went over the councils head and convinced the chief of security that an emergency meeting must be called, telling him that you had definite proof that Nobby here was a dangerous threat to the ship. All because of what Rambo said this morning. Is that what you are saying?"
"Er, yes. But I.." started Randy defensively,
"Do you know what you are Randy?" asked Andy, Randy looked at him questioningly, "You're a waste of perfectly good semen, that's what you are."
"How dare you!" shouted Randy, Nobby had began his giggling again.
"How dare I, I'll tell you how I dare," shouted Andy even louder, " I dare because I spent nearly two hours this afternoon being grilled by security wanting to know why I had allowed someone so dangerous aboard the ship. I spent two bloody hours being told that if it wasn't for you, the danger would never have been spotted; I even had a message from the deputy minister back home asking for my resignation if your theories were right. That, my stupid friend, is why I dare say what I said."

"Are you suggesting that the dog was lying, because if you are, then you're wrong. I checked the computers read out's, and they indicate that he was telling the truth," said Randy.
"and if you cared to check the read out's for the meeting with Nobby yesterday you will also notice that the computer verified that he was telling the truth, at least as far as he knows it." replied Andy
"Excuse me," broke in Bill, "are you saying that the information that Nobby gave yesterday was in some way false?"
"Not exactly," said Andy, "but a lot of the facts he gave us were incorrect."
"There you are," blurted Randy quickly, "I told you he was deceiving us."
"But I never.." began Nobby,
"Nobby didn't lie to us, he told the truth as he knows it. Unfortunately, his knowledge of the history of his planet is somewhat lacking. On the other hand, Rambo's view of the world he lives in is even less reliable, he told the truth as he knew it, but again it was wholly inaccurate. That is the reason for our calling off the meeting early. Obviously, they couldn't both tell such different accounts of the truth, and both be right. We cancelled the meeting to give ourselves the chance to check each set of answers and hopefully come up with a solution to the problem, which, if you had bothered to look further into the computer records, you would have found our explanation."
"If the dog was telling the truth when he said that the human was the owner of the Earth, then he must have

had reason to believe so. I want to know that reason," demanded Randy
"Why don't we ask him, he should be outside. I took the liberty of calling on him to be available just in case the need arose to question him," replied Andy smugly.
Nobby turned as the door behind him opened, he was about to get up when Bill placed his hand on his shoulder and gently held him down. Rambo was accompanied by a female Dolphoid that Nobby hadn't seen before; they walked side by side to the table and seated themselves to the far side of Bill.
"Thank you for coming, Rambo." said Andy cheerfully, "and of course you too Jill."
"No problem mate." barked Rambo
"Good," said Andy, "we would like to ask you some more questions if that's alright with you?"
"Fine, carry on, ask away." replied Rambo.
"Where do you live?" asked Mandy before Randy could.
"Oh, er, hang on I know this one. Er, is it the Earth?"
"And who owns the Earth?" asked Randy sharply.
"Easy, Nobby does," said Rambo. Nobby was about to complain when Bill asked a question.
"Can you describe the Earth for us please?"
"Er, yeah ok. It's not very big, and it's separated into seven different rooms with furniture in. Er, it has some windows and two doors, one at the front and one at the back." Rambo wagged his tail at a job well done.
"and that is what the Earth looks like, is it?" asked Bill
"Er, yeah. Well, I think so," said Rambo doubtfully
"You think so, but you're not sure are you?" coaxed Bill.
"Er, no not really." Rambo stopped wagging his tail. Bill got up and moved over to the wall to the left of the large

table. The computer screen appeared at his touch and he keyed in some commands. On the screen, two images materialised, one of the Earth the other of a house. Bill turn back to Rambo,

"Rambo, can you please tell us which of these pictures is a picture of the Earth is. Is it this one," he pointed to the planet, "or this one." he pointed to the house.

"That's the one!" Barked Rambo as Bill pointed to the house.

"Are you sure?" asked Bill

"Yeah, that's where I live," replied Rambo

"And do you know what this other picture is?" said Bill pointing at the planet.

"A ball? I love balls. Lovely chewy things they are"

"And who told you that this," he pointed at the house again, "was the Earth?"

"He did." replied Rambo, indicating Rasputin with his nose.

"No I didn't," said Rasputin indignantly

"Yes you did, you asked me if I knew where I lived and then told me it was called

Earth, and her there," he indicated Mandy, "confirmed it when I asked."

"I can't remember telling you that a house was Earth," Mandy said.

"Computer," said Bill, "Play back the recording of this morning's meeting please."

"Is this necessary?" asked Andy.

"Well, it is one way of either confirming whether or not Rambo was misled into believing that the Earth was the house in which he lived."

They all sat in silence while the recording played, only Rambo got excited when the part came on confirming that Rasputin had indeed told him that where he lived was called Earth and that when asked Mandy had confirmed it. Nobby sat in awe, his mouth slightly agape at the way Rambo had defended the female Dolphoid at the beginning of the recording. It was obvious that he was lying, but it still amazed Nobby about how little he knew about his own dog. They all watched in silence until the recording had ended. There was a subdued hubbub of frantic conversation from the councils side of the table, the only member who seemed not to be involved was Randy. He sat back in his chair, his dark, brooding eyes darting between Nobby and Rambo, a hateful malevolence filled his thoughts. These two vile creatures were lying, and he knew it, yet despite all his attempts to expose them, it was he that had suffered. They had turned everyone against him, making him look a total fool and the worst part was that the human openly mocked him by laughing at his misfortune. But he would have the last laugh, he would make them pay, make them suffer in the way he had suffered. A small evil smile skirted the edges of his mouth, his time would come.

Andy brought the meeting back to order with his customary throat clearance, and when he had every ones attention, he turned to face Randy.
"Now, we have a situation here which has two possible outcomes, one being that you continue your futile and pointless campaign against the characters of our guests, which will give me no option other than to have you arrested for misuse of power, unnecessary harassment of

visitors and sowing the seeds of suspicion and prejudice for you own personal amusement. Or choice two is that you apologise unreservedly to our guests for your unwarranted actions. Also, you apologise formally to the council as a whole and as individuals. As well as this you will issue a statement in which you will claim all responsibility for the unnecessary use of emergency powers, stating that the action you have taken were not in any way sanctioned by this council and that the council had no knowledge what so ever to your intentions. Copies of this statement are to be sent to the head of ships security and the deputy minister's office back home. These are your choices, and it is for you to decide on what course of action will be taken next."
Andy stared directly into the eyes of Randy, challenging a response. The whole room's attention was upon the weasel featured Dolphoid, who in turn sat in silence and stared at the table top, weighing his options carefully. After two minutes of contemplation Randy stood and bowed to the council, and then he turned and bowed again to Nobby and Rambo.
"Ladies and gentlemen, and venerable guests," he said, " I would like to formally offer my sincere and humblest apologies to the huma.., er Nobby and Rambo for any unnecessary and damaging remarks that I have made against you. I had no right to cause you to be subjected to this kind of treatment. My suspicions were groundless, yet I let my personal prejudices cloud my better judgement. I alone am responsible for the situation in which you have been placed, and my actions should not be reflected upon the good nature of the rest of the council. I stand before you a truly sorry individual who

wishes that you can find it in your hearts to forgive me for my rashness and over enthusiasm to find a dark side to everything. I truly now believe that you are good, honest individuals and I will no longer allow thoughts of anything otherwise to enter my mind. Once again I ask, undeservedly, for your forgiveness and to us a chance to let bygones be bygones. I am completely at your mercy." Randy lowered his head and out stretched his arms in Nobby and Rambo's direction. The council shifted their attention to the opposite side of the table, towards Nobby and Rambo. Nobby shuffled awkwardly in his seat under their combined gaze. He leaned over to Bill,
"What happens now?" he whispered to Bill.
"You have to stand and either accept or refuse Randy's apology," Bill whispered back.
"Oh, right. Er, what do you think I should do?" asked Nobby still whispering, He noticed that Rambo was also talking to his Dolphoid companion over to Bills right.
"Personally I think you should accept." replied Bill.
"And if I don't?" enquired Nobby
"Then Randy will become your sworn enemy and under Dolphoid tradition has the right to challenge you to a duel, which would result in one of you being dead at the end of it," said Bill casually.
"I accept." blurted Nobby rising to his feet quickly.
"You are willing to accept Randy's apology?" asked Andy a little disappointed.
"Oh yes, definitely." confirmed Nobby nodding his head vigorously.
"Your acceptance has been noted, you may sit back down," said Andy. Nobby sat.
Randy continued to stand in the same stance as before.

"What's he waiting for?" whispered Nobby to Bill
"Rambo," said Bill simply.
"Oh yeah, I forgot about him," replied Nobby. He saw Rambo stand in his chair and place his fore paws on the table.
"Right," said Rambo, " er, although I'm not quite sure as to what it is that this bloke has supposed to have done because personally, I haven't suffered in any way or if I have I didn't notice. So if he wants me to accept his apology, then who am I to argue."
"You are accepting Randy's apology?" asked Andy.
"That's what I just said." replied Rambo.
"Your acceptance has been noted, you may sit down." intoned Andy. Randy lowered his arms and raised his head,
"Thank you," he said, " I am indebted to you both for you have shown me the errors of my ways. I am at your service, for you have shown greater tolerance than I." Randy turned to face the rest of the council. "I wish to retire to my quarters where I shall personally write a letter of apology to each member of the council and the head of security. Also, I shall contact the minister's office and take responsibility for my actions."
"Permission to leave the meeting is granted." said Andy on behalf of the council.
Randy bowed to the council and then to both Nobby and Rambo before leaving. As the door closed behind Randy, Andy cleared his throat,
"Well, I suppose that concludes the meeting. Once again I would like to apologise to both our guests and I would like to invite them to join us on an official tour of the ship, which is to include a visit to the bridge, an honour

normally bestowed only on V.I.P. visitors. How does that sound?"
"Er, smashing." said Nobby.
"Yeah, ok," said Rambo
"Good, good. That's settled then, we shall meet back here in one hour from now." said Andy rubbing his chubby hands together, " That will give us time for a quick bit to eat." at this he rose to his feet and bowed slightly before turning to leave. One by one the other council members did the same. Soon there was only Nobby, Bill, Jill and Rambo.
"Let me introduce you to Jill," said Bill, "She has been Rambo's advisor and companion during his stay." Nobby stood and offered Jill his hand,
"Pleased to meet you." he said, " I hope he hasn't caused you any trouble?" Jill's cheeks flushed red for an instant.
"No, no he has behaved perfectly," she said, a little too quickly for Nobby's liking. He turned his attention to his dog,
"And I think you and me need to have a bit of a chat," he said.
"Perhaps later," interrupted Bill, "I suggest that we freshen up first and then we can have a get together after the tour."
"I agree." replied Jill, "we are a bit pressed for time at the moment." She stroked Rambo's head affectionately.
"Yeah, we've got things to do." said Rambo, " so see you later." He hopped off his chair and waited for Jill to follow. They walk out together and Nobby couldn't help but feel a pang of jealousy as they did. There was a secret between them that he wanted to know about, Rambo was his dog, and if anyone should be sharing a

secret with Rambo, it should be him. Bills voice interrupted his thoughts,
"I'll walk you back to your quarters," said Bill
"Er, no it's ok, I can remember the way." Nobby forced a small smile, "I'll have to start finding my own way around anyway."
"Are you sure?" asked Bill rising to his feet.
"Yes, no problems. If I get lost, I'll ask a policeman."
"Alright then, I shall call on you later," said Bill, Nobby nodded and Bill made his exit. Nobby remained in his chair for several minutes before leaving himself, his mind was totally occupied by thoughts of the unusual relationship that had grown between Rambo and Jill. Something didn't seem right, he pondered the situation as he made his way through the corridors as he walked to his quarters. Why had Jill lied on the computer recording of the previous days meeting, why had she blushed when he had asked about Rambo's behaviour. His thoughts were so preoccupied that he almost completely failed to notice he had a visitor sat on his bed as he entered his quarters.

CHAPTER TEN

"Are you alright, you look a bit pale?" asked Bill. Nobby shrugged his shoulders; he had a vexed expression on his face,
"I'm not sure, physically I feel fine, but I also feel like there is something important that I should tell you, although I can't for the life of me remember what," he replied quietly. They were stood in the corridor outside the bridge of the ship, Andy had gone in ahead of them to inform the captain that they were here. The tour party consisted of Nobby, Bill, Jill, Rambo, Andy and old Dick the octogenarian Dolphoid, who insisted on coming along as he and the captain's grandad once served together in the army. Bill and Nobby stood slightly away from the others, a manoeuvre exacted by Bill to allow he and Nobby a chance to talk privately. The Dolphoid had noticed that Nobby seemed a little confused when he had called on him earlier, as though he wasn't expecting anyone. Throughout the rest of the tour Nobby had hardly spoken two words, merely nodding or shaking his head if asked anything, he seemed to be avoiding direct eye contact with any one and had shown scant interest in the tour.
"Do you want to see a doctor?" asked a concerned Bill, Nobby shook his head.
"I don't think so, I don't feel ill. It's more like a feeling of Deja vu, as though I know what to expect to find behind that wall." Nobby pointed to the wall that Andy had disappeared through only seconds earlier, "I seem to have a quite clear picture of it in my head."

"Can you describe it?" asked Bill, his interest aroused. The field of psychic phenomenon had always been a fascination to him. In his spare time, he had read of many cases of Deja vu, where people who had never travelled from their home towns could describe in great detail, places in far off distant countries. Sometimes they would describe buildings that were no longer there or local people that had died a century earlier. Even though he seriously doubted that Nobby could know what was beyond that wall, he felt that he would be failing in his duties as a scientist if he didn't at least ask.
"Not perfectly, it's a bit sketchy. But I think the room is designed in a tier formation, three in all. That entrance brings you out on to the middle tier. On the top tier is the Captain's chair, which is large and made out of a black leathery material. Also on the top tier is a semi circular bank of computer consoles, which are mainly used for the purpose of ships defence."
"I thought you said it was a bit sketchy?" joked Bill, Nobby's face showed no humour.
"Am I right Bill, is that what it's like?"
"I don't know, I've never been on the bridge, but we will soon see. What else do you think is in there?"
"Well on the next tier down is another large semi circle of computers; these are mainly for monitoring probes and collecting information from outside sensors and radars. On the bottom tier are the navigational computers, also in a semi circle, and the whole front wall is dominated by the view screen," said Nobby, his eyes were blank and distant and his voice held no emotion.
"And you can see all this in your mind?" probed Bill

"Not exactly see, no. It's more like someone has described it to me a thousand times and I have built up a picture of it from that information. I couldn't even begin to describe the shapes or sizes of the computers or the colours of anything. Yet I can imagine the captain's chair." replied Nobby
"How long have you been able to imagine the bridge in your mind?" asked Bill
"I don't really know, I can't even remember thinking about it before, but the closer we got to it, the clearer the images became. Also, the closer we got, I began to have a strange feeling that I should be warning you of something, but again I can't remember what. Does that make sense?" Nobby's eyes pleaded with Bill for an explanation.
"You're asking the wrong person, I'm a scientist, my job entails making sense of the impossible. I wouldn't worry too much about it though, what you are imagining is probably just what you expect the bridge to look like," said Bill as reassuringly as he could.
"Yeah, you're probably right," replied Nobby unconvincingly. Before anything further could be said the entrance to the bridge opened revealing Andy and another
Dolphoid whom Andy introduced as the ship's captain, "This is captain er, oh, I'm afraid he hasn't got an adopted Earth name." stumbled Andy.
"Just captain will be fine." said the captain with a broad smile which displayed the majority of his ferocious looking teeth, "Please come in, and I will show you around," he said stepping to one side to allow entry. Jill and Rambo went in first, followed closely by Dick. The

old Dolphoid stopped in front of the captain, his frail stooped body dwarfed by the muscular build of the captain. Dick prodded the captain in the chest a couple of times with a gnarled finger,
"How's your grandad then, boy?" asked Dick with a rheumatic wheeze. The captain regarded the wizened figure before him,
“He's been dead for fifteen years, but thanks for asking anyway." he replied politely.
"Dead eh, what about your granny?" asked Dick who had become accustomed to finding out that his friends had died.
"She's fine, thank you." replied the captain curtly
"Wouldn't happen to have her data phone number would you?" said Dick with a wink whilst nudging the captain's ribs with a bony elbow.
"I shall tell her that you have asked about her." said the captain ushering the old relic through the door way. Next up were Nobby and Bill. The two Dolphoids shook hands and exchanged greetings,
"Allow me to introduce our guest," said Bill turning to Nobby, "This is Nobby." At his introduction Nobby forced a smile, the captain took an involuntary step backwards and withdrew the hand that he was about to offer.
"Er, yes very good, er please come in." offered the staggered captain. Bill and Nobby stepped past the captain and were surprised to find themselves in a long narrow network of adjoining corridors rather than the expected ship's bridge. They joined the other tour members and waited for Andy and the captain. The corridors were just wide enough to allow two people to

walk side by side, and even then they would have to walk shoulder to shoulder. The captain and Andy had to walk in single file to join the others, the width of the corridor would not allow for both the captain's broad shoulders and Andy's overly stuffed waistline at once.
"If you will allow me through I will guide you to the control centre of the ship." said the captain squeezing his way past every one, "If anyone has any questions please feel free to ask." he started off up the main corridor, taking them past numerous openings leading to similar narrow corridors.
"How come these corridors are so confined?" asked Jill who was just behind the captain.
"Yeah!" added Rambo for no apparent reason. The captain turned down an opening on his left and waited for everyone else to reach the corridor before explaining.
"It's basically a security system. There are forty separate corridors in this segment of the ship, only two of them lead to the bridge, the rest are either dead ends or lead you back to where you started from. They are to prevent any one suddenly rushing on to the bridge, and the reason that they are so narrow is to prevent large numbers of invading hoards from storming up them. It is practically impossible to launch a surprise attack when forced to move in single file." explained the captain, while resuming his pace.
"So, what if any undesirables decided to just simply beam on to the bridge, these corridors would seem pretty pointless in the face of modern technology?" countered Jill.
"You tell him girl!" remarked Rambo.

"That is true," said the Captain with a smile, "so, that is why the whole of the bridge is enveloped in an electron deflective transfer shield, which as you may be aware is impenetrable to transferral, disruptive, x ray, radiation and tractor beams."
"I didn't know that." admitted Andy and judging by everyone else's expressions neither did they.
"Well it is hardly surprising really considering that the only three people on the ship who are aware of it are myself, the ships engineer and the chief of security." replied the Captain smugly.
"We know about it now!" said Andy
"Yes, you know of its existence, and many people do, but what I meant was that only three people aboard the ship know where the electron deflecting emitter is situated, that is the real big secret, if no one knows where it is then logically no one can tamper with it."
"It's hidden behind the back panel of the food dispenser on deck fourteen." interrupted Nobby in a way that suggested that it was common knowledge to absolutely everyone in the known universe. The Captain stopped dead in his tracks, causing those who were following him to collide with each other.
"Who said that?" he bellowed at the collected hubble of bodies in the narrow corridor. Everybody was looking around at each other and muttering that it wasn't them. Only Bill seemed to know exactly where he was looking; he was looking directly at Nobby, who had raised his hand to attract the Captain's attention.
"What the hell are you doing?" urged Bill in a hushed voice, but before Nobby had time to reply the corridor suddenly became full of security men armed with laser

rifles. "Shit" uttered Bill as he, Nobby and the rest of them were forcefully ushered back down the corridor at gun point.

"So how did you know the where a bout's of the electron deflector?" asked the Dolphoid dressed in black, he had introduced himself earlier as the chief of security, no name just his title. Nobby was beginning to tire of the question; he had been asked it about twenty times in the last hour, but no one believed his answer.
"I've already told you I don't know. It was just a lucky guess." The security chief at the table opposite Nobby, his dark piercing eyes were scrutinising every movement Nobby made, searching for some facial expression that would give him a clue as to the truth.
He rubbed his glove clad hands together making the leather like material squeak as he did so.
"Who do you work for?" he asked
"Nobody, I was unemployed before I came here," answered Nobby.
"So who are you working for now?" asked the security chief again.
"Nobody, I just said."
"No, what you said was that you were unemployed before you got here, which implies that since coming here you have been employed by someone, so who is it?" said the Chief coldly.
"What I meant was back on Earth I didn't have a job, and since being here, I was told that if I decided to stay, I would be given a job, to earn my keep, so to speak.

That's all." Nobby said with a deep sigh, he could feel an almighty headache coming on.
"So who has offered you a job?" asked the Chief
"No one yet, apparently I'm here as a guest at the moment, and until they have finished with me, I don't need to work. But I have expressed a preference to work with the animals that are kept in the loading bay behind the kitchens if that's any help to you," said Nobby hopefully
"None at all. So how did you know the location of the electron deflector emitter?"
"I've already told you numerous times, I have no idea. When the captain mentioned it the image of the food dispenser on deck fourteen came into my mind. To be honest
I don't actually know if I have ever been to deck fourteen, let alone seen the dispenser there." replied Nobby honestly
"You haven't," said the security chief, "I've already checked, that is why I know you're working for someone else, and it's vitally important that I find out who."
"I am not working for any one, honest." pleaded Nobby
"Okay, let's put all our cards on the table," said the chief trying a new tactic, " I don't believe that you are any threat to the ship's security, but at the same time you are privy to some extremely delicate information, which I know you didn't just lucky guess at. So therefore so one must have told you or at least mentioned it while you were in ear shot. It is a matter of utmost importance that we ascertain who that individual is. Information like this can be used to disable the ship's systems, so any light you can shed on the subject, no matter how seemingly

trivial, could help us to find the person who is really responsible for possible espionage. Do you understand?"
Nobby nodded.
"I didn't even know what the deflector thing was, I honestly had never heard of it until the captain mentioned it, and when he did this image of the food dispenser just popped into my mind." said Nobby quietly, shaking his head " I've no idea why."
"Well I believe you, and the computer confirms that you are telling the truth as you know it, as far as you can't honestly remember any one mentioning it before, but that doesn't mean that nobody has, just that if they did you can't remember it. Now this brings us to yet another problem." said the Chief almost casually.
"What now?" asked Nobby wearily.
"Apparently you gave a detailed description of the bridge to...er," he paused for a moment while he checked his computer, "to the Dolphoid you know as Bill, is this true?"
"Well I told Bill that I had a strange feeling of knowing what the bridge looked like, although it wasn't in any great detail," replied Nobby
"But alas it was too accurate for someone who had never been aboard a ship like this one before. So again we face the problem of where you acquired this knowledge. Are you a psychic by any chance?"
"I don't think so."
"No, neither do I, so where did your knowledge come from, that is our dilemma. When did you first begin imagining what the bridge looked like?"
"I don't know, I can't ever remember thinking about it at all. It was just the closer I got to it the more I was sure of

what to expect. I think at first when I knew that we were going to visit the bridge I started thinking about what I expected to see, using images from television programmes like StarTrek and Starwars as a basis, I suppose. Maybe it just stemmed from that!" answered Nobby hopefully
"Or maybe someone was feeding you the information." said the Chief abruptly.
Nobby was a bit perplexed at this statement.
"Nobody told me anything," he said defensively. The security Chief smiled.
"I believe you," he said, "At least nobody said anything to you face to face, but perhaps you were receiving information by means of telepathy, therefore giving you the impression that they were your own thoughts."
"I didn't hear any voices in my head if that's what you're implying." replied Nobby.
"No, I wouldn't imagine you would have, whoever sent you these images were being very careful. They most likely visualised the bridge and passed the information on to you, but for what reason." the Chief ponder rhetorically.
"I didn't see any images." said Nobby while the chief was thinking.
"What do you mean?"
"Well as I told Bill earlier, I had no real idea of what the bridge looked like, it was more of, say, a verbal description that had been repeated to me many times until I knew it off by heart. I didn't know what the computers looked like, or what colour everything is, I just somehow knew that the bridge was designed on a

three tier system, and what each tier was responsible for. I still have no idea what they look like,
I just know they are there and what they do. It's as if I have read about it somewhere, and whatever I read told me where things were and what they did, but not what colour, shape or size of them. Does that make sense to you?"
"No, but it does give us something to go on." replied the chief thoughtfully.
"It does?" questioned Nobby.
"Yes, if someone is sending you this information about the lay out of the bridge, but are not giving you any definite descriptions of the objects with in it, then we are possibly looking for somebody who has either access to only schematics of the bridge or has been given the information from possibly a third party. On the whole, I think that we are looking for someone who has never seen the bridge themselves." he turned his attention to the computer on his desk and began tapping in data, Nobby sat silently and watched him work. After several minutes the Chief looked up at Nobby again.
"Right," he began, "there are at present six hundred and fifty three individual aboard this vessel, out of them only forty eight of them have had access to the bridge. That leaves six hundred and five individuals who haven't seen the bridge, out of them only a further twenty seven have access to the bridges schematics, but only twelve of them have had reason to access the data. So, for the time being, I think we should have a chat with these twelve as a starting point at least." He stood up and began heading for the door.
"Er, what about me?" asked Nobby

"What, oh sorry, yes er, you are free to go, but I would appreciate if you didn't discuss any of this with any one for the time being. Obviously you will constantly be monitored, and a member of security staff will accompany you if you decide to go anywhere, just for your own protection of course."
"Of course!" said Nobby sarcastically. At this, the security Chief nodded slightly and left. Nobby leant back in his chair and put his feet up on the table, he rubbed his hands over his face a couple of times and then over the stubble on his head. He had always dreamed of a more exciting life, but somehow this was taking things to the extreme. All these years he had waited for Lady Fortune to come his way, and when it finally came down to it, all that turned up was her daughter, Miss Fortune.

"Pleases state your requirements" intoned the computerised food generator in Nobby's quarters. Nobby scratched his head and thought for a moment.
"Er, can you make Earth style food and stuff?" he asked finally.
"I am able to access all Earth recipes and reproduce them!" informed the computer.
"Anything at all?"
"Yes, the food generation unit is capable of synthesising over sixteen million different combinations of edible forms of nourishment." replied the computer with a hint of pride.
"Even drinks?" asked Nobby.

"Yes, I have a menu of 1.4 million drinks of both alcoholic and none alcoholic variety's."
“Right then," said Nobby rubbing his hands together, "I'll have a pint of lager and some cheese and onion crisps please."
"Thank you, please wait a moment for your order." said the computer cheerily.
Nobby stood and waited in anticipation, normally he didn't drink as he tended to end up being arrested for one reason or another, but after the last couple of days, he had come to the conclusion that the only way to make sense of anything was to get completely toilet hugging drunk. With any luck, he may even derive some satisfaction from it by throwing up all over the security guard that had been pretending not to follow him, since his meeting earlier today with the security chief. The food generator buzzed, and Nobby watched as a plate sized hole appeared within the unit, and his order rose up from it. The food unit buzzed again,
"Your order is now ready, please enjoy." chirped the computer. Nobby gazed at his order and after a second or two elected not to take it.
"Er, computer!" called Nobby.
"Yes, how can I be of service?" replied the computer happily.
"It's about my order." began Nobby,
"Would you like another one?" interrupted the computer.
"Er, no not exactly, it's just that there is a small problem with this order."
"Really, Please wait one moment." said the computer, the food unit began to buzz again and Nobby's order rotated slowly as the computer checked it. "I have

examined the order and cross referenced it with the Earths data bases, and I conclude that the lager is an exact duplicate of the planets best-selling brand, and it has been served at the correct temperature. The cheese and onion crisps are also a duplicate of the planets leading brand, and they have been produced to exactly the same standard as found on Earth. I cannot find anything wrong with either product." returned the computer.
"Well I'm sure that you took great care in reproducing both the lager and the crisps and I'm sure that they would be perfect if it wasn't for the fact that they are both in the same glass." answered Nobby with a sigh.
"That is what you ordered." said the computer in an annoyingly jolly manner.
"No, it wasn't!"
"Please wait," said the computer, Nobby was about to complain when he was cut off by his own voice, " I'll have a pint of lager and some cheese and onion crisps, please." said the computers recording of his words.
"Ah," said Nobby, "That is my order, but I didn't want the crisps in a glass with the lager."
“I see," said the computer, "and in what do you wish them to be served?"
"Well, normally they come in a plastic bag."
"Please wait." said the computer again. Nobby watched the food generator again as his previous order disappeared back down the hole that it came from. The food unit buzzed for several seconds and once more the hole re opened and from it rose a crisp packet.
"Your order is ready." informed the computer. Nobby scrutinised the food units offering.

“Er, where's the lager?"
"It is in the plastic packaging as requested." answered the computer joyfully. Nobby leant against the wall beside the food unit and sigh as deeply as humanly possible.
"Computer." he said wearily, "Are you just trying to annoy me or are you very stupid."
"I am programmed only to do as requested, and I am capable of performing fourteen million separate calculations per second." replied the computer happily.
"Ok then, listen very carefully, forget the crisps, just pretend that I never mentioned them ok?" said Nobby slowly and purposefully.
"If that is what you wish."
"Yes, it is." said Nobby without hesitation, "That is exactly what I wish. Now is it possible to have from this fine piece of apparatus, which is known as the food generator, a pint of lager, nothing else, just a pint of lager? Plain and simple lager, any brand, I'm not fussy, no crisps, no nuts, no pork scratching's, nothing. Just lager, on its own. Do you think you can manage that?"
"Please wait." intoned the computer. Once more the food unit buzzed into life and Nobby watched his packet of cheese, onion and lager crisps disappear back into the serving area of the machine. After a few more seconds of buzzing a sudden stream of frothy golden liquid issued forth from the food generator in a graceful arc that glided straight down onto the floor. Nobby watched his order foam and bubble on the ground before him. When the flow stopped the computer made an announcement,
"Your order is ready, just lager as requested," it said with a gleefulness of a job well done. Nobby remained silent

and stared balefully at his drink spreading across the floor. He turned slowly and strode purposefully from the room. He strode purposefully back into the room less than a minute later with a fire extinguisher and began smashing the food generating unit into pieces with it. Or at least he was until the security man jumped on him.

"It seems that you can't keep yourself out of mischief." said the security chief across the desk to Nobby. Nobby didn't answer; he just continued to stare aimlessly at the floor. "Wanton destruction of government property is a serious offence. Do you know what the sentence for vandalism is?" Nobby didn't look up but shook his head.

"Well at the very least," began the chief, "you could end up serving five years on the shit farms of Oltega four or even worse, you could end up on Hulan two, in one of their gonad thrashing centres."

"It wasn't my fault." said Nobby without looking up.

"Apparently it never is, but at the moment we have more important things to worry about haven't we?" asked the chief. For the first time since being dragged here by an overzealous security officer, Nobby raised his head.

"We have?" questioned Nobby.

"Oh yes," replied the chief almost sounding happy about it, "We have. Our little investigation into telepathic involvement has drawn a blank, none of the suspects shows any signs of telepathic ability, and each one has an alibi as to their movements at the time of your sudden psychic insights. So now we need to look elsewhere."

"Where?" asked Nobby unhappily
"You!" stated the chief quite simply. "You are after all the only clue we have, so we are going to perform a little experiment."
"We are?" spoke Nobby timidly, he didn't like the sound of this.
"Oh yes, indeed we are, so if you would like to follow me.." said the chief turning towards the door.
"Where?" asked Nobby with rising from his seat.
"Back to the bridge, see if we can jog some memories, ok ?"
"I suppose so," replied Nobby practically dragging himself from the chair to join the chief. As they left the security office three armed guards fell in behind them, their fingers poised ready on their triggers. This was becoming a regular occurrence Nobby thought to himself. The guards held position a few yards back while keeping pace with Nobby and the chief. As they walked along the corridors, Nobby let out a string of silent farts just to annoy the following escort. When Nobby looked over his shoulder the guards seemed to have fallen back slightly, he suppressed a giggle.

After a short journey in the lift, where Nobby was prodded menacingly in the back by a laser gun from the silent but disgruntled guards, they arrived at the entrance of the corridor that leads to the bridge.
"Do you feel anything?" asked the chief.
"Hungry," replied Nobby hopefully

"This is neither the time nor place for flippancy." warned the chief. "Can you remember anything?
"No, sorry I can't." replied Nobby shaking his head to emphasise his words.
"Never mind, come along." the chief had opened the door way and was half way down the corridor before Nobby caught up with him.
"We'll just keep walking and as soon as you remember anything, say so ok?" instructed the chief, Nobby muttered agreement and plodded along behind him.
After turning many different corners, they came up against an apparent dead end.
"This is the last barrier between us and the bridge, can you feel or remember anything now?" asked the chief searching Nobby's eyes for an answer. Nobby looked at the wall ahead of him and then the guards behind him, the only thing he did feel was fed up, but he declined to mention it.
"No, sorry. It's all a blank," replied Nobby with a shrug.
After several seconds of silence, the chief nodded and opened the door to the bridge. Nobby took a deep breath and followed the chief in. A sudden wave of panic hit Nobby, and he began to stagger backwards. He would have most likely crashed to the ground if the two security guards hadn't caught him and held him up.
Almost instantly the chief had hold of Nobby shoulders and was shaking them gently,
"What is it, Nobby, What do you feel?" an air of urgency joined his words. Nobby shook his head to try and clear his thoughts,
"I..I don't know, I need to.....er, it's a warning," Nobby mumbled quickly, his eyes staring blankly ahead of him.

"We need to know, Nobby. What's a warning, who's in danger, think!!" shouted the chief. Everyone on the bridge had stopped to watch the unfolding drama at the entrance way, the captain jumped from his chair and rapidly made his way to the scene.
"I need to warn you.., There is something I'm supposed to tell you ... I can't remember what it is,....something I don't want to do, but have to." rambled Nobby wildly, his eyes were beginning to bulge in panic, and he was struggling desperately against the two guards that held him. The chief had seen men panic like this before and he did what he always did in these situations. He gave Nobby a hefty slap. And surprisingly it worked a treat. Nobby stopped babbling and struggling instantly, he stared in disbelief at the chief,
"What....what happened?" he managed to say before his legs gave way. He hung limply between the security men.
"Nothing," lied the chief, "just calm down and relax." he said.
"I need to sit down." gasped Nobby breathlessly. The two guards lugged Nobby over to the nearest chair, which was still occupied by a member of the bridge crew. The captain nodded to his crew man to move. As he raised himself from the chair, Nobby darted forward with remarkable speed and agility which took everyone by surprise. He grabbed the shocked crewman by the arm and spun around, flinging him straight into the two guards and the chief, knocking them all to the floor. In what seemed one easy movement Nobby slid into the vacated chair and began to key instructions into the computer consoles keyorb. Almost instantly the glimmer

of a force field appeared around Nobby and the ships warning alarms began to ring. The two security men were on their knees and firing their weapons at Nobby. They some stopped when their lasers began ricocheting off the force field and bouncing around the bridge. Nobby ignored the shots and continued working at the computer; his expression was vacant and emotionless. He worked the keyorb without looking at it, as though it was something he did every day. On the screen before him on the console, hundreds of lines of code appeared as he typed.
"What the hell is he doing?" shouted the captain over the noise of the alarm. Quickly he sprinted to his chair and began using his own computer to try and stop Nobby. The chief was quickly beside him watching the information on the screen, his eyes widened as he read.
"This can't be true." he said looking at the captain, but the captain's expression told him it was very much true.
"It took him four seconds to erect a force field around himself." said the captain reading his computer screen; the colour had drained from his face.
"Quick close him down!" shouted the chief
"I can't, he's bypassed all the security shutdown codes. The bridge is effectively isolated from the rest of the ship. He's shut down all communications and transferred all ship functions to his console. He has complete control of the ship." the captain practically screamed. The chief moved his gaze from the captain, over to Nobby and slowly back again.
"Exactly what are you saying?" growled the chief.
"We have effectively lost control of the ship." replied the captain, his voice quavering with panic.

"MOVE." bellowed the chief pushing the captain from his chair. The captain didn't argue, he stood dumbstruck and watched on uselessly as the chief began keying in security override codes into the computer. Sweat was standing out on his brow and beginning to drip from the tip of his snouty nose. He mopped the sweat away with the sleeve of his uniform and resumed his frantic attempt to stop Nobby. He keyed in the last couple of digits of the security codes and hit the enter button.
"Security codes invalid, all input from this console will be terminated." informed the computer.
"WHAT!!" cried out the chief in fury as the screen went blank, he stood up quickly and drew his gun and shot the console. His face was red with rage, his blood was beginning to boil. He looked around the bridge, as far as he could see all the other computer terminals were also blank. He slammed his fist down hard on the top of the recently shot console and cursed many hundreds of generations of Nobby's ancestors. Quickly he turned and pulled the arm from the Captain's chair, revealing three different coloured buttons. He stabbed at the red one, and the chair moved to one side. Beneath the chair was an opening which led down to a maintenance access tunnel beneath the floor of the bridge.
"I..I..didn't know about that." stuttered the captain at seeing the opening
"Nobody did except me." shouted the chief, lowering himself to climb into it. he was about half way down when the computer stopped him.
"Warning," it said calmly, "weapons overload, full discharge in ten seconds."
The chief almost jumped out of the hole

"What the fu.." he began
"Five seconds." informed the computer, "Target locked," it added. The image of the Earth appeared on the bridges view screen. Everyone on the bridge, including the captain and the chief found themselves staring involuntary at the screen, each one of them transfixed and unable to do anything.
"Commencing full weapons discharge." announced the computer. The whole ship shuddered as hundreds of beams of laser energy burst forth from the banks of the weapons arrays at the front of the ship. Everyone on the bridge stood immobile as the beams of energy hurtled toward the unsuspecting planet. Suddenly the whole bridge was bathed in a brilliant white light; several crew members cried out as the glare blinded them temporarily, others dived for cover in fear that the blast would reach them. Then as suddenly as the glare had begun, it ended, as the view screen went dead. The bridge was silent apart from the subdued moans of the blinded crew members, the chief stood motionless and stared unblinking at the blank view screen, his entire body was damp with perspiration, his mouth was dry and his senses were numb. He had witnessed death many times in his life, but never the death of an entire planet, over two hundred thousand billion separate individual life forms gone in an instant, God only knows how many different species of plant life. An icy cold shiver ran down his spine as he realised that in a way he was responsible for all that death, if only he hadn't insisted on bringing Nobby to the ... suddenly his thoughts snapped back into place. Nobby, where was Nobby. He looked over to where he had last seen him. He had gone.

Quickly, but still on shaky legs, he made his way down to the lower tier. As he drew around the bank of computer terminals he spotted Nobby. He was slumped on the floor next to the console he had been at. Nobby lay motionless as the chief approached. Several others had begun to gather round Nobby still form. They moved aside as the chief neared, he stopped short of Nobby and glared at him with hateful, malevolent rage, slowly he raised his weapon and aimed it at Nobby's head.

Bill had been sat at his desk, working his computer. He had become increasingly worried about Nobby's visions of the bridge. It wasn't until after he had spoken to the security chief that Bill learned just how accurate Nobby's description been. Nobby was also spot on as to the where a bout's of the bridges secret jamming device. Bill knew this information was not available anywhere, so it was impossible that Nobby could have known about it, but somehow he did, and that was worrying Bill as much as it was worrying the security chief. Bill was pulling all the information he could regarding paranormal activity for the Earths computer networks, paying close attention to any references about Deja Vous and other "been here before" phenomenon. He had been working away for several hours when the ship juddered, and his computer link with the Earth ended abruptly. "Damn!" he said to himself. He keyed in instructions to re establish the computer link. After a couple of seconds the computer screen flashed the message that it was unable re establish the link.

"What!" he said out loud in dismay. "Computer." he said opting to try the verbal command, "re establish information link with Earth."
"Unable to perform the command." stated the computer. Bill leaned back in his chair.
"Why?" he asked
"There will be no further communication with Earth." answered the computer impassively
"On whose authority?" questioned Bill
"No one's authority, the Earths computer network has been terminated," it replied.
Bill furrowed his brow, the computer wasn't making sense.
"Explain the last statement." demanded Bill.
"Earths computer network has been terminated, the Earth has been terminated." the image of a planet engulfed in flames materialised on the computer screen. Bill stared at the image in stunned silence. His mouth opened and closed several times before he could speak,
"Is that the Earth?" he asked quietly.
"Affirmative." answered the computer. Bill sprang to his feet and ran from the room, he sprinted down the corridor, almost colliding with several people as he did so. He reached the end of the corridor and found the door to the observation lounge already open. Gingerly he entered the room, it was already full of people. Nobody turned as he entered, their eyes were fixed on the view from the observation port. Bill followed their gaze. His heart sank as his eyes fell upon the sight of the Earth, which for reasons unknown to any one present, had suddenly become little more than a ball of fire.

CHAPTER ELEVEN

A deadly hush had descended around the bridge, as crew members, security staff and the captain all held their breath as one. The security chief stood over Nobby's prone body, his firearm pointed directly at Nobby's head. His hands trembled as an overwhelming rage raced through his veins. Never before in his life had any one ever made him feel this way. It wasn't the fact that Nobby had just destroyed an entire planet and countless untold lives; it was that he had been fooled by him. The chief prided himself on the security of the ship, almost nothing happened with out his knowledge; he had kept a watchful eye over every body. He had spotted problems in the making and quickly nipped them in the bud before anyone noticed; he had averted numerous threats to the ship, without a second thought. Yet today he had brought this human onto the most security sensitive part of the ship and couldn't see the danger.

He put his finger on the trigger mechanism and tried to hold his aim steady. His hand was shaking too badly. He brought up his other hand and used it to steady his aim. He took one final look around the faces in the room, nobody tried to stop him.

He checked his aim one final time and said a silent prayer. His placed his finger back on the trigger and gently began to squeeze.

"OY!!" boomed a loud voice. The chief instinctively turned the gun in the direction of the voice, ready to fire. He dropped the gun in shock when saw that the view screen had come back on, and in view were about several hundred or so Imperial warships encircling the burning planet. Quickly the image was replaced by that of an ugly fat lipped beady eyed greenish alien,
"Oy! cloth ears, I'm talking to you." bellowed the alien.
"Er, can we help you?" answered the chief nervously.
"Did you do this?" demanded the alien loudly
"Er, do what exactly?" asked the chief knowing full well what the alien was talking about.
"This!!" the image of the burning planet returned to the screen for a moment.
"Ah yes, well we can explain." began the chief trying to stall for time.
"Did you or did you not destroy this planet!" shouted the ugly large mouthed alien.
"Well, er..."
"Just answer the question stupid." the alien practically screamed. The chief didn't take kindly to the aliens tone, he decided to try and bluff the alien.
"Do you know who we are?" shouted the chief, adopting an arrogant air. The alien jolted slightly at the Chiefs sudden change of manner. He thought for a second before answering.
"No, who are you?" he asked in an almost pleasant manner.
"We are representatives of the United Union of Galaxies, and this is the starship The Traveller." replied the chief

"Oh, well in that case representative of the united union of galaxies," said the alien nicely, "You're all nicked!" he shouted with a broad smile.
"But we didn't do...." stuttered the chief, his arrogant poise forgotten.
"You are being placed under arrest in accordance with Chapter six, paragraph nineteen, clause E, sub section Delta, amendment Q of the Empires possession laws." informed the Alien.
"And exactly what does that mean?" asked the chief meekly.
"Oh, er hang on a second," said the alien, he disappeared from view for a moment.
He returned with a large book. "right then let's see." he flicked through several pages," ah, here we are. Basically, it means that nobody is allowed to destroy any of the Emperors planets without prior permission, in writing. So there you are." He slammed the book shut, "So surrender your vessel or be destroyed."
"And..er then what, I mean what happens once we surrender the ship?" inquired the chief.
"You will be transported to Empire headquarters, where you will stand trial and then you will be shot."
"Hang on, what do you mean shot, what if we're found not guilty?" the chief was beginning to panic, things were not looking good.
"You'll probably be shot anyway, don't worry about it, it's just a formality." replied the alien with a smirk. The chief stood speechless. The captain spoke up instead.
"Er, excuse me, but er, we have a list of planets that belong to the Emperor, and I
believe that this planet wasn't on it." he said.

"Yeah, well he hasn't had it long, you should have checked with the empire record department."
"And exactly where is that?" asked the captain
"I don't know, it's a secret." said the alien
"Oh," uttered the captain miserably, he flopped into the nearest chair and sulked.
"Now, what's it to be, surrender or be destroyed?" asked the alien. The captain looked at the chief, and the chief looked around at the crew, their faces gave him the answer.
"Prepare to come aboard," he said sadly. The view screen returned to the images of the flotilla of war cruisers, circling the Earth and glowing ominously in the reflected flames. The Chief shook his head and released a long sigh, he looked at the captain and his security men. He could see in their eyes that they were waiting for him to make the first move as to what to do next.
"I suppose we'd better go to the transferral lounge and await our er, guests." he said finally.
"What about him?" said the captain pointing a shaking finger at Nobby. The chief turned to look at Nobby.
"Pick him up." he said to the two security men, "we can throw him out of an air lock on the way." Without question, the two guards heaved Nobby's scrawny body up between them and began heading for the door.
"On second thoughts," began the chief, "take him to sick bay and keep him under guard." Once again neither security man questioned the order, they both gave a small nod of compliance and left.
"I think your original idea was better." said the captain
"Yes, but seeing as he caused the problem, I only think it fair that the little bastard takes the blame, don't you?"

answered the chief. The captain smiled wryly as he followed the chief out through the door.

"Wake up, I've got something important to tell you." said Jill shaking Rambo gently by his shoulder.
"Huh, what.." yawned Rambo with an accompanying fart. He squinted out of one eye to see who had disturbed him. "Oh, hiya babe," he said
"There is something I need to tell you." re issued Jill
"Can't it wait till later?" yawned Rambo ignoring the urgency in Jill's voice.
"No it can't." snapped Jill irritably. Rambo opened both eyes and yawned again.
"Okay, okay, keep your nose wet!" said Rambo with a laugh, because this was an extremely funny thing to say in dog terms. He stood up and gave himself an invigorating shake and scratch. By the time he had finished Jill had seated herself on a small stool near Rambo's squeaky toy collection. Rambo plodded over and stood before her.
"So, what's so important that can't wait then?" demanded Rambo.
"I think you had better sit down." answered Jill.
"Sit down, SIT DOWN!!" barked Rambo with annoyance, " Thirty seconds ago I was fast asleep, and you told me to get up, and now that I'm up your saying get down again!! What's the matter with you? Have you gone mad?"
"Shut up," spoke Jill calmly. "There has been a terrible accident."
"Am I injured?" asked Rambo

"Er, no."
"Well, in that case, I'm not interested either," said Rambo gruffly
"But it involves you." replied Jill firmly
"Look I've been here all day; I'm not involved in nothing. If you don't believe me, you can ask that comspewter thing that keeps telling me not to piss in the corners." barked Rambo defensively.
"The Earth has been destroyed, Rambo," said Jill bluntly
"Well, I've not been anywhere near it, so there's no point trying to blame me for it."
"No one is blaming you for it." replied Jill.
"You just said that it involved me."
"It does, don't you understand?" snapped Jill again, she slid from the chair and onto her knees, bringing her face down to Rambos level. Rambo cocked his head to one side as she stared intensely at him.
"Er, no sorry, I don't understand." he said with a wag of his tail.
"Right come here," said Jill as she grabbed Rambo's ears and pulled him forwards until his nose was touching hers. "Listen, the Earth, that's the planet Earth, the planet Earth that you live on, has been totally and utterly destroyed. Now the reason that it involves you is because the Earth is your home planet, the planet on which you live. Got it!" Rambo was wincing in discomfort as Jill emphasised each word with a sharp tug on alternate ears.
"Ow, ow give up, listen to me Jill, babe, I understand now. You were concerned about my feelings, but it's alright see, I don't live there anymore I live here now, so it doesn't matter does it. Ow, ow" yelped Rambo as Jill shook his head with his ears.

"I don't believe you, I really can't believe what you are saying." shouted Jill, her eyes filled with tears, "An entire world has been destroyed, and all you can think about is yourself, don't you care about the billions of lives that have been lost?"
"Ow, ouch look I didn't know anybody else." pleaded Rambo feebly. Jill stared hard into Rambo's eyes, Rambo wagged his tail hopefully.
"You're despicable," spat Jill releasing her grip on his ears, she pushed him away roughly. "You didn't even bother to ask how it happened."
"Er, Well I was just about to ask," lied Rambo. "That question was on my lips when you grabbed my ears, but the pain made me forget, honest." he gave Jill his best sorrowful doggy look. Jill glared back at him.
"You're not really interested," she growled at him
"Oh, I am, I'm really interested me, I think it's important that I know all there is to know about, er what's its name getting destroyed, and all that," replied Rambo as convincingly as he could, which unfortunately wasn't convincing at all.
"It was blown up." Said Jill coldly
"Oh dear, oh deary deary me, now that is just terrible, that's er, awful news it really is, er, quite distressing." Rambo fell over and rolled about a bit trying to look distressed.
"I suppose you would like to know who did it?" asked Jill sarcastically. Rambo stopped his distressed rolling for a moment.
"You must be able to read my mind," he said quickly. Jill shook her head in despair; she rose to her feet,

"Well seeing as you're so interested it was your friend Nobby." Rambo thought about this for a moment.
"Aye well, I did tell you he was a clumsy fucker; he nearly skewered my knackers once with an electric knife because he didn't put the blades on proper..." Rambo didn't get to finish what he was saying, he suddenly found himself on the other side of the room and in considerable agony. Through blurred and pain streaked eyes he saw Jill leave the room.
"Computer," he groaned feebly, "call the R.S.P.C.A, some ones just mashed me knackers."

"He's coming around," said the doctor monitoring his computer readouts from the recovery bed.
"What was the matter with him." asked Wellod, the big lipped green alien of the Imperial planetary protection fleet.
An hour had almost passed since he had transferred aboard, he had been greeted by the ship's captain and the chief of security who had gone to great pains to place the blame on this one, unconscious, individual. Wellod stared in disdain at the rousing form of Nobby, and even though he had seen the computer play back of the events leading to the premature end of the Emperors newly acquired planet, he found it difficult to imagine that the scrawny humanoid before him was able to fool an entire ship's crew and overpower the security systems. He listened intently as the doctor spoke.

"Well on initial diagnosis, everything points towards post hypnotic overload syndrome." answered the doc
"So what does that mean exactly?" queried Wellod. A question both the Captain and the security Chief wanted to ask as well.
"Well to put it in simple terms.." The doc emphasised the word simple with a smile towards the Imperial alien. The Imperial alien smiled back, missing the point entirely.
"..What appears to have occurred is that our patient here has been the victim of a hypnotic over load, caused by a probable deep founded hypnotic suggestion resulting in his mind acting in a predetermined manner on receiving a specific stimulus."
"Er.. self hypnosis?" asked the chief hopefully. Otherwise Nobby would have to be classed as innocent and under Imperial law that meant that he as security chief of the ship would have to take full responsibility. Unless the real culprit could be found.
"No, not to this degree, it would be impossible to implant such a strong suggestion on oneself." replied the doctor, dashing all the chiefs' hopes.
"So who is responsible then?" demanded Wellod looking at the security chief.
"I'm afraid that's something my instruments can't tell me." answered the doc.
"I will launch a full investigation straight away." Interrupted the security chief, "and as soon as we have found the culprit we will, of course, inform the Emperor and then you can come back then and take it from there...."
"Silence, your vessel will be taken from this place and escorted to the imperial home planet, no one is permitted

to leave the vessel or attempt to make contact with any other planets. You may carry on with your investigation, and if no one has been found responsible for this crime by the time we have arrived at our destination, then the captain and security chief will bear the full responsibility of all the charges. If you needed my assistance, you can contact me aboard my ship, good day gentlemen you have two days." At this Wellod turned and left the sick bay. The doctor, captain and Chief watched him leave, as his huge frame disappeared through the doorway a frail voice interrupted the silence.
"Excuse me.." it said. They all turned and found Nobby half sat up on the examination bed. The doctor returned his attention to the computer.
"How do you feel?" asked the doctor with out looking up from his read outs.
"What happened, the last thing I remember was...." Nobby's facial expression suddenly changed to one of panic. He turned to face the security chief, "Quick there is going to be an attempt to take over the ship and destroy the Earth, you have to stop him!!" babbled Nobby excitedly. The chief looked Nobby over once before answering.
"Stop who?" asked the chief. Nobby opened his mouth to answer and then closed it again. He thought about it for a moment,
"Er, …me apparently." Nobby said softly, "Sorry, have I missed something?" He asked as he looked from face to face with the three Dolphoids.
"Here drink this, and we'll explain everything," said the doctor handing a beaker of liquid to Nobby.

"Oh cheers," remarked Nobby to the doctor, he took the drink and after a quick sniff gulped it down eagerly. He smacked his lips in appreciation. "That was nice, What was it?"
"Truth serum. We need answers quickly, and we haven't the time for playing games." Said the doctor simply.
"What is the last thing you remember before waking up here?" interrupted the security chief, Nobby turned his attention to him, he felt a strong sense of deja vu.
"Er, I.. He's just given me some truth serum," stated Nobby suddenly
"Yes I know." replied the chief.
"Why?"
"Because I told him to, that's why." said the chief.
"But you can't do that!" said Nobby shuffling up on the sick bay bed, trying to edge away from the three Dolphoids.
"Yes we can, and we did, so if you will just..." Began the chief
"No you can't" shouted Nobby, "It's in the Jennifer Confection."
"Geneva convention." Corrected the security chief, "And it doesn't cover being held prisoner by aliens and force fed truth drugs."
"Shit" sighed Nobby quickly resigning himself to the fact that he was well and truly up the proverbial creek in a leaky canoe, with no visible means of propulsion. "Ok then, what exactly does this truth serum do ?"
"Er, it makes you tell the truth!" said the doctor
"Well that's handy considering what it's called," replied Nobby with a smile. All three Dolphoid winced slightly.
"How long before it starts to work?" asked the Chief

"Well I'm not an expert on human physiology, but I would guess more or less straight away." the doc answered.
"What is your name?" asked the chief turning to Nobby.
"Oh, I suddenly feel all giddy," replied Nobby swaying slightly. The Chief looked back at the doctor questioningly.
"I have never administered this particular drug to a human before," stated the doctor defensively, " I surmise that as the drug suppresses his abilities of inventive thought, he may experience a slight sense of pseudo intoxication."
"Meaning?" demanded the chief
"He will probably feel like he has been drinking a lot of alcohol, but will at the same time be unable to fabricate stories or exaggerate the truth." replied the doctor with a sigh, he hated having to explain things in simple terms for the likes of burly and thankless individuals like the chief.
"What is your name?" demanded the chief of Nobby again.
"Aren't you ugly," answered Nobby with a giggle. "I do feel all peculiar."
"What is your Name?" asked the chief again.
"Oh, don't tell me I know this one, er, Bobby! No, Nobby, that's it, Nobby, not Bobby at all."
"Who is responsible for destroying the planet Earth?"
"Er, yeah sorry about that, but I believe that it was me, but not to worry, I'll pay for the damages." slurred Nobby while trying desperately to keep hold of the bed he was sat on, everything kept zooming in and out of focus.

"Did you plan the takeover of the bridge yourself?" questioned the chief standing before Nobby and watching him sway. He looked over again at the doctor who checked his computer readouts and nodded.
"Oh no, not me, I can't even set the video. It must have been someone else." giggled Nobby moment before falling off the examination bed. The chief and the captain lifted him back up, and the doctor gave him a quick check over.
"He's fine," said the doctor
"Who helped you overcome the bridges defences?" asked the Chief
"Ah, well, I can't quite remember your honour." slurred Nobby. "But I think it was the man from Atlantis. Or Flipper. Or perhaps it was both, Sorry I can't seem to give a monkey's." added Nobby with a giggle. The security chief stepped forwards and slapped Nobby soundly across the face with a leather clad hand.
"What the hell do you think you are doing?" shouted the doctor pulling the chief away from Nobby.
"He's stalling, and quite frankly we don't have the time for this." replied the chief. He had two days to extract a full confession from Nobby or anybody else for that matter. His concern was not with how he got a confession, just as long as it absolved him personally of any blame what so ever.
"I don't give a damn!" sneered the doctor in the direction of the chief, while examining the growing red welt across Nobby's face. "This is the sick bay, and I give the orders in here. We have no idea what damage could have been done to this humans brain by the hypnotic

suggestion, slapping him around is not going to help, understand!!"
"It's alright darling" replied Nobby before the chief had a chance to, "I enjoy a bit of rough, but I'm not paying any more than twenty pounds, you saucy little giddy kipper you."
"I think that perhaps you should come back later," said the doc to the chief. "You'll get nothing from him in his present state, we'll have to let the serum wear off a bit."
"Don't you worry about me, you silver clad temptress." interrupted Nobby grasping his crotch area, "There's enough here for you and both your sisters."
The chief considered his options; eventually, he nodded agreement to the doctor and turned to leave. The Captain shrugged his shoulders at the Doctor and followed the security chief.
"No, come back I love you," shouted Nobby while managing to fall from the examination table for the second time. The Doctor turned to Nobby's crumpled form on the floor.
"Come on Nobby; let's get you back into bed." He said bending to retrieve his patient. Nobby lifted his head to face the Doctor and cocked a missing eyebrow.
"Ok then you smooth talking little nymph, but we'll have to be quiet, my dad's asleep in the next room." grinned Nobby, and then passed out. The Doctor scratched his head in confusion; it had been a strange couple of hours. He took the blanket from the bed and draped it over Nobby's snoring body.
"Computer, I am going back to my quarters. No one is to leave or enter this room, inform me the moment the

patient regains consciousness." With one final look at to sleeping Nobby, the Doctor left the room.

The security chief sat at his desk, his eyes glued intently to the view screen of his computer. He had been sat staring at the computer for more than an hour now. "Come on, give me a clue," he said through gritted teeth as he watched for the eighth time the computers play back of the earlier events on the bridge. He had watched the scene again and again from every available angle, he knew there was a clue in there somewhere, but he was damned if he could see it.
"Computer, scan logs for this time sequence for any telepathic or even paranormal activity." asked the chief, he knew he was clutching at straws, but he willing to give anything a go at the moment.
"There was no telepathic or paranormal from within the bridge section of the ship recorded at this time frame." replied the computer after several seconds.
"Hmm," murmured the chief. "How about telepathic or paranormal activity's emanating from beyond the bridge?" once again the computer remained silent for several seconds.
"Telepathic messages would be unable to pass through the bridge areas electron deflectors osculating magnetic energy field. The effects of paranormal phenomena on the bridge areas electron deflector is unknown due to the uncertain and arguable parameters within which a subject could be classified as paranormal." intoned the

computer. The chief rubbed his chin absently as he thought.
"Was any telepathic activity recorded at all, anywhere on the ship during this time sequence?"
"Affirmative." answered the computer. Suddenly the chief sat forward in his chair, at last maybe this was the lead he was looking for.
"What was the location of the telepathic activity?" snapped the chief.
"Deck six, section four." informed the computer instantly. The chief rubbed at his chin again.
"The science blocks," he muttered to himself. "Was the activity part of a controlled and monitored experiment?"
"Negative, there is no logged permission for any such activity." The chief felt his hopes rise slightly at the computer's answer; at last, he was getting somewhere.
"Identify the individual or individuals responsible."
"The individuals are identified as Groonhoot Malinki and Broppchet Proot." returned the computer.
"Who?"
"Groonhoot Malinki and Broppchet Proot." repeated the computer.
"Right, and what do we know of er, these individuals?"
"Both Malinki and Proot came aboard as voluntary subjects when the ship was docked in orbit around their home planet of Kurhud, Catalogue number 997 cvm/22b. They agreed to stay aboard and be examined provided that they were allowed to go to the toilet whenever they wished and that they wouldn't be forced to fight any forms of cheese."
"Fight cheese!!" Interrupted the Chief. "Did you say fight cheese?"

“That is correct." replied the computer. " Before agreeing to remain they required assurances that even if a full scale cheese war broke out, they wouldn't be forced to fight any, and I quote especially them with hard skins on or those that smell off, but aren't. end quote" The chief furrowed his brow and once again rubbed his chin.
"Are they stupid or something?" he asked.
"Yes, very much so. They have a combined I.Q of sixty two." replied the computer.
"Well," remarked the chief, "whatever their I.Q, they are our prime suspects at this present time. Have a team of security men bring them in for questioning."
"I believe that that would be a waste of time and effort." answered the computer.
"Oh, you would, would you?" sneered the chief. "And exactly why would we be wasting our time?"
"Although both Malinki and Proot are gifted with telepathic abilities, unfortunately, neither of the pair are aware of the fact." replied the computer. Once again the chief rubbed his chin and let out a sigh as his slumped back into his seat.
"Sorry, you lost me there. How can they not know they are telepathic?"
"Both Malinki and Proot are, to say the least, simple creatures. Their level of intelligence is similar to that of the legendary happy love people of the planet Peace, in the star system Catalogue number BB945MK01A."
"The who of where?" interrupted the chief.
"The happy love people of the planet Peace."
"Never heard of them, what have they got to do with our two suspects?"

"The happy love people were also simple people. They were all descended from two fierce, warlike tribes known as the Who are you looking at? Tribe and the Oy, you just spilled my pint tribe. Both these tribes had been locked in a savage battle for over two thousand years, a relentless war that swept the whole planet dividing its inhabitants into either one or the other tribes. Untold billions of lives were wasted, and the lands stood scarred and ruined from the endless onslaught of warfare. Their future was a bleak and unsavoury one, or at least it was until someone had the idea of instead of fighting let's love each other instead. At first, the idea was met with dubious scepticism, but an inter tribal exchange system was set up to test the theory. Twenty individuals from each tribe were put together and ordered to make love instead of war. The tests proved to be a success, and the war was replaced with love, and both tribes merged together and became the happy love people." explained the computer.
"And what relevance has this on our two suspects?" inquired the chief.
"After so many years of war, the now reformed tribes embraced love as a total way of life. Anger, hatred and selfishness were completely forgotten after several generations. But unfortunately, that was to become their down fall. Their love extended to the animals that also inhabited the planet, and it was decreed that all living creatures were sacred and that none should be harmed. So as a result the whole population of the planet became vegetarians, which worked well for several decades until some bright spark suggested that plants were also

technically speaking living things and therefore should be bestowed the same rights as animals."
"And what happened then?" asked the chief after a short paused once he realised the computer wasn't forth coming with the information.
"Everybody agreed that plants should also be regarded as sacred, and a short while later the whole population of the planet starved to death." replied the computer matter of factly.
"Oh." was the chiefs simple reply, " But I still can't see what all that had to do with our problem.
"Malinki and Proot are from a planet with a similar history, several centuries of all-out war followed by a sudden reversal of feeling. Although their planets adoption of peace wasn't as extreme as the happy love people's, but the principle is the same. Tests have proved that neither Malinki nor Proot understand the concept of hatred or anger. All they ever want to do is clean and sing, and apparently, their greatest fear is as I said before, fighting cheese."
"Brilliant, our only real lead turns out to be a couple of operatic janitors with terminal cheese o phobia." grumbled the chief miserably. His options were looking a bit thin, even though that human Nobby had done the deed, technically he couldn't be held responsible. And as chief of the ship's security he himself would have to bear the responsibility, an honour he didn't cherish. "Well, in that case computer, I fear that I don't know where else to start looking."
"Perhaps you could start by questioning the only other individual aboard the ship apart from yourself who would know the code red security override codes."

suggested the computer. Suddenly the chief's full attention was on the computer screen, it had not occurred to him to find out how Nobby had overridden the ships systems; he had been to wrapped up in just finding someone to blame other than himself.
"Only the ships security chief is privy to that information" stated the chief. "not even the captain is aware of its existence. The code red security override code is there only to be used by myself to regain control of the ship via any available console in case of mutiny or other forceful takeover of the ship. The code is not written down anywhere, it is passed on only by word of mouth direct from the security council, it is impossible for anyone other than the security chief to have it." The chief drummed his fingers on the table top as he spoke, something he often did when his anger began to rise. He was angry at the fact that he hadn't considered the question of how the ship had been overrode, but even angrier at the possibility that someone other than himself had the ships ultimate override code
"You are correct in saying that the chief of security is the only person to have access to the codes." replied the computer. The chief slammed his fist down hard on the desk top causing everything on it to shudder.
"DON'T PLAY WITH ME." he screamed. "If only the security chief has the code, how could anybody else have it. You have already said the someone else has it, and at the same time you are saying that the information is only available to the security chief, I am the security chief of this ship!!" added the chief accentuating his words with several more fist poundings.

"You are indeed the chief of this ship's security," returned the computer unfazed by the Dolphoid's temper. "But you are not the only security chief aboard this vessel; there is a security operative higher ranking than yourself aboard the ship."
"WHAT!!" bellowed the chief, he grabbed the edges of the computer monitor and brought his face close to the screen. He bared his razor like teeth in a twisted snarl and spoke softly, yet menacingly to the computer. "Are telling me that there is a government spy on this ship?"
"There is indeed an operative from the governmental security division aboard this ship." answered the computer, impervious to the Chiefs threatening tones. The chief felt his grip tighten on the monitor; he heard the structure of it creak under the pressure. A thousand questions ran amok in his mind, but one stood alone from the rest.
"WHO?" he demanded
"Unfortunately that information is still classified at the present moment." The chief resisted the temptation to slam his fist through the screen; it wouldn't help matters, although it would probably feel good. Instead, he stood up straight, placed his hands behind his back and slowly began to pace the room. "Ok," he said after a few moments, "why is there a spy aboard the ship?"
"It is standard procedure on all long range exploratory missions." replied the computer.
"Really, and exactly what is their purpose?" asked the chief, he continued his slow deliberate pacing around the room.
"To protect the home world from any threats which may result from the exploratory nature of these missions."

"I see," said the chief, absorbing the information. "And would this spy have anything to do with our present situation?"
"That is correct." replied the computer simply. The chief sensed a chill pass through the length of his body. The sinister undertones of the computer's reply were beginning to make him worried.
"Well, in that case," he continued as calmly as possible, "Suppose you tell me everything you know or at least everything you can about it then."

"Oh my god, I don't feel well," said Nobby for the fifth time in the last two minutes. He was sat on the edge of the sick bays examination bed, clutching a large plastic bucket, into which he had already deposited several technicoloured yawns.
"You will be alright in a few minutes." answered the doctor from his desk further down the room.
"You said that a few minutes ago." whined Nobby dejectedly.
"You'll be fine, don't worry." replied the doctor.
"Oh, yeah that's easy for you to say. You haven't got loads of truth serum in you." snapped Nobby.
"And neither have you." said the doctor gesturing towards the bucket. Nobby glanced at its contents and then suddenly wished he hadn't. He placed the bucket on the bed beside him and then put his feet on the floor to test his legs. The first time he tried to stand up about ten minutes ago he found that his legs were still unconscious and refuse to be revived. He slowly pushed himself from the bed, gradually increasing the weight on each leg.

After a moment or two of standing unaided Nobby decide to try a step or two. He found that his legs responded happily to his request.
"Er, excuse me doc, but how long am I going to have wait here, it's just, well I can't stand you. Er, I mean I think you're ugly. Shit!" Nobby quickly put his hand to his mouth to stop himself talking. He looked sheepishly at the doctor. "Sorry I er,.."
"Don't worry it's just the effects of the truth serum." said the doctor reassuringly.
"Unfortunately you will not be able to stop yourself from saying what you really think."
"Even so," began Nobby, "I shouldn't have said that I don't really think you're ugly, well actually yes I do. Fuck!!" he exclaimed.
"Don't worry about it." reasoned the doctor, "I suppose in your terms I would appear quite er, different." Nobby shrugged and nodded feebly at the doctors understanding. Nobby hadn't meant to insult the doc, As far as he knew the doctor could be considered as a dashing hunk, in a Dolphoids point of view. But none the less, to Nobby he was just an overgrown fish in a boiler suit.
"I'm sorry all the same." apologised Nobby. "But I was supposed to be questioned, and considering the effects of the truth serum, I thought now would be as good a time as any."
"Well, I would agree with you, but while you were asleep the chief called to say that he didn't need to question you." said the doctor.
"Oh right, does that mean that I can go then?"

"Yes, but unfortunately you will be escorted back to your quarters by two security guards, and you will have to remain there until the meeting later." replied the doctor
"What meeting?" asked Nobby.
"The one that the chief has called for, in three hours' time. Apparently, you are the guest of honour." answered the doctor with a smile that didn't appeal to Nobby.
"Oh, I see. Sounds ominous." sighed Nobby. "By the way doc, do you have a name? Just something I can call you other than Doc."
"You mean an Earth name?" asked the doctor, Nobby Nodded. "Well, I really never gave it much thought before. I suppose it wouldn't hurt to have one if it makes it easier for you." Again, Nobby nodded rather than answer vocally. The doctor studied for a moment.
"Truth is Nobby I don't really know any Earth names, perhaps you could choose one for me."
"It would be a pleasure," replied Nobby choosing his words carefully. "How about Crippen?"
"Crippen!" repeated the doctor.
"Yes, Crippen, he was a very famous doctor back on Earth."
"Oh, in that case, Crippen it shall be then." replied the doctor sounding the name to himself a couple of times.
"I suppose it will grow on me."
"Smashing, can I go now, then, Crippen?" asked Nobby suppressing a smirk.
"Yes, but you'll have to have a security escort I'm afraid."
"That's alright, I'm getting used to them." said Nobby truthfully.

CHAPTER TWELVE

Nobby had only been back in his quarters about six minutes when the computer informed him of Bills arrival.
"Oh, brilliant timing," said Nobby through clenched teeth to himself, as sat on the toilet straining over an unnaturally stubborn channel trout. "Tell him to wait a couple of minutes, I won't be long." he uttered with a sigh as he and last night's dinner finally parted company.

Two minutes later, after having his ring piece scrubbed, cleaned, disinfected and perfumed by the toilets automatic hygiene system, he was sat on his bed talking to Bill.
"I can't understand how you did It," said Bill wringing his hands together with worry, his brow furrowed in concern. "They say you completely disabled all the ships security systems and took control of the ship in ten seconds."
"Three seconds." correct Nobby absently.
"Three seconds!" repeated Bill in awe. "How?"
"I really haven't the foggiest, Look, Bill, there's something that's been puzzling me, and you might be able to help me understand it," answered Nobby placing his hand on Bills shoulder.
"Sure, anything. What's the puzzle?"

"A couple of days ago you told me we were travelling at a fantastic speed towards another so called twin planet, yes?" questioned Nobby. Bill looked a bit perplexed but agreed.
"Yes that's right." he said
"Well, this is the problem, if we were supposed to be hurtling through space, away from the Earth, how come we were still in orbit around it at the time of me blowing it up just a couple of days later? do you see my problem."
"Ah yes, that indeed is a curious happening, and unfortunately I don't know the answer." remarked Bill, "All I know is that everyone involved in the exploratory part of this mission received a memo stating what the advance probe had discovered and subsequent alterations to the mission planned course. Up until a couple of hours ago I was still under the impression that we were still on our way there."
"So in reality," spoke Nobby, "if we were travelling to that other planet as we were supposed to be doing, none of this could have happened?"
"That may be true, but what are you getting at?" asked the Dolphoid
"Well, obviously I didn't just accidentally destroy Earth, somehow someone made me do it, I don't know how but the doctor mentioned something about hypnosis. But however they made me do it isn't really important right now, the important fact is that for me to be able to do what I did, it was vitally important that we be somewhere near the Earth So whoever is really behind this must have the power or authority to alter the ship's course. Do you follow what I am saying?" Bill regarded

Nobby for a moment, he wiped away the sweat that had developed on the end of his snout like nose before answering.
“Not 100%, but bear with me a moment." he replied, his brow furrowed with thought.
"Let’s see, what you are saying is that if someone had planned for you to do this, which I honestly believe they have, and then any alterations to our flight plans would have in effect thwarted their scheme. Unless somehow they have enough influence or rank to be able to order the ships return to this position. Is that right?"
"Spot on," said Nobby with a relieved smile. Bill was surprised to find that he didn't flinch. "So, all we have to do," continued Nobby, "is find out who gave the order to return here and that is our real culprit,"
"Computer," said Bill before Nobby had the chance to ask him. "Who gave the order to return the ship to its current orbit?"
"That information is classified." returned the computer. Both Nobby and Bill looked at each other quizzically.
"Ok, what reason was given for the necessity of the ships return." tried Bill.
"All information regarding these matters are classified." answered the computer. Bill decided to change tactics.
"Computer, put me through to the security chief," demanded Bill
"The security chief isn't taking any calls at the moment." replied the computer.
"Tell him I know who is responsible for the destruction of the Earth." lied Bill. The computer remained silent for several seconds, Bill was about to repeat the last bit of

information when the security chief voice boomed through the computer's speakers.
"What!!" he bellowed, "Who am I talking too?" Bill stood up before he answered; straightening his uniform just in case the chief could see him.
"I am.." at this point Bill let out a piercing screech which was his name. The sound rang painfully through Nobby's ears.
"So you know who is responsible for the planet Earth's destruction do you?" sneered the chief. Bill felt his legs begin to shake and his mouth go dry at the chiefs obviously unpleased tones
"Well, actually no we don't," answered Nobby instead. " But with your help maybe we could find out.
"Listen friend" the last word was spat out by the chief "You have caused us enough trouble today, and believe me when I say that I am not in the mood for playing games. Now either you tell me who is responsible or I shall come and personally shoot you."
"Ok then," began Nobby. "The person responsible for the destruction of the Earth is the same person who gave the order to return the ship back here." There was a short silence following this statement, and Nobby suddenly realised that he could in fact just have revealed this information to the very person who gave the order. After all, he was the ships security chief, he would know all the ships security codes, he has the authority to give orders to the captain, and it was him who had taken Nobby personally to the bridge. Last night's supper began to make its presence felt in Nobby's bowels.
"Is that it?" eventually returned the voice of the chief

"Er, y..y..yes." stuttered Nobby nervously. "But I could be wrong." He added quickly
"No, you're not wrong." came the stark reply. Nobby was about to start panicking, He had visions of the chief bursting through the door at any moment with a laser gun and shouting You may have discovered my secret, but you won't live to tell. The only thing that stopped Nobby fearing totally for his safety was the utter despondency in the chief's voice.
"You mean you already know?" asked Bill who felt a little braver since Nobby had already done the hard bit.
"Yes and no." was the chief simple reply.
"Yes and no!" repeated Bill. "What's that meant to mean?"
"That is all I can say on the subject at the moment. I will explain the situation in full at the meeting later." at this, the computer beeped to signify that the chief had ended the transmission. Bill turned to Nobby,
"Well at least we know that the chief has the situation in hand," he said more cheerfully than necessary after seeing Nobby's gloomy expression.
"I wouldn't be too sure," replied Nobby. "He seemed a bit disappointed that we didn't actually know the perpetrator's name." Bill pondered for a moment and then shook his head slowly.
"No.," he said, "I don't think he knows either."
"So, what now?"
"When's the meeting?" asked Nobby
"In a little over two hours," replied Bill after consulting a small credit card sized object from his pocket. "Fancy something to eat?"

"No, not really, I think I'll just stay here and have a quick wank, Er... I mean grab forty wan...shit!!" said Nobby jumping from the bed. "bollocks." he added while slapping his fore head.
"Are you alright?" asked Bill with concern, "Shall I call for the doctor?"
"No, it's alright. It's just the doctor gave me some truth serum earlier and, well I can't stop saying things that perhaps I shouldn't." explained Nobby as diplomatically as possible.
"Oh right," smiled Bill. "In that case, I shall leave you to have a ..er, rest. I'll call by later to pick you up for the meeting. Sweet er, dreams." he said as he made his way to the door. Nobby declined to answer on fear that he may say something he really regretted. After Bill had gone, Nobby returned to his bed and flopped on to it. He turned on to his back, laced his fingers together and put them behind his head, out of harm's way.

"Look I've already said I'm sorry." pleaded Jill, "What else can I do?"
"You could kiss them better for me." answered Rambo indicating his throbbing testicles that were at present neatly wrapped in an ice pack administered by the ship veterinary surgeon.
"NO!!" replied Jill bluntly
"A rub then?" enquired Rambo hopefully.
"I said no, and that's final."

“Ow, ow, ouch," replied Rambo writhing around in mock agony. "The pain, the terrible pain, ow, ow."
"And you can pack that in. The vet said that it is nothing more serious than minor bruising. Besides, he gave you a pain inhibitor, so I know you can't feel anything."
"It's the mental torment." answered Rambo placing his paws on his head. " Oh the torment, the agony of er, my, er,..brain." he overacted. Jill sighed and settled herself down in a chair, this could take a long time.
"What mental torment?" she asked without much sympathy.
"Oh, er, the, er mental torment of, er, maybe not being able to father puppies. Yeah, that's it. Not being able to have pups, that'll do for a start." said Rambo working it out as he went on.
"Well regardless of the state of your testicles, it would be impossible for you to father any puppies anyway." stated Jill.
"What are you trying to say?" asked Rambo indignantly. "There was nothing wrong with my little puppy factories until you volleyed them. In fact, I bet I could've got a bitch up the duff just by looking at her, that's how powerful they were. They were my pride and joy; I gave them a damn good licking every day."
"And exactly how many bitches have you made pregnant then?" asked Jill sarcastically.
"Oh er, well none actually, but that wasn't my fault, given a chance, I would have been frotting away at anything that stopped still long enough." said Rambo defensively.
"So, in reality, you have no idea whether they worked or not?" chided Jill

"Of course they worked." Snapped Rambo
"How do you know?"
"I just do alright, not that it matters now, they'll probably never work again thanks to you," growled Rambo sulkily. Jill sat forward in her chair, placed her elbows on her knees and her chin, as such, on her interwoven fingers.
"Ok then, just imagine for one moment that your testicles are in perfect working order, and the vet assures me that they are. Exactly who would you mate with?" she asked
"A bitch of course," said Rambo with a wag of his tail.
"Rambo there are no bitches, you are the only member of your species left."
"Since when?"
"Since the Earth was destroyed."
"Oh yeah, I'd forgot about that. Oh well, their loss," said Rambo flippantly. "What's for dinner then?". Once again Jill sat back and sighed deeply.
"Rambo, The Earth has been destroyed; you are the only one of your kind left. Doesn't that bother you?" she asked.
"Er, are you going to kick me again?" replied Rambo shuffling to a safe distance.
"No."
"Well in that case not really, apart from I'll never be able to hump that Labrador from down the street. She kept pissing outside my gate, egging me on, she was gagging for it. She could have had it as well if it wasn't for that Nobby. By the way, how is he, been put down yet?" asked Rambo hopefully

"The last I heard he was in sick bay," answered Jill deciding not to pursue the matter of Rambo's lack of interest in the world's destruction.
"Oh really, I hope it's something fatal." barked Rambo with amusement.
"You don't really mean that, surely," asked Jill
"Oh don't I?" mocked Rambo. " In fact, if he were to get eaten by a, er, er, a big thing that eats people, I wouldn't give a chuff, and that's the truth."
"Don't you have any feelings," Jill asked gruffly
"Yes, I have lots of feelings, trouble is they are all concentrated around my knackers at the moment," replied Rambo with a sarcastic bark. Jill stood up suddenly, and Rambo instinctively ran for cover.
"I am going now." She said calmly, "I will be back in a while to take you to a meeting."
"What meeting?"
"A meeting that has been called, by the ship's chief of security, for everyone who had any professional or personal interest in the planet Earth." replied Jill as though reading the words from an official letter.
"And what's that got to do with me?" asked Rambo.
"Planet Earth was your home planet."
"Yeah, maybe so, but I didn't have any interest in it." barked Rambo. Jill closed her eyes and shook her head. She turned and left the room without saying anymore. The door materialised behind her leaving Rambo on his own. He carefully had a scratch behind his ear with his hind leg, trying desperately not to rattle his delicate love plums too much. Once satisfied that the offending itch had been sated, he turned his attention to the computer.
"Oy, computer." he barked.

"Yes Rambo." came the instant reply.
"I want to ask you a question," said Rambo
"Please feel free to ask." answered the computer cheerily
"Right, er have you got any bitches in this place?"
"Please define bitches" replied the computer
"You know, hot to frot fur bags. Red hot four legged love cushions." enlightened Rambo. The computer fell silent for several seconds.
"I am unable to find any reference to which you require in the ships data banks."
"Ok then, er let's see." pondered Rambo. "Right, what type of animal am I?"
"You are a quadruped of the canine variety."
"Good." enthused Rambo, "Have you got any more of them, but without bollocks?"

"Did you have a good er, rest?" enquired Bill as he and Nobby made their way to the dining hall, where the meeting was to be held.
"Oh you're ever so funny Bill," said Nobby sarcastically. He took a quick glance over his shoulder at the two security men following them both at a not so discreet distance. "Why are those two still following me?" whispered Nobby, Bill looked around at the ensuing escort.
"Well, you did not so long since destroy an entire planet. Maybe they are celebrity stalkers." joked the Dolphoid. "Or maybe they are following you, Bill?"
"Now why would they be following me?" asked Bill light heartedly.

"It could have something to do with the fact that there is a huge rip in the back of your uniform and your arse is hanging out."
"WHAT, WHERE!!" said Bill loudly while instinctively grasping his back side and checking his clothing for any damage.
"Ah, got you." laughed Nobby. Bill looked puzzled for a second before the penny dropped
"That was a joke, wasn't it?"
"Yep." replied Nobby with a broad smile. Again, Bill didn't flinch.
"I see, yes very good. You did indeed get me." chuckled Bill. "I must say it's nice to see you in such a cheerful mood again. It must have been that little er, rest you had earlier."
"Shut up," said Nobby in mock anger. They both laughed together, like naughty school children swapping dirty jokes. They both looked at their security escort and simultaneously broke out in gales of laughter at the guard's bemused expressions. Bill and Nobby both felt the days stresses lifting with the laughter and without words, the look in each other's eyes told them that more of the same was needed. After several moments Nobby managed to add some more fuel to their merriment.
"I don't fancy yours much." He said indicating the beefiest of the two security men.
"Can I share yours then?" giggled Bill
"No he's all mine." At this Nobby turned and blew the security man a kiss. Both security men looked at each other questioningly and then tightened their grip on their weapons, just in case.

"Hey I've just noticed something Bill!" exclaimed Nobby seriously
"What?" asked Bill looking around the corridor.
"The truth serums wore off." smiled Nobby
"Oh good, you must have sweated it out while having your little rest." Giggled Bill, with a knowing wink.
"You cheeky bugger!" laughed Nobby, as he placed his arm around Bills neck and gave it a playful squeeze. Seconds Later he was laid out on the floor with a security man kneeling on his chest and a laser weapon lodged firmly up his nostril. The weight of the security man prevented Nobby from both talking and breathing, but there again Nobby realised that judging by the facial expression of the man on his chest, his assailant cared little for small talk or the fact that his victim's lips were beginning to turn blue.
"Get off of him now and that's an order!!" Nobby heard Bills raised voice but his scope of view was very limited, he saw the guard on his chest quickly look round at Bill, and the expression on his face suddenly changed. A second later he had removed himself from Nobby's chest and was stood to attention. Nobby drew in a deep breath and began coughing and spluttering. Bill appeared beside him and he felt himself being eased up into a sitting position.
"Are you alright?" asked Bill worriedly.
"W..what happened?" gasped Nobby, his coughing preventing him filling his lungs properly.
"Sorry I should have known." apologised Bill, "But they thought you were attacking me."
"Oh." gasped Nobby trying to get to his feet with Bills assistance. "I suppose it could have looked that way. "

"You were very lucky," remarked Bill
"Oh was I really?" replied Nobby sarcastically
"Yes, they have orders to shoot."
"Christ!!" said Nobby not so sarcastically. "Why?" he added
"Well after what you did earlier, who knows what else you might have been hypnotised to do," explained Bill grimly. "The security of the ship is too important."
"So what you're saying is, that for the rest of my time on this ship I am going to followed everywhere by a couple of trigger happy guards?" said Nobby angrily.
"Well yes and no." answered Bill, "Truth is we could all be executed in a couple of days anyway, so I wouldn't worry about it too much if I were you." Nobby stared into the Dolphoids eyes for a couple seconds, letting the words sink in. Then out of the blue he laughed, which surprised Bill immensely.
"You know something?" began Nobby, "You nearly had me there. I nearly fell for it. Executed in a couple of days, you're a funny guy Bill."
"I'm not joking Nobby, what I say is true. At this very moment, we are being escorted to the home planet of the person who owned the planet Earth. Some kind of self styled Emperor who claims to own various planets and is very protective of them. He is a very powerful person." Bill tried to explain, but Nobby wasn't taking him seriously.
"Bill mate, you're milking it. I'm not falling for it." said Nobby with a half-smile. It has to be a joke, he thought to himself, yet neither Bill's nor either of the security men's face showed the slightest bit of humour. "You are joking, right?" he asked with a sudden dry mouth. Bill

shook his head solemnly. Nobby began to realise that many things had happened that he was unaware of, dreadful thing that were the consequences of his actions. Even though he had technically been cleared of the Earth's destruction, he was still responsible for the biggest act of mass murder possible. Up until now he had regarded the fact with little consequence, natural ability to accept the absurd had kicked in, as it had on many other occasions in his life. His brain had effortlessly separated him from the shocking truth, cushioning his conscious and quickly displacing his guilt and substituting it with self-pity.
"I.. " Began Nobby but his words were drowned by tears. The weight of countless billions of lives bore down on him quickly and heavily. Racked with remorse, he slumped to his knees, sobbing deeply. Unable to speak and tormented by sudden realisation, he began to beat his fists upon the floor, each impact echoing a silently screamed curse with in his thoughts.
He was unaware of how long he had pounded the floor, he was only vaguely aware of the doctor arriving. He was only aware of the hypo spray being pressed against his neck for a second before everything went blank.

When Nobby next opened his eyes, he was surprised to still find himself on the corridor floor, flanked by his personal security men.
"He should be okay in a moment." he heard the doctor say from somewhere out of sight.
"Hey Crippen, is that you?" inquired Nobby rising to his knees, shuffling around to face the source of the voice.

"Yes, Nobby. " replied the doc. "How are you feeling?"
Nobby deliberated over the answer for a moment.
"Well now that you mention it, I feel unnervingly fine and dandy, which should worry me, but I don't seem to be able to give a fuck!" responded Nobby with a shrug.
Bill gave the doctor a worried glance.
"Well I have given you an anti depressant, Nobby." explained the doctor, "It's nothing to worry about, and it will just stop all the nasty thoughts for a while." Went on the doc, speaking in a manner that resembled that of trying to sweet talk a child.
"Oh right," said Nobby. "Er, is there any side effects that I should know about?"
"Well. Only that you may feel euphoric and a little spaced out for a while."
"Is that painful?" questioned Nobby
"Not at all." reassured the doctor.
"Right you are then Crip, me old pal." responded Nobby.
Bill stood silently behind the doctor, he never was a great believer in the use of such drugs, and the sudden mood swing he had just witnessed in Nobby caused him concern.
"Er, may I have a word in private," Bill asked the doctor, taking his elbow and leading him to one side out of earshot.
"Will you excuse us a moment Nobby." He said over his shoulder to Nobby.
"Yeah, sure. I'll just chill out here with Cagney and Lacey." He replied indicating his security escort.
Once out of range Bill spoke to the doctor.
"Was that really necessary, pumping people full of potions and serums is not always the best answer."

"What else was I to do, you could see for yourself he was hysterical." defended the doc.
"He wasn't hysterical. He was just venting his anger and frustrations; he's been through a great deal these last few days. The stress of it all just caught up with him.
He should have been left and given time to come to terms with what has happened."
Bill spoke quietly yet firmly.
"I agree, but unfortunately time is not a luxury that we have. There is a meeting about to start in several minutes and the security chief is quite insistent that Nobby is to be present." replied the doc just a firmly. He placed his hand on Bills shoulder and softened the tone of his voice, " Listen, if we manage to work our way out of this, I promise I will give him all the help and counselling he needs, but until then my hands are tied."
Bill heeded his colleague's words.
"I'm sorry, I wasn't blaming you." He said. "I just don't know how much of this he can take."
"Don't worry, I will be there to keep a close eye on him." answered the doctor sympathetically. "Come, we have a meeting to attend," he added gesturing down the corridor. Bill nodded and they both made their way back over to Nobby.
"Hiya." He said as they approached. "Crippen, I need to ask you a question."
"Er, ok sure." replied Crippen
"These two security men, were they genetically designed to be this big and muscular, or are they freaks of nature that have been put to good use?" Both guards shot Nobby a glance, but remained stood to attention.

"Perhaps we can discuss this at another time." interrupted Bill, "I believe we have more engaging matters to attend to."
"Yes that's correct." agreed Crippen, "Come, we can all walk together." He added hinting towards the dining area.
"I suppose." moaned Nobby and set off with his four companions to the meeting.

The dining area was alive with gossip and speculation, crowded to capacity with everyone who had a professional interest in the now dead planet. Scientists, historians, geographers, cartographers, anthropologist, etc.. There was even a large contingency of bodies that had absolutely nothing at all to do with the extinct planet, but didn't want to miss out on anything important.
The tables of the dining hall had been replaced with row after row of chairs, set in a semi circle before a small raised platform, which had been suitably installed with a large monitor screen and a speaking lectern.
Every time the doors opened the room fell quickly silent for a second or two before the cacophony of voices resumed when it was apparent that the person entering the dining area wasn't the security chief. A whole spectrum of universal life forms had gathered together for the meeting, including the majority of Dolphoids, some shiny yellow skinned reptilian methane breathing swamp dwellers, from a marshy planet known locally as Harse! There was even one or two translucent jelly like

bipeds which smelt faintly of boiled eggs and had the uncanny ability of being able to join together to form an even bigger jelly monster if threatened. In fact, there was every conceivable type of hairy, scaly, lumpy, dimpled, feathered, bluish, greeny, pink, opaque, bi ped, tri ped, quadra ped, tentacled, tall, small, skinny, fat intelligent life form present. Every seat in the room was taken, except half a dozen in the front which had been reserved for special guests, one of whom was at that very moment in the adjoining kitchen finishing off his eighth helping of Gelkick.
"It's still too salty!" belched Wellod, captain of the imperial war fleet, in a deliberate attempt to upset the cook. He had so far complained that every portion he had eaten was in some way faulty. Such as it was too cold, too sweet, too slimy, too little or even too purple. On each occasion, the cook had nodded acknowledgement and re present Wellod with yet another dish of the Dolphoid speciality, which he ate eagerly before complaining. There had been nothing wrong with any of the dishes he had eaten, in truth, he had enjoyed each one immensely, it was just, more than anything else in the universe, he enjoyed being a bastard to any one he considered lower than himself, which as far as he was concerned was almost everybody.
"Perhaps you would like to try something else instead?" asked the cook nicely.
"No, I don't think so, I've eaten enough rubbish for one sitting." replied Wellod pushing his plate away in apparent disgust.
"Good." interrupted the chief swiftly, wanting to avoid any kind of confrontation. He smiled apologetically at

the cook who just raised his eyebrows slightly and nodded.
"We should really be getting on with the meeting, everyone's ready." he added.
"I'm not." grunted Wellod, "Where's the nearest toilet, I think you've poisoned my guts." he said punctuating the sentence with a rumbling trouser rattler of a fart.
"Er, through that door there." said the chief pointing the way and trying not to breathe through his snout.
"Right, I won't be long, so don't go have the meeting without me." called Wellod over his shoulder as he made his way to the little green aliens room, quacking a fart with every step. The chief waited until Wellod had left the room before speaking to the cook,
"Er, I don't suppose you have any air freshener in the kitchen, do you?"

Nobby, Bill, Crippen and the two security escorts entered the main dining hall at much the same time as Wellod was entering the toilet. All five of them stood in the doorway surveying the hundreds of eyes that had suddenly locked on to them. Nobby became quite unnerved, although not at the idea of hundreds of people staring at him, but more at the absolute silence that almost instantly fell upon the room as he entered. Fortunately, the feeling didn't last long, as the happy drugs administered by the doc rapidly made everything seem just fine and dandy.
"Er, perhaps we should find our seats?" suggested the doc timidly

"No," said Nobby firmly, "let them stare a bit longer," he added at a level loud enough for everyone to hear. Almost as one, the occupants of the room looked away and hushed conversations slowly began.
"Well done" whispered Bill.
"Thanks, Where are we sitting?" Nobby asked still loudly.
"I believe that there are some seats reserved near the front," replied Bill. Nobby was going to reply, but he had spotted a most unusual thing. At one end of the room a strange and impromptu Mexican wave had started, one line of seated people began to quickly get to their feet. There were many cries of "hey" and " What the..". Both Bill and the Doc had spotted it as well and had side stepped slightly as the security men stepped forwards for a closer look. Suddenly the wave which had originally been going in a straight line along one row of seats, changed direction and began to move diagonally in a line that seemed to be heading Nobby's way. More astonished cries accompanied the directional change. The wave was almost upon them, Nobby turn to look at Bill and Crippen, and as he did so, he failed to see Rambo come shooting out from under the seating, but to make up for not seeing Rambo, Nobby certainly felt Rambo as his teeth sank satisfactorily deep into Nobby buttocks. Now Rambo wasn't a big dog, he was normally only knee high to Nobby, but today he had lunged at Nobby and had managed to jump high enough to reach Nobby's backside.
Unfortunately for Rambo, and equally Nobby, he was now a couple of feet of the floor dangling from Nobby's arse, without any leverage to be able to pull himself free.

Nobby screamed in agony and spun around to see what was the cause of the pain, only he found nothing there, yet the pain suddenly increased as he had spun. Rambo quickly realised his predicament and began to scrabble urgently at the backs of Nobby's legs. Nobby screamed again as something began to rip his arse and legs to shreds, his screams were short lived as almost immediately he found himself face down on the ground being held down by one of the security men. Without warning the pain intensified greatly, and then as quickly as it had started, the pain virtually stopped. Working as one the security men had rushed forward knocking Nobby to the ground, and as one pinned him down the other grasped Rambo firmly and yanked him roughly from Nobby's buttocks, causing Rambo to leave behind a couple of teeth. Nobby heard the slight buzz of the transferal beam as he instantly found himself in the sickbay, face down on a bed. He felt some one spray something on to his wound, something cold yet soothing.
"Is that you Crippen?" He said weakly. He felt very tired all of a sudden.
"Shh," replied the doctor. "You've lost quite a bit of blood." Nobby then heard the hiss of the hypospray and then all was dark.

"What about my teeth?" growled Rambo though his new muzzle. Jill on the other side of the cell door looked down in disdain at the now chained up mongrel.
"Never mind your teeth, what about Nobby?" she practically growled back.

"Oh, yeah." chuckled Rambo, "I wish I could have seen his face. I bet it was a picture."
"IT ISN'T FUNNY." emphasised Jill coldly.
"Oh, yeah that's right, feel sorry for him. He's only lost a chunk out of his arse. I've lost some teeth and my chance of ever getting a shag, but no one's felt sorry for me. He blows up an entire planet and he gets tea and bloody sympathy, I have a piss in the corner and I get a bollocking off the bloody computer and sprayed and disinfected by the hygiene droids." barked Rambo angrily.
"That isn't true and you know it." replied Jill
"Oh, isn't it." mocked Rambo. "Well how come after killing millions of people he's free to walk around, yet I bite just one person and I'm dumped in here." He indicated with his muzzled nose the prison cell that he had been dragged into a short while earlier. "Now tell me, does this seem fair to you?" He pulled himself as close to the cell door as his chain would allow and looked Jill straight in the eye. She faltered for a moment, almost not being able to keep his stare.
"What you did was wrong."
"Yes, perhaps it was, but what he did was a squillion times wronger, yet he's not locked up and chained up like me." whimpered Rambo woefully. He sat himself down heavily and sighed. Once again Jill began to feel sorry this scruffy looking and uncouth dog, after all, most of what he said was almost true. She reached her arm through the bars and touched Rambo gently on the head. He didn't respond, he just carried on looking miserable and dejected. She swallowed away the lump

that had developed in her throat as she began stroking him.
"The reason Nobby wasn't locked away.." she began softly and soothingly, " ..was because it was established quite early on that Nobby wasn't in fact responsible for his action. What he did, he did unwillingly and unknowingly."
"Aye, I thought he'd have an excuse somehow." moaned Rambo. "He always has."
"You mean this sort of thing has happened before?" Stroked Jill.
"Oh yes, only not on this scale before."
"Such as?" asked Jill, a sudden interest with in her had been aroused.
"Well a long time ago, Nobby decided to have a go at playing baseball, But, seeing as he had no friends he had to improvise a bit. So, what he did was throw the ball he was using on to the roof of the house and hit it when it came back down, only things don't quite work the way Nobby plans them. He used a soft sponge ball to avoid causing any damage, which after a couple of goes got itself lodged in the guttering on the neighbour's side of the fence. The neighbours weren't in, so Nobby got a ladder went round and climbed up to dislodge it. Only the ladder was several feet to short so he went back home for his base ball bat. He then climbed the ladder again and began swiping at the guttering with the bat. After several failed attempts, he had a brain wave, he decided that if he was to throw the bat at the guttering from the top of the ladder he would have a better chance of success." Rambo paused for a moment to scratch.

"What happened then?" prompted Jill after a moment or two.
"Well he threw the bat upwards; it hit the plastic guttering, rebounded back onto his forehead and ricocheted through the upstairs window. Nobby was knocked unconscious and fell from the ladder. A couple of hours later the neighbours came home to find Nobby covered in blood at the bottom of a ladder. Now anyone else would have been in serious trouble, but not Nobby. The neighbours knew Nobby was a bit of a twat, but he was quiet and kept himself to himself. So when they found him like that, they saw the broken window, presumed Nobby had disturbed a burglar and had been clobbered for trying to stop them. So instead of being called a clumsy idiot and being made to pay for the window, he was called a hero and rewarded with a bravery certificate from the local neighbourhood watch group."
"You mean he never told the truth."
"Well he did try when a reporter from the local paper came round, but the reporter ignored him because the burglary story was more exciting. So Nobby just shut up and left it at that." replied Rambo. Jill was still stroking his head absently.
"Do you think that Nobby could be lying now?" she asked
"Oh, I don't really know, I haven't heard what he has being saying. All I know is that with Nobby not everything is always as easy or straight forward as they usually appear. I have seen Nobby cause many incidents, albeit accidentally, and has somehow come out of it all looking like a victim."

"Rambo, are you suggesting that he has more to do with the situation than he is saying?" enquired Jill, she had stopped stroking Rambo now, her hands were rubbing together nervously as she had listened.
"Look babe, I'm tired and I'm going to have a kip." said Rambo moving away from Jill and Hopping onto the small bed. "Nobby isn't my problem anymore, just don't take everything for granted just because things look a certain way. Now leave me alone I'm tired." Rambo sprawled out on the bed and closed his eyes. Jill watched the dog for a few moments before leaving, she wanted to stay and talk more but there were things she needed to check out. With one final look at the sleeping Rambo, she left the prison area with numerous doubts and questions formulating in her mind.
As the door quietly closed behind her, Rambo opened one eye and surveyed the area. All clear, he sat up and smiled to himself, Jill had believed everything he had said, and that is exactly what he had hoped for. Although the story he told her was true, he omitted the fact that Nobby did actually confess to his actions and subsequently paid for the window to be replaced. Rambo decided that he had done a good job with Jill and to celebrate he was going to give his gonads a long slow cleaning. Only when he tried he got his tongue trapped in his muzzle. He spent the next two hours struggling to get it free.

"Ladies, gents and beings of a non or asexual nature." began the security chief, "I would like to apologise for the unforeseen delay in the starting of the meeting.

Everything is now under control and for anyone that may care, I am assured by the doctor that the human is fine." the chef spoke the final words with a sneer, if Nobby had snuffed it the chief could have piled the blame on him and hopefully that would have been the end of that. But as it was, Nobby had survived and now he had the unenviable task of explaining the arcane truth to his fellow crew members and that god awful Wellod, the commander of the Imperial so called protection fleet. The pale green reptilian like skinned Wellod sat next to the chief at the podium. His bloated quivering lips twisted into what could only be described as a smile as the chief mention the incident with Nobby. Wellod was amused by other people's suffering, he always had been, it was the reason he had joined the imperial fleet in the first place. Initially he wanted to be a member of the secret police because they were allowed to torture people, but alas his over enthusiasm was frowned upon by his superiors who decided that he would be better suited patrolling the very outskirts of the empire, out of harm's way. He had been patrolling this sector of the empire for almost a year and up until now absolutely nothing had happened. He and his fifteen man crew had just policed the area aimlessly, hoping and praying for something to shoot at other than stray asteroids. Then out of the blue this ship full of Dolphoids shows up and starts using imperial owned planets as target practice, Wellod thought it was his birthday.
He rubbed his hands together in glee and gave the order to ready all weapons to fire at will at the interplanetary vandals. His chubby, nail less fingers hovered millimetres away from the fire button, poised ready to

strike, and he would have done if a couple of hundred more warships hadn't suddenly popped out of time warp and took up positions around the burning planet.
"Commander Wellod," blurted the intercom, "This is commander Flunch of the third Imperial patrol fleet. I have instructions from the Emperor."
"Where the hell did you come from?" asked the disgruntled Wellod, viewing the armada of vessels circling the burning planet. "I didn't call for assistance."
"We received your report about the planet incident, and the Emperor wishes the criminals to be brought home and made an example of." replied Flunch over the radio.
"Which report?" asked Wellod, "I haven't sent a report."
"Er, it's the one that you send tomorrow." said Flunch matter of factly, he was used to the confusion caused when travelling in time warp.
"But how.... oh right, you time warped it here didn't you?"
"Correct, the Emperor dispatched us the day after tomorrow, so that we could get here now to stop you killing everybody aboard that ship, which incidentally by the time we had set off, you had already done so."
"I have already done what?" questioned Wellod.
"Destroyed the ship," answered Flunch
"No I haven't." replied Wellod indignantly, " Look it's still there!"
"Yes, it's there now, but it wasn't when we set off in two days time. So now we are here, we have prevented you from blasting the ship, which ironically if you hadn't have destroyed the ship we wouldn't be here now."
"But I haven't destroyed the ship, so how come you're still here?" posed Wellod.

"What do you mean?" Flunch asked over the ship to ship video link.
"Well, I haven't blown up that ship. Therefore, I will not be sending a report back to headquarters, which in turn cannot be read by the Emperor, who will not give you instructions to come here and prevent me doing something that I haven't done anyway. The long and short of it is, in reality, you can't possibly exist in this time period because the event which caused you to be here hasn't happened and therefore all subsequent events related to the original action should, in theory, cease to be."
"I didn't know you were as well versed in the theory of time paradoxes." said an amazed Flunch, he had been briefed before the mission and was lead to understand that commander Wellod was not the sharpest tool in the shed. "I am quite literally taken aback at your perception. Have you been studying temporal time paradoxism in your spare time?"
"Er.. no." replied Wellod, "I have just watched an episode of Stellar Voyage where the same sort of thing happened, and the rescue team from the future disappeared into the realms of lost time." There was a short silence from the video link.
"Oh, I see." returned the rather suddenly unimpressed Flunch. "Well to answer the question, on our return home we will once again have to return back here just to balance the equilibrium of time, therefore making everything equal again."
"So you're not going to be swallowed up into a time warp worm hole and be destined to spend eternity having

your molecules torn to pieces in a perpetual state of agony?"
"No!" replied Flunch sharply, "Anyway your orders are to arrest the criminals and transport them back home. The matter is in your hands."
"Can I torture them a bit first?"
"No, just take them home, in one piece. We will act only as an escort." at this Flunch discontinued communications. Wellod smiled to himself and rubbed his hands together. There could be a promotion in this. Even now, a day later his thoughts were on his probable rise in rank, and possibly even a medal. This is a shame because if he had listened to what the Security chief was saying, he may have lived to collect one.

CHAPTER THIRTEEN

"There is no easy way of explaining this," began the chief, "so I shall be as blunt as possible. if anyone should become offended by what I have to reveal, then I am very much afraid that you shall have to learn to live with it." He eyed the packed mess hall and noted the looks of concern and trepidation on the faces of those present. He was surprised by the volume of people crammed into the makeshift conference room. He had expected only personnel who had an active interest in the destroyed planet to attend. Somehow it seemed that everybody and their pet globular mucous monkeys had suddenly taken a passing interest.
"As you will all be aware the planet we were recently studying, Earth as it was known to its natives, was completely destroyed in a bizarre and tragic turn of events. Events which at first glance seem relatively straight forward enough. But on closer inspection, by just scratching below the surface a more sinister and odious truth is revealed." At this, the buzz of whispered conversation began its rounds through the room, comments and theories given birth and allowed to take wing amongst the expectant audience. The chief stood silent, letting the hubbub die down under it's on steam. He looked sideways to where Wellod was seated only to find him deeply engrossed in a large portion of Sulphuric slime slug sausage, which on most planets is used as a deadly poison, yet to Wellod's race, it was considered a

good dessert to have after several heaps of Bull horse scrotal fungus and chocolate sauce. The chief returned his attention back to the amassed assembly and waited for absolute silence.
"Ladies, gentlemen, others and those of you who may be unsure, our brief, yet scrupulous investigation has led to the discovery of a traitor amongst us." Once again many small pockets of conversation broke out through the crowd; before they could all merge into one huge noise, the chief continued his oration.
"Not only is there a rotten apple in this barrel," he gestured with his arms to indicate that by barrel he meant the ship. "Not only is there a rotten apple here, but it appears that the apple was placed here purposely." the chief paused to allow his words to sink in, and judging by the crowd's response they had done just that. The surge of discussion rose dramatically and once again the chief waited patiently until the swell of voices abated. Wellod looked up briefly from his food when the chattering had began, but after realising it wasn't a threat, he returned his attention back to his slug sausage. Several minutes passed before the chief resumed.
"People, friends and loyal crew members, I am afraid we have been betrayed by our own government and left to take the blame." The audience stood stunned momentarily, none could believe what they had heard, yet they all knew the security chief well enough to know that he wouldn't make such statements without absolute proof. Slowly the silence was broken as a thousand questions wanted answering at once. A frantic scrabble to be heard began, not unlike a presidential press conference.

The chief raised his hands to quell the crowd and restore order. "Please be patient," he shouted over the babble, "I will try to answer all questions as I explain, Please settle down. I am not willing to shout over the noise. If you are not quiet, I will have no choice than to eject unruly individuals." He stood with one hand raised, palm facing forwards in an expression for the crowd to hush. The crowd fell silent, thousands of eyes trained on the chief in expectation. The chief nodded, "Thank you." he said to the audience. "I will now go through the events leading up to and including the destruction of the Earth, using computer recreations and actual security video recordings made at the time. I will present the evidence as I found it, no dramatics, no thrills, just hard evidence. I think the evidence will speak for itself, but I will endeavour to answer any questions afterwards." at this, the lights dimmed, and the screen on the wall behind him glowed into life.

"How are you feeling?" asked Bill. Nobby stared blearily eyed at his Dolphoid friend; he was still slightly dazed from the anaesthetic the doctor had administered earlier.

"Is that you Bill?" Nobby asked.

"Yes, how do you feel?"

"I feel like someone has bit my arse." admitted Nobby.

"Someone did, as a matter of fact," replied Bill

"Oh!" was Nobbys surprised answer. "It wasn't you was it?"

"Er.. no."

"Thank God for that, I was beginning to worry." said Nobby with much relief, "what happened then, It wasn't Crippen was it?"
"Who?" said Bill, confused?
"Crippen." repeated Nobby, "The doctor, that's what I have nick named him."
"No, not the doctor, it was your old friend Rambo I'm afraid." explained Bill.
"Rambo!" exclaimed Nobby, "What the bloody hell has that damned dog got against me?" Nobby tried to sit up, but the pain prevented anything more upright than laying on his side. Bill helped Nobby readjust his position while answering.
"Apparently you ruined his sex life."
"But, he didn't have one," replied Nobby scratching his head
"Exactly, and now there is little chance that he ever will."
"I suppose the same could be said for me as well." sighed Nobby. "Although they say you can't miss what you never had."
"Who said that?" asked Bill
"Er, I don't really know, probably someone who never had to go without a shag. Maybe some sarcastic piss taking philosopher who was up to his plums in kipper land every night of the week. Truth is I don't care who said it, but whoever it was they were wrong. I can understand Rambo's anger, I just wish he'd realise that it wasn't my fault."
"Truth is.." began Bill, "there is still hope for both of you." Nobby raised a stubbly eyebrow of interest.

"Really?" he said, "I thought there were no humans left, tell me more."
"Well strictly speaking you are correct, there are no humans left, but there are plenty of humanoid species around to whom you would be sexually compatible, if not reproductively compatible," said Bill optimistically.
Nobby mulled the idea over in his head for a moment.
"Bill, that is a frightening thought."
"Is it? I'm sorry, I was just trying to cheer you up." apologised Bill.
"But.." continued Nobby, "the most scary part was the fact that it sounded appealing for a moment." he said with a shake of his head.
"Inter species sexual relations is quite a common phenomenon. Frankly I can't see what you find scary about it." said Bill, "there are so many races out there that are almost nearly human."
"Such as?" asked Nobby dubiously.
"Er, well there's the Oomarli people of Komporst, yes the Oomarli people, they're almost totally human." smiled Bill
"And exactly how different is almost totally human?" queried Nobby, he reached over to the bed side table for the glass of water there.
"Hardly noticeable at all really," answered Bill uncomfortably
"How different?" demanded Nobby
"Well they're a tad taller, But I hardly.."
"How much taller?"
"Er, about four foot taller." squirmed Bill under Nobby's gaze
"Four foot taller!!" exclaimed Nobby loudly.

"And they have beaks," said Bill quickly and quietly
"What?" spluttered Nobby around his drink of water, "they have what?"
"Nothing ." lied Bill
"You said they had beaks!"
"Only small ones, hardly noticeable through the fur."
"Fur!! Right, that's enough," protested Nobby, "I don't wish to know any more about alien sex. I mean I'm grateful that you've tried to cheer the situation up, but personally, I don't think that sex would be the same with another species."
"The same as what?" asked Bill
"Well, the real thing of course," said Nobby indignantly
"The real thing?"
"Yes, the real thing, sex with a human."
"How would you know?" asked Bill.
"Yeah, that's right, rub it in. So what if I'm a semi virgin!"
"A what?"
"A semi virgin." reiterated Nobby.
"I see." mused Bill "and what differentiates between a virgin and a semi virgin?"
"Consciousness and the ability to actually remember the deed," answered Nobby with a sigh. "Although I still have, or at least had, the police reports to prove it."
"I've got it!" exclaimed Bill suddenly, taking Nobby by surprise.
"Got what, is it catching?"
"The Lispodians of Shytepile six." Bill said
"You've gone off on one again, Bill."
"No, listen. The Lispodian people are humanoid, in fact when we first discovered them we thought that they were

the same species that once lived on our planet. The species we have since discovered were human."
"You mean they're humans?"
"Well almost."
"How almost?" asked Nobby with a raised stubbly eyebrow.
"Externally identical, internally, well you will probably never father children. Their insides are arranged differently, that's all. Genetically speaking there is only a three percent difference between you and the Lispodians." assured Bill. Nobby was having none of it.
"Do they have feathers?" he asked blandly.
"Er no."
"Scales?"
"No"
"Extra limbs or eyes?" continued Nobby
"No nothing like that, they are as human as you can get without actually being human," replied Bill. Nobby re adjusted he position again, bringing his face inches away from Bills.
"And do you think we would be, er you know, sexually compatible. Never mind the reproduction bit, I mean their bits and pieces are where they should be aren't they? I'm not going to find their minges half way up their backs, or find out that the females have bigger dicks than me."
"Rest assured Nobby, externally they are as good as humans, apart from the smell you would probably never notice the difference."
"Well I suppose I could always have a look first, that is if we are not all executed before then." answered Nobby with more cheerfulness than the situation required.

"Oh yes," said Bill "that reminds me, you're off the hook as far as destroying the Earth is concerned. The Security Chief has identified the real culprit."
"What smell?" question Nobby absent mindedly
"Smell?" repeated Bill.
"You said that I would get used to the dipstickians smell."
"Lispodians," corrected Bill
"What ever. I don't want a smelly bird. Ugly, to a degree, I can cope with, but I don't want an old biffer that smells like ten pounds of last month's haddock."
"You are not in a position to be overly fussy."
"Are you married Bill?" asked Nobby, Bill was taken back a little by the question.
"Er, No. why?" he replied
"Well if you were, would you prefer a wife that smelt faintly of roses or boiled cabbage?"
"Ok I see your point, But your pickiness could be stopping you having a hell of a time." mocked Bill.
"Anything beyond abject misery could be classed as a hell of a time for me. I thank you for your concern, but I will reserve judgement until I'm drunk or desperate, whichever comes first." smiled Nobby. At that moment, the doctor re-entered the room carrying a large box resembling a picnic cooler box.
"Is it lunch time, Crip?" asked Nobby
"Er, no. But it is for you." replied the Doc
"Oo! lovely, what is it." beamed Nobby eagerly while trying to sit more upright with a little help from Bill. The doc placed the box on the table near Nobby's bed and popped open the two locks. The box hissed as a plume of dry ice type mist escaped from beneath the now loosened

lid. Both Bill and Nobby watched with trepidation as the doctor removed the lid and delved into the swirling fog of the box. Slowly he lifted from the mist a greyish half moon shaped object that resembled a lump of sweaty putty.
"There, what do you think of that?" said the doctor with obvious pride. Nobby and Bill looked at each other in bemusement.
"It's er,.." began Bill
"Lovely." lied Nobby on Bills behalf, "In fact I don't think I've ever seen one quite like it." he added truthfully. The doctor regarded their forced smiles and puzzled expressions.
"You've no idea what it is, have you?" said the doc with dismay. Slowly both Nobby and Bill shook their heads and shrugged.
"I'm sure that it is a perfect example of er, what ever it may be." smiled Bill diplomatically
"Yes." added Nobby, "It's fantastic in an unknown subject kind of way."
"Look, I appreciate that perhaps it doesn't appear to be much, but gentlemen what you are looking at is nothing short of a miracle of modern technology." sneered the doctor.
"Yep, that's exactly what I thought it was." said Nobby to Bill. Bill couldn't suppress his smile, so he pretended to cough, trying to spare the doctors feelings.
"You said it was for Nobby?" he said
"That's correct," replied Crippen
"I'm not really hungry, but thanks all the same," Nobby said quickly, remembering the horrid stuff that the Dolphoids consider as good cuisine.

"It is a buttock," Crippen informed them as he placed it back in the box.
"Hmm, sounds delish' but as I said I'm a bit podged." replied Nobby pushing out his belly and rubbing it for effect.
"It's not for eating, Philistine. It's for transplant." It was obvious from his tone that his patience was running out.
"For me?"
"Yes"
"Do I need one?" questioned Nobby
"You have recently lost almost 65% of one buttock, resulting, in my opinion, the need for a replacement."
"But it doesn't feel that bad," said Nobby nervously. He gently felt his mangled arse.
"I mean there's not much pain or anything."
"Believe me, if you weren't dosed up on nerve suppressants it would hurt like hell." Crippen smiled for the first time after saying this. Nobby felt uneasy, he wasn't sure that he liked the idea of a transplant.
"Will it hurt, the operation I mean?" he asked.
"Not in the slightest, it will almost be instantaneous. It will be grafted at a molecular level."
"It's the wrong colour," Bill added to the conversation.
"At the moment, yes, but once it has blood flowing through it, it shall soon turn the right shade," Crippen explained.
"Will it do the same job as the old one?" asked Nobby.
"Job?" queried the doctor, "what job?"
"Filling out my Y fronts for a start."
"What is it made of?" Bill asked looking into the box at the sweaty grey lump.

"I cloned it from a sample of Nobby's D.N.A, so there is no chance of any rejection."
"Er, when are you planning on doing this transplant?" Nobby said nervously.
"Now." replied Crippen casually, "it won't take a moment. All you need to do is lay on your front and expose your backside."
"Hey watch it, my mother warned me about people like you." quipped Nobby, "are you sure it's not going to hurt." he continued as he turned over to expose his bum.
"I assure you I won't feel a thing." Crippen smiled. He took the replacement buttock and placed it in a contraption that looked some what like a micro wave oven. The doctor fiddled with a couple of dials on the machine then walked back over to Nobby. He removed the dressing on Nobby's backside, revealing the wound. Bill winced at the sight. Nobby saw his reaction.
"What's the matter, Bill?" he asked.
"It looks rather nasty."
"The wound or my arse?"
"Neither, I was referring to your face," Bill said with a smile.
"Oh you're so funny, why don't you go and lay on a plate with some chips." tarried Nobby.
"Brace yourself." interrupted the doctor from over near the micro wave oven thing.
"Not much of a chat up line is it?" Nobby said to Bill. Before Bill could answer, there was a slight crackle followed by a pop of displaced air. Right before Bills eyes, the wound was replaced by the pallid grey lump of new arse cheek.

"Aarrgh!!" screamed Nobby jumping from the table.
"Jesus friggin' Christ," he added for good measure.
"What's going on?" shouted Bill to the doctor. Crippen looked stunned.
"It shouldn't hurt, I numbed it all, the nerves shouldn't be able to register any pain." all the while Nobby was hopping around clutching his new buttock and cursing. Bill stepped forward and grabbed him by the shoulders.
"How bad is the pain?" He asked calmly
"No Pain.." gasped Nobby through gritted teeth. Bill looked into his tear filled eyes
"I don't understand, Nobby."
"It's f..f..fucking f..f..freezing cold." Nobby said rubbing his bum cheek vigorously.
"Ah yes," began the doctor. "Sorry about that, but the graft had to be kept a just above freezing point. It wouldn't have taken properly otherwise, it'll warm up in a moment."
"You could have warned me," growled Nobby
"Sorry." smiled Crippen, "It slipped my mind."
"How's it look?" Nobby asked Bill while thrusting his arse threateningly in the air.
"Lovely, a stunning work of art, now could you please put it away, it's getting disturbing," muttered Bill with embarrassment. Unperturbed Nobby rounded on the doctor.
"How's it look then Crip?"
"Positively picturesque as far as posteriors go. Here look for yourself." The doctor touched the wall which dutifully disappeared to reveal a full length mirror. Nobby stepped forward and turned his back on the mirror. He strained his neck to look over his shoulder at

his reflection. Apart from the rapidly fading greyish colour of his cheek, he couldn't see any scars or teeth marks; in fact, there was no physical sign of any damage at all

"That amazing, unbelievable," said Nobby in awe. "Crippen I could kiss you."

"I rather you didn't if you don't mind." The doctor stepped out of arms reach.

"You couldn't make me a bigger penis could you if you're not too busy that is?"

"I'm sorry, but I can only clone what is already there." replied the doctor

"How about cloning what I have and stitching them both together then?"

"Absolutely not. The process is for emergency use only and not for vanity or purely cosmetic reasons. It is not for personal gratification." declared the doctor

"I bet you've used it. Show us your dick."

"W..what!! I never.. How dare you." splutter the doctor wildly

"Calm down, just kidding." laughed Nobby. "No I think you've done an amazing piece of work there," he said indicating his arse in the mirror.

"Yes I must agree on a splendid job." added Bill.

"Thank you." blushed Crippen, "I was just doing my job."

"Just one thing." asked Nobby "any chance of some clothes now."

"Is he alright to leave now?" Bill asked the doctor. Crippen checked his instruments.

"How does it feel now, Nobby?" he asked without looking up.

"Well it seems to be tingling a fair bit."
"Good, that means that the blood is flowing freely. I can see nothing more that needs to be done, you are free to go." the doctor said cheerfully.
"Thank you." replied Bill on Nobby's behalf. "Come Nobby lets find you some suitable attire."
"Yeah and some clothes as well." beamed Nobby. He walked up the doc and put out his hand to shake. The doctor took his hand and shook it. Nobby turned and winked at Bill.
"That's quite a bulge he's got in his pants, I think he was lying to us, you know!" said Nobby just loud enough for the doctor to hear before the door closed behind them as they left the sick bay.

Wellod clutched his guts and waddled around in a desperate attempt to find a toilet. He had left the meeting almost an hour earlier and insisted on looking around the ship. The security chief was going to assign a security detail to guide the Imperial captain around, but Wellod demanded to tour the ship unaided. He had insisted that someone of his intelligence would have little difficulty in finding his way around. Also it was extremely hard to pinch anything when flanked by security men. Although at this very moment he could have done with a guide, the umpteen helpings of purple stuff he had devoured had travelled the length of his alimentary canal and at present was trying to reach his underpants. He had wandered aimlessly around what seemed like thousands of identically bland corridors, too proud to ask for help.

"Rats cocks!" he grumbled to himself as he turned a corner into another dead end.
Frustrated and desperate he looked up and down the corridor, there was no one around, not even one of those annoyingly happy probes that had tried to help him earlier. Although they had stopped pestering him after he had told several of them to piss off. With one last quick look around Wellod began to unbuckle his trousers, he was just about to crouch down and drop a load when a voice broke his concentration.
"May I be of assistance." the voice said. Wellod hitched up his pants and turn to see who had spoken. Just a few feet away stood a thin, sickly looking Dolphoid.
"I was er, just er.. And then, er.." stuttered Wellod nervously, "I er..er. Do you know who I am?" said Wellod changing tactics. The Dolphoid seemed unphased.
"Yes, I know exactly who you are. You're the great Captain Wellod, the hero of the Imperial fleet." the Dolphoid replied. Wellod regarded the pale, ill looking creature before him. He thought for a moment about what the Dolphoid had just said and as the words sank in his ego began to inflate.
"Yes that is correct I am the great, er.. I mean Captain Wellod." he boomed loudly
"and who may you be?"
"Just someone who could help you catch the real culprit and send you home a true hero." answered the Dolphoid calmly
"Hero, eh. I like the sound of that my friend. Perhaps we should talk some more."

"I agree, but first perhaps you would like to relieve yourself of your er, burden, so to speak?" The Dolphoid pointed a thin finger at Wellods unfastened trousers.
"Yes, where is the little runt's room." asked Wellod with some considerable embarrassment.
"If you would follow me, we can talk on the way." said the Dolphoid indicating the way forward.
"So you know who the real culprit is then?" asked Wellod as the strode down the corridor.
"Didn't you attend the meeting earlier?"
"Er, yes. Why?"
"Well the security chief disclosed the culprit's identity at the meeting." the Dolphoid informed Wellod.
"Oh, yes. I was er, busy and er..missed the name." coughed Wellod
"Well it's all academic really isn't it?"
"Is it?" answered Wellod after a moment. "How?" he added when he realised that the Dolphoid wasn't going to tell him freely.
"Well, they know who the villain is, but they don't know where he is."
"Oh, that." bluffed Wellod. "Look is it much further." he said with a loud fart.
"Almost there now." The Dolphoid smirked. "The thing is, I think I know where the rogue is hiding and together we could capture him."
"Where is he?" demanded Wellod who could see a promotion dangling before him.
"All in good time, we are here now." said the Dolphoid stopping suddenly.
"Where?" asked Wellod looking at the blank walls. The Dolphoid touched the wall, revealing a room beyond it.

"In here. The little Runts room, as you requested."
Wellod looked into the room.
"Where's the pot?"
“Once the door closes behind you the receptacle you require will emerge from the floor. We find it more hygienic that way." answered the Dolphoid
"Oh right then." at this Wellod strode into the room and waited. He never got to have the dump he so desperately needed, because moments after entering the room the air lock in front of him opened, shooting him into space and to his death. Back on the ship the Dolphoid Nobby knew as Randy, shook his head,
"Fool." he said simply as he listened to the air lock shut behind the ejected Wellod.

"What do you mean dead?" bellowed the security chief to the two guards who had roused him from his sleep. The senior of the two men stepped forward,
"He was found floating past the observation deck," he said while saluting
"With his trousers down." added the second guard timidly.
"He was reported by the cleaners down there." the first guard said.
“For mooning." said the other quickly.
"MOONING!!" boomed the security chief, "We have a dead, semi naked, Imperial war fleet captain floating around the outside of the ship and someone reports him only for mooning??"

"Yes sir, that's correct." answered the first security man
"Are you stupid or something?" the chief asked menacingly, staring into the guard's eyes.
"No sir, b..but the cleaner are." he stuttered back.
"Yes." added the other guard from behind the first.
"They complained that he smeared his backside on the window and that they would have to go outside and..." he stopped talking when he saw the enraged expression in the chief's eyes. The chief stood clenching his fists before the two nervous security men. Suddenly he snorted loudly and spun on his heels, the two men instinctively ducked for cover.
"Where is the body now?" demanded the chief while searching in his wardrobe for clothes.
"Sick Bay" said the cowering security men.
"Does the rest of the imperial fleet know of Wellod condition?"
"No sir, there has been no contact."
"Well keep it that way. Where's the doctor?"
"In sick bay with the body." replied the senior guard relaxing slightly.
"Tell him to contact me the moment he can ascertain the cause of death. I'll be in my office." ordered the chief. He stepped into his boots and for the first time turned back to face his men since his initial outburst. "what are you waiting for, GO!" he snapped at the waiting guards. After a brisk salute, they practically fell over each other to leave. As the door closed behind them the chief barked out orders to the computer.
"Computer, I want to know every step that Captain Wellod took after leaving the meeting. I want to know who he talked to, what he said, who saw him and where

they saw him. In fact I want to know absolutely everything about everything and I want it ten minutes ago. Have it ready in my office for when I get there." he demanded as he stormed from his cabin and into the corridor. Dark rage coursed through his body and it showed on his face. As he stomped purposefully along the corridor people avoided his gaze and gave him a wide berth. At the end of the corridor, he entered the lift, and everyone else in it got out at the next available floor. As he reached his floor the door of the lift open and several individuals began to step in until they saw the Chief's murderous expression. Very quickly they all found somewhere else more important to be. The chief strode out of the lift and into the corridor of what is the security centre of the ship. There were numerous security men milling around in the corridor, each one saluting briefly before carrying on to where ever they were headed. He reached the end of the corridor the wall before him opened revealing his office. As he walked in, a large display screen on the far wall flickered to life showing a schematic display of the ship. A red dot was flashing on the edge of the diagram of the ship. The chief strode over and stared at the flashing dot.
"Air lock P:676, floor 4, laundry department." the computer informed the chief.
"Is that his last known position?" he asked.
"Affirmative. He entered the air lock and was sucked into space within four seconds."
"How? The air locks can't be operated from inside them without an override code?"
"Person or persons unknown activated the air lock from the corridor." the computer intoned.

"And I suppose it's the same person unknown who has been causing all our other problems?" sneered the chief
"correct." returned the computer
"So why say persons unknown when we know who it is?" demanded the chief
"Security protocol 897 k/23.For their own safety and that of government, the subject is to remain anonymous and invisible until further instructions are given." the computer recited.
"Damn" spat the chief "I hate the idea of having a spy on board, especially one that is supposed to be on our side. Why this ship?"
"it is standard procedure on all exploratory missions." answered the computer
"Yes we've been through this already." the chief muttered as he remembered the several hours before the meeting as he and the computer played a guessing game where the computer could not give a straight answer.
"I suppose you know where he is then, our person unknown?" the chief eased himself into his chair and got comfy. Past experience told him this could take some time.
"That is correct, but to all else he is invisible."
"And exactly what does that mean, invisible?"
"Probes will pass him and instantly forget him, doors will open for him, and their memory will be erased." replied the computer. The chief pondered for a moment, a glimmer of an idea was forming in his mind
"Computer" he said "show me a list of all doors that have been opened since the incident at airlock P:676, and display who they opened for." he turned to his monitor and studied the lists, each entry displayed a time

followed by a name. Silently he read through the names. About twenty names into the list he encountered a blank space beside a time.
"Who entered the laundry warehouse at time index 29/54.7" he asked
"Persons unknown" replied the computer.
"The same persons unknown that we are looking for?"
"I cannot answer that question" the computer said flatly
"Cannot because you don't know or cannot because you are not allowed to?"
"The latter statement is most accurate." The chief scratched his snout thoughtfully as he continued to study the blank spaces on the door list. He raised his eyebrows as a pattern in the blanks emerged.
"Computer dispatch a unit of ten men to the sickbay at once. Seal all doors between the science labs and the hospital; he's heading towards the sick bay."
"He can override the doors." the computer informed the chief.
"Yes, I know, I'm just trying to slow him down. Show me a schematic of the medical deck." Instantly a large area of the wall displayed the plans for the deck. After a moments study the chief spoke. "inform me immediately if any of these doors.." he said pointing at the diagram "..are opened, you can do that?"
"Yes" was the swift reply
"Good, inform the doctor that I am on my way." at this the chief heaved his bulk from the chair and stomped into the corridor.
"You, you, you and you, follow me." he barked at the first four security men he saw outside. Without

hesitation, the four men fell in behind him, and together they stomped off.

"I tell you he's not here." said the doctor for the third time. He was face down on the floor. "He just left as you entered," he added. The pressure of the boot pinning his head to the ground lessened slightly.
"Where's he gone now?" asked the owner of the boot bluntly. The doctor turned his head a fraction and looked up at his assailant.
"I don't know, maybe his quarters. He didn't say."
Crippen turned some more, and his former crew mate removed his foot from the side of his face.
"Get up," said Randy with some disdain. He gestured for the doctor to move over to his desk. Slowly the doc rose and made his way to the desk and seated himself in his own chair. Randy put away his laser weapon, a small pen like tube with enough power to pierce through a foot of solid steel, he sat opposite the Doctor and absent mindedly picked fluff from his clothing. Gone was the regulation silver/grey uniform that was sported by everyone else, it had been replaced by a black uniform with a gold collar and cuffs. Crippen recognised the two pairs of crossed keys insignia that was embroidered onto the collar of the uniform. It was the symbol of the internal military security service, a secretive branch of the security force dealing in intelligence, espionage and all manner of other underhand nastiness. The doc cleared his throat in the uncomfortable silence.
"S..so," he stuttered "it is true what they said about you at the meeting earlier."

"Yes, almost every word, I thought the chief had worked it out pretty well, considering." replied Randy with a wry smile.
"You heard the meeting?"
"And saw." said Randy leaning towards the doc, "I was there," he whispered for no reason other than to unnerve the Doctor. The Doctor looked into Randy's eyes expecting to meet a piercing gaze, he wasn't prepared for the totally blank and vacant expression he met. Randy looked confused and lost, as though he knew where he was but not why or how he had got there. Crippen decided to try and keep him talking.
"Are you okay, you don't look too well? Perhaps I should take a look at you." he reached towards his diagnostic scanner at the side of the desk. Randy grabbed Crippen's arm and firmly but gently moved it away from the scanner.
"No." was all that Randy said, his voice seemed suddenly tired and weak. The doctor noticed beads of sweat on Randy's face and snout. Crippen also became aware that the hand that still gently held his arm was trembling. He made a quick mental diagnosis without his scanner.
"When did you sleep last?" he asked Randy softly. The other Dolphoid shrugged ever so slightly
"I er, I don't know." Randy muttered in reply, "maybe yesterday, or the day before."
"You're exhausted, you need to sleep." cooed the Doctor.
"They won't let me," said Randy in a strained manner. The doctor studied Randy for a moment, watching his chest rise and fall as his breathing deepened and the

sweat on his brow ran forward to join with the accumulated sweat on his face and neck.
"Who are they??" he asked calmly in a low voice. Randy flinched and drew his hand from Crippen's arm, a sudden sharpness returned to his eyes; he glanced around the room before rising from his chair.
"No one, forget it." he snapped. He dug his hand into the pocket of his uniform and drew out the laser weapon again. He looked at the doctor and raised the laser.
"I'm sorry." he said "but I can't let you live. I will make it quick."
"NO," said the doctor loudly. His heart began to pound frantically in his chest. "Please, I can help you; you are not well I can tell. Maybe if you let me I can help you, just don't shoot."
"I'm sorry." was all Randy said, with a final shake of his head he re aimed his weapon.
"HOLD IT RIGHT THERE" boomed a voice from behind him. Slowly and calmly Randy lowered his weapon and turned to the source of the voice.
"Well, well, well." mocked Randy "aren't you the clever one." the chief and seven of his men stood in the door way of the sick bay. Randy surveyed the eight weapons trained meaningfully on him and he had no doubt in his mind that they would fire at the least provocation.
"Put the weapon down" demanded the chief.
"What this one?" teased Randy wiggling the laser tube between his two thumbs, his eyes never leaving the chiefs for a second.
"Put the weapon down." reiterated the chief.
"And if I don't, then what?" replied Randy calmly.
"We will open fire."

"I don’t think so." sneered Randy. "You need me alive to take the blame, the Emperor will have you killed if you can't produce the person responsible. He can't make an example of a corpse." he continued playing with the laser tube. The chief took three slow paces forward until the nozzle of his weapon was just inches from Randy’s snout. Without breaking eye contact the Chief moved the nozzle of his weapon to Randy’s shoulder.
"How about I just blow a couple of pieces off you instead. I'm sure the emperor wouldn't mind if you had an arm missing."
"Maybe not, but I'm afraid we will never find out." Smiled Randy, he clicked a button on the tube and before the Chief could react there was the slight hum of a transferal beam and Randy was gone.
"Damn!" spat the chief. "Computer, lock off all transferal actions and tell me who initiated the last transfer from the sick bay."
"all transferal functions have been halted." replied the computer. "There have been no transfers in sickbay from this vessel."
"Are you saying that the transfer came from outside this ship." asked the chief.
"Affirmative."
"Where?"
"That information is classified." answered the computer. The chief shook his head and put away his weapon. He looked at the doctor,
"You ok?" he asked
"I think so, yes. What's going on?" the doc asked in return.
"I think we have a shadow." he said grimly.

"A shadow?" repeated the doctor.
"Yes. A small stealth ship with disruption camouflage. It attaches itself to a large ship and blends with its background. They were used by the government to enter foreign planets or systems that they had been refuse access. The small one or two man vessels hid near forbidden borders and waited for ships entering the forbidden zone, and latched onto them and passed through the systems unnoticed." explained the chief.
"and we have one?" asked the doc
"I Believe we have." said the chief with a nod "from our own government at that"
"But why?" questioned Crippen
"Am not sure, but I'm beginning to think that it is standard practice on these long term projects. A sort of insurance policy." the chief sat on the edge of the doctor's desk. "You alright?" he asked Crippen
"Yes fine, just a bit shook up." replied the doctor. He ran his medical scanner over himself just to make sure, "Insurance against what?". The Chief let out a large sigh before answering,
"The unknown and the unexplainable. I really don't know. Whatever it was it has landed us in the shit up to our necks."

CHAPTER FOURTEEN

"So let me get this straight." said Nobby through a mouthful of cheese sandwich. He had declined the suggestion of jellied crabs brains, or char grilled algae and stuck to something simple. Bill sat opposite Nobby in the canteen tucking into a large helping of rubbery looking red balls in a foul smelling clear sauce.
"What you are saying is that er.. Randy is the real culprit."
"Not to put too fine a point on it, yes." answered Bill mid chew.
"Right, got it, it was Randy all along, not me."
"That is correct."
"Ok then," said Nobby thoughtfully in to his sandwich. After a moment or two of silence Nobby put his sandwich down and cleared his throat. "Er..Bill!"
"Yes Nobby" Bill responded
"There is just one thing bothering me."
"What's that?"
"Well, I have no idea who this Randy character is," admitted Nobby. Bill put down his eating utensils and looked in to Nobbys eyes.
"Remember the meeting we had with the council when you first got here, well he was one of the council members."
"Was he the one with large tits?" asked Nobby

"Er.. no that was Mandy, she is a female hence the large er..glands. Randy is a male that is why I referred to him as a he"
"Just wishful thinking on my behalf then!" sighed Nobby. "But why? I mean why did he want me to destroy the Earth?"
"He is a member of the Governments internal security force. His job is to safeguard our planet from so called disruptive influences." Bill explained "and unfortunately the existence of your planet was deemed threatening."
"Threatening! how? we don't even have the ability of space travel like you."
"No, that is true, but either Randy was following orders or he decided on his own that your planet threatened the religious culture of our planet." explained Bill, "you have to understand that the theory of humans ruling our planet before we did is still a touchy subject with the majority of the population. Religion dictates that all Dolphoids descended from two individuals that were taken by God from the sea and placed into a magical land of plenty. They find the theory of humans being rulers of the planet quite ridiculous."
"But you said that the knowledge of human history was known on your planet." countered Nobby. His earlier interest in his sandwich lost as he tried to make sense of Bills words.
"Our planet is heavily controlled by the church, much of the findings of archeologist and scientists like myself are suppressed and hidden. The average person on the street would know little or nothing of Human existence. Long term exploratory voyages like this one are often funded by the church just to stop us scientist from talking

publicly about our planets true history." admitted Bill, his appetite also lost.
"And for that the Earth was destroyed?" asked Nobby sadly
"It appears that once the church heard of your planets existence the order was given to er.. suppress any information regarding its location and inhabitants"
"In other words, blow it up?"
"Well normally it just means classify all data regarding such finds and brief all concerned parties." replied Bill apologetically
"You mean this has happened before?" snapped Nobby
"No, not like this. I, er..we hoped that a find on this magnitude would persuade the church and authorities to accept the facts and recognise the role that humans played in our planets history." Bill answered quickly.
"Well it looks as if they weren't ready to accept. Bit of a costly gamble on your behalf, and the population of Earth." mocked Nobby
"We believe the action of destroying the Earth was that of Randy alone. He must have thought that this was the quickest and easiest way to stop the significance of the find having any effect back home."
"So where is he?"
"We don't know, somehow he has left the ship. But not before murdering a member of the imperial war fleet."
"Things aren't getting any better are they?" muttered Nobby shaking his head.
"You must hate us." asked Bill quietly, he shrugged, "I can't say I blame you if you did." he looked at Nobby with sorrowful eyes, Nobby met his gaze.

"I don't hate you, not personally, but I do hate the system of religion that would condemn a whole planet to death simply to protect its out moded ideals"
"I agree, as a scientist I believe what I see and on many occasions the scientific community has come up hard and sharp against the authority of the church. Many scientists have been exiled and some have even mysteriously disappeared altogether."
"So why do you persist?"
"The truth Nobby, the truth. God only knows what else the church could be hiding. Some things need to be exposed, but the church has greater power than the government." Bill looked at his plate and pushed it away. "I suppose this is hard for you to understand?"
"It's not as difficult as you could imagine, we have had our fair share of religious dictatorships over the centuries." A sudden clatter of feet at the far end of the mess hall distracted their attention. They both watched as a the chief and several heavily armed security men made their way towards them. Bill rose to meet the chief.
"Is there a problem?" he asked as the chief drew near.
"We need to get Nobby to safety." he grunted
"What's happened?" Nobby spluttered rising from his seat
"Randy has attacked the Doctor, he was looking for you." replied the chief, "Now if you will follow me, we have a room prepared for you."
"Prepared in what way?" demanded Bill. Both he and Nobby began to walk in the direction the chief indicated, they were instantly flanked by security men as they walked.

"The room has had a security disbursement field erected, along with transferal re alignment scanner and weapons interceptor." replied the Chief as if this was nothing unusual.
"Is all that really necessary." asked Nobby, who didn't actually understand a single word that the chief had said.
"We arrive at the Emperors home world in less than eight hours; we need you intact to verify our story. Your mind holds the answer to this situation, and if we are to get through this we need you alive." barked the chief with little compassion.
"And I just thought you liked me." mumbled Nobby not really wanting the chief to hear.
"Is there any news on the whereabouts of Randy now?" asked Bill as they passed into the corridor.
"We have reason to believe he is in a stealth ship attached to our hull. As yet the sensor sweeps have shown nothing, but then again that is what the stealth vessels are for." answered the Chief without turning his head, Bill and Nobby were having a little difficulty in keeping pace with the marching escort.
"A stealth ship?" questioned Bill, more to himself than to anyone in particular.
"Where on Muck did he get a stealth ship from out here?" he continued
"We are presuming that it has been with us since we left home, possibly standard procedure on these kind of voyages. Nothing would surprise me after the past couple of days." The last statement had a hint of sadness in the words and both Nobby and Bill recognised the sense of betrayal that hid behind them. They arrived at the lift where two security men were all ready and

waiting. One of the men stepped forward and saluted at the chief
"Sir." he began "there is a message for you from the ship of Captain Wellod."
"I will deal with it later, any further developments in the search?"
"We have men on the outside of the ship performing a touch search. if it's there sir, we will find it." replied the security man with much confidence.
"Good, when you find it, log its position but remain radio silent, if he is listening in we don't want to frighten him off."
"Yes sir!" said the security man with another salute. Both he and his companion turned and left. Nobby, Bill, the chief and their escort entered the lift and headed to the security deck of the ship.
"Where are we going?" asked Nobby. The chief regarded the human with much disdain before answering.
"For your own safety you are to be placed.." the last word was heavily pronounced as if to give the impression that he actually meant locked away. "..in a secure living unit in the brig area." the chief informed Nobby as the lift door closed and began its journey.
"Oh, I see. Can I bring some personal things from my room?" asked Nobby.
"If you tell me what it is you require, I will see to it that they are brought to you."
"Well I could really do with my er, my er.. I definitely need my.." Nobby looked around the lift into the occupant's faces. He shrugged his shoulders "I just realised that I don't actually possess anything."

"You will find the room most comfortable. It has everything you will need." replied the chief with no regard to Nobbys feelings.
"It is only for a few hours, I will stop with you if you like?" Bill placed his hand on Nobbys shoulder. Nobby smiled and nodded, but didn't speak.
"Here we are." said the chief unnecessarily as the doors opened. The corridor was bustling as uniformed Dolphoids hurried up and down quickly. The chief turned to his men,
"Escort our er, guest to his new quarters and secure the area. I will be in my office." at this he turned a walked briskly up the corridor as Nobby and Bill was guided in the opposite direction.

"This is Second Officer Queeb of the imperial fleet, To whom I'm I addressing?" demanded the green skinned alien on the chief of security's intercom screen. The chief sighed, he knew there was no easy way to break the news he had.
"I am the chief security officer of the starship Traveller."
"Where is your Captain?" answered the alien, his tone indicating that he didn't wish to speak to any one of lower rank.
"I out rank the Captain in times like these." he spread his hands apart as he spoke and shrugged as he uttered the last word.

"I see." replied Queeb, not totally convinced. "Where is commander Wellod?" he added sharply. The chief steeled himself against his chair, his mouth suddenly dry. He breathed deeply and cleared his throat.
"Well, the thing is, I'm afraid there has been an incident." The chief paused letting the information sink in and allowing himself time to compose the next part of the news.
"Incident?" repeated Queeb cautiously, "what kind of incident?" he asked emphasising the word by splitting it in two, so it became inci dent.
"Well to not put too fine a point on it.." the chief paused and cleared his throat once more, although unnecessarily, "..I am afraid it is my sad duty to inform you of your Commanders untimely demise." said the chief in a diplomatic tone, hoping it would be taken better. The Imperial second officer just stared blankly from the screen at the chief. A few moments of awkward silence passed. The chief looked back at the alien, waiting for a response, still nothing. It was several moments later that the chief realised that the Second officer of the imperial fleet had not understood his statement, And obviously he wasn't ready to admit as much.
"I'm afraid your Commander is dead." the chief said simply. This time there was a reaction from Queeb. He raised his flabby eyebrows and thoughtfully rubbed the place on his face where his chin would have been had it not been so bloated and fat.
"Dead you say." still rubbing his chin, "Are you sure of this?"
"Yes positive."

"And exactly how did this happen?"
"Er, I believe he accidentally fell out of an air lock." the chief decided not to tell the whole story just at the moment; he sensed that it wouldn't help any.
"An air lock?" Queeb repeated for no real reason. "And he is definitely dead, not just seriously injured or something?"
"He is definitely 100% dead, I can assure you." confirmed the chief. He noticed a faint smile on Queeb's bloated lips. The alien rubbed his hands together vigorously.
"And his death was an accident you say?" asked Queeb distractedly.
"Well, the thing is..." began the chief
"Good, good." interrupted Queeb, "I shall fill out a report to that effect."
"Second Officer Queeb, I must.." started the chief
"That's Commander Queeb from now on." snapped the alien from across the screen.
"Sorry Commander." returned the chief, noting the speed of promotions in the imperial fleet.
"Was there something else you wish to add regarding Wellods death?" asked Queeb.
The chief noticed the sudden drop of title from the mention of the dead former commander.
"Er, no. Nothing to add." he replied.
"Good. We will be arriving at our destination in around 6 hours. I hope you will be ready in time." Queeb said with a bloated smirk before ending the transmission. The chief stared at the blank screen for a moment or two before shaking his head slightly

"Scary" he muttered to himself. He leaned forward and pressed a section of his computer screen, the screen glowed into life.
"Update on search." he said bluntly, before sitting back in his chair. He waited several minutes before his door beeped, indicating someone wishing to enter.
"Come" he said sitting upright to meet the caller. As the door opened two uniformed security officers marched in briskly, they stopped at the desk and saluted sharply. The chief quickly returned their salutes and looked at them questioningly. The taller of the two Dolphoids responded to the chiefs unspoken query.
"We have located and secured the shadow. The vessel was unoccupied, but had signs of being used recently." he spoke briskly, but clearly.
"Security scans and searches have yet to reveal our targets where a bout's." said the second man. "All door codes have been changed to a fluctuating pattern system and all transferal capabilities have been temporally shut down to all floors other than this one. All unauthorised transferals will automatically be shunted into the brig area."
The chief regarded his men closely, he saw the well disguised nervousness in their eyes, but he knew each man was too well trained to let their feelings interfere with their work. He nodded to both men.
"Well done, carry on and updated me as soon as there are any developments." he said for want of anything better. Both men saluted and left without waiting for the chief to return the gesture. Alone once more the chief leant back and swung his feet up onto the desk.

"Computer." he said, the computer blipped in response indicating its readiness. The chief settled back into his chair and placed his hands behind his head. "Music, Classical, slow and low." he muttered. Almost instantly the soft swell of a full orchestra broke the silence, the chief smiled to himself, it was one of his favourite composers from back home. At this moment in time home seemed like nothing more than a distant memory, a far away dream, and more frightening was the fact that maybe he would never see it again.

"You lied to me. You deliberately tried to make me believe that he did it on purpose" she scolded "you tried to distort the facts and twist the truth so it seemed like something else, didn't you?"
"Yep, I did." he said truthfully
"Don't bother trying to deny it either." she snapped back immediately, then after a moment of thought and recognition she spoke again. "Oh, right. But that doesn't change anything."
"So why bring it up then?" asked Rambo, watching Jill pace up and down the room.
He had had his muzzle removed earlier after getting his tongue stuck several times.
He had solemnly promised not to bite anyone again, and it was a promise that he intended to keep, especially after the ships vet recommended the removal of his teeth if he couldn't be trusted to act civilised.

"Well, because it's .. er..it's. Just because. Ok?" flustered the female Dolphoid. She glared menacingly at the dog, daring him to contradict her as she paced up and down. Rambo didn't even consider returning a reply. He was too busy trying to resist the urge to drag his arse across the floor to stop it itching.
"Don't you have any morals?" her voice interrupted his thoughts.
"Am I supposed to have some?" he asked in return. She fixed him with a cold steely stare,
"Yes." she almost spat.
"Well in that case probably not then." shrugged Rambo in a dog like way. Jill stopped pacing and looked for a chair. She sat down at the opposite side of the room to Rambo but angled the chair to face him. She decided to try a different approach.
"It has been proven beyond a shadow of a doubt that your friend, Nobby is totally innocent." she spoke much calmly than she felt.
"Even so." said Rambo "that doesn't solve the problem, does it?"
"Which problem?" asked Jill suspiciously after a moment of thought.
"No bitches" he answered simply with a wag of his tail. Jill breathed in deeply through her snout like nose and silently counted to ten before exhaling.
"Do you like me?" she asked plainly, her voice dull and flat. Rambo cocked his ears up in response to the question.
"Er, yeah. You're alright" he said. "For a fish," he added unnecessarily. Jill ignored the remark.
"Doesn't it bother you then that soon I may be dead?"

"Are you ill?" asked Rambo. Jill sighed
"Not just me everyone on the ship."
"Is it catching?" he said backing away from her. Jill's eyes narrowed to slits, and she slammed her fist down hard on her thigh, resulting in nothing more dramatic than a dull thud.
"Are you really that stupid?" she bellowed at the scruffy dog. Her outrage attracted the attention of the guards out side the cell like room. They looked up from their posts and assessed the situation instantly. A quick glance at the dog and then at the Dolphoid told them all they needed to know. They relaxed again, although keeping a wary eye on the cells. Rambo thought carefully about the question and made sure his love pods were safely tucked under his body before answering.
"Possibly, I'm not sure," he replied honestly. Jill shook her head in despair, her fingers clutched involuntary at the material of her boiler suit around her upper legs. She took a moment to collect herself, a few deep inhalations calming her rising anger, no not anger, more frustration at this dog's total lack of grip on the true situation.
Although she sensed a deeper intelligence in the mangy mutt, Rambo was either keeping it well hidden or truly was unaware of it. She wanted to know if Rambo knew more than he let on, or was he truly doomed to his own simplicity.
"Where are you from?" she asked gently. Rambo was a little taken back by her sudden change in tone and manner. He cocked his head sideways and sniffed in her direction.
"Here?" he said hopefully

"Before here," she responded calmly.
"Er, somewhere else?" again he wagged his tail for good measure
"And what was it called, this place where you are from?"
"Home!" he exclaimed eagerly, "I know that one." frantic tail wagged only earned him a raised eyebrow from the Dolphoid.
"Yes, very good," said Jill without enthusiasm. "But that place had another name, can you remember what it was?" Rambos ears pricked up at the question, a look of understanding crossed his face. His tail wagged so quickly Jill actually felt the draught.
"Yeah, I remember." He said excitedly, "It was called.."
"Yes, Rambo, it was called what?" Jill sat forward in her chair mentally coaxing the words from the canine's mouth. Rambo continued
"It was called.." he repeated for effect,
"Yes.." Jill uttered softly. With a final triumphant wag of his tail, he stood and barked out aloud,
"Nobby's house!!" In his jubilation, he failed to notice that Jill had hung her head and was supporting it in her hands, elbows on knees. Her recent eagerness gone, her body slumped. Rambo was still running in circles chasing his tail with delight and yapping happily as the sounds of sobbing reached his ears. He stopped in his tracks, the tip of his tail nipped between his front teeth, and looked in the direction of the sobbing. He dropped his tail and took a couple of wary steps forward. He was stood before Jill, watching her body spasm as the sobs forced their way out of her lungs. Rambo remained silent, not understanding the change in the Dolphoid. After several minutes the sobbing subsided, and Jill

opened her eyes. Rambo was sat with his nose only inches away from her face, as she opened her eyes Jill was treated to a close up of Rambo. He wagged his tail expectantly, and Jill raised a faint smile. Rambo leant forward and gave her a lick on the nose. Jills Eyes began to well up with tears again. Tenderly she reached forwards and placed her arms around Rambo, who stiffened for a moment, she gently drew him nearer and hugged him to her bosom. Rambo relaxed and wagged his tail. Jill hugged him tightly, not too tightly, but firmly

"You really are a stupid dog aren't you?" she whispered through her tears.

"Yep that's me!" said Rambo happily.

"Come on Nobby it's almost time."

"Huh, what?" replied Nobby sleepily

"Time to get ready," said Bill softly. "We dock in about half an hour."

"Rah!" exclaimed Nobby before yawning. "Did I nod off?"

"Not so much drop but landed heavily with a thud." smiled Bill in a vicious looking toothy way. Nobby noticed Bill had changed and was wearing a slightly different uniform, Although identical in style it was not silvery grey but a deep black, in fact it was so black you couldn't see the folds of the material. The collar on this uniform was white with a tiny red insignia of a flying bird.

"Nice threads," said Nobby as he arose from the uncomfortable cot bed, once again he yawned and

accompanied it with an all over body stretch and various oo's and ah's as his joints creaked and muscles flexed.
"Threads? where?" replied Bill trying to look behind himself at the rear of his uniform, he quickly ran his hands over his uniform back.
"No, not real threads, It is just a figure of speech." Nobby yawned, he approached the small wash basin in the corner of the make shift quarters. He proceeded to run some water to wash with.
"Oh, I see. Was it some sort of joke?" Bill asked still checking his uniform.
"No, it just means nice clothes." Nobby splashed his face with water, the coldness shocking his body into alertness. He shivered inwardly and shook his head vigorously making a small "bbrr" noise. Bill looked towards Nobby, he saw the shudder run through Nobby's body.
"Are you ok?" he asked
"Yep, fine" Nobby dried his face with a small towel.
"you look very smart."
"Thank you, it's my dress uniform. For special occasions only."
"Trying to make a good impression?"
"Well despite the circumstances there are certain protocol's that must be adhered to."
"Right. I'll just go in this then," said Nobby indicating the gown he was still wearing from the sick bay. Bill laughed.
"Well despite the fact that it suits you I thought that maybe that would be more appropriate." He pointed a finger toward the other side of the cell, Nobby followed the direction of the finger.

"Oh wow!" gasped Nobby.
"Hope you like it."
"It's.. It's fantastic." Nobby moved toward the uniform hung near the cot bed. Like Bill's it was deep black, but with a pale green collar and a white insignia depicting a broom.
"I'm afraid it is only a domestic's dress uniform, but it was all that was available." said Bill apologetically.
"It's fine, honest" Nobby replied truthfully. He held the uniform up against his body.
The legs dragged along the floor, and the crotch area was parallel to his knees. "I suppose it will adjust?"
"Yes. The boots are beside the bed." Bill pointed towards them, Nobby nodded and began to put on the uniform. Bill coughed nervously and turned away as Nobby unrobed.
"What does the bird mean?" asked Nobby pulling on his clothes
"Bird? What bird?" questioned Bill
"The one on the collar."
"Oh, that one," said Bill unconsciously raising his hand to feel the insignia. "It represents that bird of knowledge and wisdom."
"What's that then?" Nobby gasped slightly as the uniform adjusted around his scrawny form.
"It is from an ancient story of a bird that left its home and dared to explore the world outside its own nest and in the process gained knowledge from its travels and on its return used that information to make its own world a better place."

"Is that how you see yourself, going out to seek knowledge and returning to use it productively?" asked Nobby
"Well in a way I suppose, yes. I always thought that by exploring the past we could try and make sense of the future."
"Not quite worked that way this time has it?" Nobby said with out any malice
"No I am afraid it hasn't." an awkward silence fell between them. Nobby looked up at Bill, he had his back towards him but he could see his head hung low. He decided to change to topic.
"Any news on what's his name?"
"Who?"
"Er.. Randy."
"No not yet, but I believe they have found a small one man vessel that he has used."
Bill looked behind himself furtively, not wishing to embarrass Nobby, or himself, by catching his companion unclothed. Nobby was sat on the bed pulling on the boots to the uniform. Nobby looked up and met Bills gaze.
"Is he still on the ship?"
"I don't know, He could be, and there again he could have left. Truth is we just don't know."
"Oh well, perhaps he has fucked off for good." exclaimed Nobby getting up from the bed.
"Eloquently put, but don't rely on it, we must be on our guard at all times." warned the Dolphoid, "we don't know what he is capable of."
"Ok. So what is the plan for today then?"
"Plan?"

"Yeah, why the posh clothes."
"Oh right. In approximately twenty minutes or so we will be docking on the northern most continent of the Imperial home world, But don't worry these suits should protect us from the cold," explained Bill pointing out the thermostatic control panel of his own suit. Nobby absent mindedly fingered his own panel
"Cold?" he asked
"Yes, it is the northern most continent, more of an ice cap really."
"Oh, why are we docking there?"
"It is where the Emperor chooses to live," replied Bill. He indicated for one of the guard outside the room to open the door.
"Must be a fairly inhospitable planet if the best place to live is basically the north pole." mocked Nobby. The guard opened the door and Bill and Nobby began to walk.
"To be truthful the planet has various temperate zones, ranging from Polar Regions to deserts and everything in between. The Emperor just chooses to live in the northern polar region." They both left the brig area silently flanked by security.
"He must be daft, or the planets greatest lover of snowmen." Joked Nobby. Bill regarded his companion with a raised eyebrow.
"The choice of area is purely strategic," said Bill
"Really, plenty of snowballs to throw at invading hordes?" they were stood before the lift.
"In a way, the northern hemisphere is protected by a natural layer of concentrated acidic gas anything that tries to penetrate it is melted. The only way to reach the

Emperors continent is via the equator." the lift opened and they all entered. "So if anyone tries to mount an attack they will either melt to death or be confronted by the entire war fleet before they got half way to the Emperors palace."
"Is he attacked a lot then?" asked Nobby, the doors of the lift opened again, revealing a different floor. They stepped out into a moderately busy corridor.
"At least only once by anyone." smiled Bill. Nobby smiled back and the security men tightened their grips on their weapons. Nobby looked up and down the corridor, they turned left and headed to the furthest end of the passage. Nobby also noticed that all the Dolphoids on this level had breasts.
"Where are we?" he asked
"This is the secretarial area, where all the filing and typing is done," explained Bill
"Oh, I see. Nice to know sexual discrimination is alive and well in the er.. what ever century you are from."
"Not really, it is just that females are naturally better listeners and undoubtedly more prolific typists," said Bill defensively
"Yep, sure I believe you," smirked Nobby as they passed several silver clad Dolphoid beauties.
"It's true," Bill said sheepishly. Nobby laughed, and Bill smiled.
"So, where are we going exactly?" Nobby enquired as they trudged down the long curved corridor.
"We are heading for the manual disembarkment platform, which is down here next to the main reception lounge." Bill said pointing along the corridor. "We have

disabled the transferral capabilities in an attempt to apprehend Randy."
"You don't half talk like a posh lawyer." Chided Nobby.
Bill stopped walking and waited for the other to do so. When they did, he stood before Nobby and distorted his snout like features.
"We go to big hall" he said in a broken English manner of a native American Indian.
"No magic beam, must find bad man." Bill continued to stand before Nobby his face twisted in a strange parody of itself. Nobby looked at the worried expressions on the security escort faces as they regarded their countryman. Nobby turned back to Bill and caught his friends wink. Nobby couldn't control his giggles any more and spluttered a half suppressed laugh, spraying spittle in Bills direction. Bill turned to the bemused security men.
"Short face gone mad." he told them still in his bad accent. Neither man looked amused. Bill realised that he was attracting a small crowd of onlookers. He coughed nervously and smiled to the small audience.
"It's an old Earth custom." Smirked Nobby. "How does it go again."
"Never mind, come on or we will be late." Bill pretended to adjust his uniform and continued down the corridor.
Nobby turned to the gathered folks,
"I am afraid he has gone a bit mad. Swamp gas fever, hardly contagious at all, really."
A murmur ran through the assembled people as Nobby turned to leave.
"You probably won't even be infected." He added over his shoulder. He caught a couple of small gasps as he hurried to catch up with Bill.

They entered the disembarkment area together, followed, a strategic distance back by the security escort. The area was little more than a glorified cargo bay, with curtains. Several large comfy looking chairs were arranged in semi- circles around small tables decked with small bowls, dishes, which Nobby presumed would be full of treats and nibbles when the occasion merited it. This wasn't one of those occasions though, the bowls, dishes, tables and chairs were not being utilised, in fact the area seemed deserted. They all stood in the doorway for a moment, expecting someone to appear and call them in or to hear a voice, a conversation that would've broken the silence.

The majority of the locality was in a gloom, only the tabled area lit from hidden lighting.

"Are you sure this is the right area?" asked Nobby scanning the surroundings. Bill looked at the two security men behind him.

"The chief told us to escort you and the human to this disembarkment lounge." Return one of the men, emphasising the word human without much affection.

"Well then, "said Bill turning back to Nobby, "we may as well make ourselves comfortable." He gestured towards the tables and chairs. Nobby nodded and they began to descend the half dozen or so steps to floor level. As they reached the bottom steps, a heavy thudding drew their attention. They both turned as one to see the source of the sounds. It took a couple of moments for them to understand what had happened.

The two security men were both slumped near the top of the stairs, either unconscious or dead. A shadowy figure

stood in the doorway, laser weapon still in hand, its features hidden from Nobby and Bill as the light from outside caused the face to be in darkness. Bill gasped and took a step backwards, Nobby gulped and also moved backward the figure stood silent and unmoving, even though they couldn't see its eyes, they could feel them watching, scrutinising them. Nobby tried to shield his eyes from the light behind the figure, hoping to get a glimpse of its face. Slowly and deliberately the figure raised the weapon towards them.
"There's no need for this Randy." said Bill his voice calm and low, the figure didn't respond." We can sort all this out, it's not too late." Again, the figure didn't respond.
Bill quickly scanned the area looking for cover, the tables were too far away and the rest of the room appeared empty. The figure trained its weapon on Bill as if interpreting his thoughts. Using the weapon as a pointer the figure indicated to Bill to stand closer to Nobby.
"You will never get away with it Randy. We are about to land; the Emperors entire personal guard are waiting for us. There is no way for you to go." Bill coaxed,
"Come on Randy give it up. This is not going to solve anything is it?"
"No" replied the figure, its voice tired and strained. "No it won't." the figure added. Bill and Nobby watched as the figure slowly shook its head.
"So why?" asked Bill.
"They ..never mind." sighed the figure. "You wouldn't understand."

“Try me, you never know,” Bill replied trying to stall for time, hoping that the security Chief would turn up soon.
“You know nothing.” spat the figure. “You wouldn’t understand.”
“You may be surprised.” answered Bill calmly.
“Oh you will be surprised all right.” cackled the figure, as it stepped forward into the light. Both Bill and Nobby were more than surprised, they were shocked. Stood in a pool of light at the top of the stairs wasn’t Randy as they expected, but the security Chief, and his eyes burned with a vicious undisguised rage.

CHAPTER FIFTEEN

"Will you stop complaining!" Jill said in an exasperated manner, she was trying to keep her voice low so not to attract undue attention from other corridor users.
"That's easy for you to say." retorted Rambo miserably as he walked along his Dolphoid companion.
"Look, do you want to be muzzled again?" Jill said while smiling and nodding to passersby.
"No."
"Well then, quit whingeing."
"But this leash is embarrassing." Rambo whinged
"It's either this or the muzzle," Jill replied, giving the lead a small tug to emphasise the point.
"It's not doing my street cred any good."
"What, and stopping earlier to lick your genitals was?" mocked the Dolphoid
"Hey, don't knock it till you've tried it. There is a certain amount of pleasure to be gained from a thorough cleaning."
"Is that why you clean yours about twenty times a day."
"Oh yes, been spying on me have you?" asked Rambo with a knowing wink.
"But.. I never." Spluttered Jill loudly, attracting the attention of several passers by's.
She blushed and lowered her voice again. "I have just looked through the computers observation log, that's all."
"Yeah, sure. Oww!!" yelped Rambo as Jill tugged sharply on his lead.

"Sorry, my hand slipped." Rambo eyed Jill suspiciously; he thought he saw a faint smile playing at the corners of her mouth.

"You're just jealous of my ability that's all. I bet you wish you could lick your dick."

"I haven't got a ...dick." Jill whispered the last word.

"Well if you did, you would probably clean it as often as possible."

"I would not!" snapped Jill, she was aware of her own blushing and she was sure that other people could sense it also.

"Oh, I see."

"See what?"

"You're one of those!" replied Rambo cryptically, Enjoying every minute of Jills obvious discomfort of the conversation.

"One of what?"

"Never mind it doesn't matter." teased the dog

"Tell me." asked Jill

"Well I was going to say..No I better not. Forget it."

Rambo found himself coming to a sharp halt at the end of the leash as Jill stopped suddenly. He let out an exaggerated yelp. He turned towards Jill to find she had squatted down to his level.

"Tell me." she demanded as he moved closer. Rambo sat down and cocked his head towards her.

"Well," he began "You said if you had a dick you wouldn't spend a lot of time cleaning it." Jill nodded agreement. "Then that means you must prefer mucky dicks."

Rambo smirked in a way that only dogs can, half snarl half drool.

"You are beyond contempt." answered Jill, unperturbed by the statement, after a lengthy pause.
"Is that good?"
"No," Jill said, "Not in the slightest".
"Are you sure, it sounds good?"
"I would appreciate it if you didn't talk about your...genitalia." the Dolphoid requested as she rose, avoiding eye contact with the tatty canine. She restarted her journey down the corridor, gripping Rambo's lead tightly. Rambo had little choice but to follow, his short legs plodding away quickly to keep up with Jill.
"Have I done something wrong?" Rambo asked after a few moments of stoney silence.
"No." was the terse reply, Jill stared ahead of herself as she navigated the corridor, trying to evade looking down at the dog. "Never mind we haven't the time. We're late already; we were supposed to be at the disembarkment area a short while ago."
"It was only a joke, I didn't think it would bother you that much." defended Rambo, ignoring completely What Jill had said.
"You just don't think about what you say, do you?"
"No can't say I do."
"Well, there are some things I don't wish to know about." They came to the end of the corridor and waited for the lift. Rambo sat next to Jills feet.
"Oh, I see. It's the dick thing isn't it?" he asked.
"That is one of them, yes." the lift opened, and they both waited for the occupants to step out before they entered.
"If I had known that not having a dick bothered you so much I wouldn't have mentioned it."
"That's not what I meant, I was.." began Jill

"In fact," interrupted Rambo, "If you like I will let you lick mine."
Several people in the corridor turned as they heard the sudden yelping coming from the end of the corridor, but the sound ended as the lift closed.

"WHAT??" bellowed the Chief slamming his fists down so hard on to the surface of the table that most things resting on it jumped a couple of inches into the air. The three security men in the room flinched at the chief's outburst.
"But you gave the order, sir." replied the highest ranking officer. The Chief glared menacingly at the Dolphoid before him.
"DO YOU THINK.." the chief began to shout, he stopped mid-sentence and inhaled deeply. "Do you think I would be sat here now asking where they are if had given the order?" he continued more placated.
"The message is logged in the files, Sir." the senior security man replied, carefully avoiding answering his superior's question. The chief's eyes burned into the officers daring him to usurp his authority.
"Show me." he said finally. The security officer nodded to one of the other two men, who stepped forward and handed him a small disc. The senior officer took the disk and moved around the desk until he was beside the Chief. He leant forward and placed the disc into the drive module of the desks computer screen. The screen came to life and displayed a menu of contents, of which the Dolphoid selected the file he required. He moved

away from the screen allowing the Chief to watch the display. On the screen, the image of the chief appeared. "Men, we will be landing at any moment." said the image of the chief. "We need to get a few things ready before unboarding. In a short while (at this point the chief let out a series of clicks and squeaks that was Bill's real name) will arrive to collect the human and take him to an unspecified location that I have discussed with him personally and for security reasons this location will not be broadcast on this computer link. Have an escort of two accompany them to the location and I will issue further orders when they arrive." at this, the message ended abruptly. The security officer moved forward to eject the disc, but the chief placed a hand on his arm. "Leave it," he said brusquely. He let go of the officer's arm and placed his hand on the desk, his fingers began to drum the surface as he thought. The officer returned to the other side of the desk and stood where he had been earlier. The drumming of the chief fingers became louder, his expression darker. The three security Dolphoids stood unmoving, not wanting to engage the anger behind those eyes.

"Computer," barked the chief, causing the others to jump slightly at its suddenness.

"Where is visitor Nobby?"

"Visitor Nobby can be located in 103 separate locations." answered the computer

"Where is the security detail assigned to him?" he demanded

"The security escort is located in 103 separate locations also." The chief closed his eyes for a moment and inhaled deeply once again.

"Right," he said to the men before him "make a list of every one of those locations and start checking them out. I want two teams one starting at the top and one at the bottom and meeting in the middle. Someone has planted 102 decoy beacons, and we need to eliminate them fast. Move." all three men departed rapidly from the room and began planning the search. As the wall closed behind them, the chief sagged into his chair. At this very moment, they were docked on the Imperial home planet, their ship was being surrounded by the Emperors military. In a short while, he will receive a message from the Emperors secretary asking them to disembark. On disembarking the Chief is expected to hand over all guilty parties or face the charges himself. At present, the Chief had neither guilty party nor a main witness. He touched the computer screen and accessed the menu file, he found what he was looking for and touched the screen again. The footage of himself he had watched previously appeared. The Chief paused the image and regarded the face on the screen.

"Now where did you get that Holo suit from?" he said rhetorically.

"So, what now, Randy?" Asked Bill.

"Er.. that's the chief." Nobby pointed out. Bill shook his head slowly but never took his eyes off the figure on the stairs.

"No. It's Randy," he replied

“No it isn't remember." began Nobby. "Randy is the skinny ugly looking twat. The one that resembled a gormless Weasel."

"Your companion is indeed correct." the figure on the stairs said to Nobby. He took another step forward and pressed a small button on the control panel of his belt. Nobby and Bill watched as the chief's features warped and twisted grotesquely for a second or two before reforming into the feature of the Dolphoid known as Randy.

"Of course, I meant all that in the nicest possible way." added Nobby with a big hopeful smile.

"Save your words human. They won't help you."

"How about money then?" enquired Nobby.

"I have no need for money." said Randy tiring of the conversation.

"Well if it's sex you're holding out for..." Nobby began to say.

"Silence Human. I have much to do and little time to do it in. Now move over into that far corner, next to the bulk garbage compactor." He indicated the direction with his laser weapon.

"Why all this?" asked Bill, "All the pointless deaths."

Randy flinched for an instant, as though he received some kind of electric shock. He quickly regained himself.

"We don't need them," he said pointing at Nobby who gave a small wave of recognition. "Don't you understand? They would destroy us, just like they destroyed themselves."

"That was history." countered Bill, stalling for time. "We have the chance to help and learn from history and improve the future."

"Nonsense. They are a virus that needed eradicating. They devastate everything they touch." continued Randy, moving slowly down the steps towards the others.
"So why not just suppress the information, debrief the crew and report home? There was no need for the deaths," asked Bill. He and Nobby both shuffled involuntary backwards as Randy, laser weapon in hand, moved forward.
"It was the only way, it's what they wanted.." Randy's body shuddered violently for a second as though a sudden nightmarish memory had invaded his thoughts.
"What who wanted?" Bill questioned.
"Them. Can't you hear them?" Randy replied holding his free hand over his ear, his eyes scrunched together for a moment, an almost inaudible gasp of pain escaped his lips.
"Are you talking about.." began Nobby, ".. the voices that are telling to do bad things.
The endless, persistent voices that follow you everywhere and just seem to get louder and louder, relentless and unyielding. Laughing and mocking, goading you, even in your sleep, to do things you don't want to, but the only way to dull their sound is to do as they demand?"
"Yes, yes." sighed Randy with relief. "You can hear them too?"
"No, it was just a guess," said Nobby. Swiftly Randy moved forward, pushing Bill to the floor with a strength that belied his scrawny frame. He grabbed Nobby by the collar of his uniform and pressed the laser weapon into his temple.

"How dare you mock me" Randy whispered into Nobbys ear through clenched teeth.
Nobby could feel the warmth of the Dolphoids breath on the side of his head.
"I have been through far too much over the past few days to actually give a flying fuck," spoke Nobby with remarkable calmness despite the circumstances. "I may not have had much on Earth, but it was home, it was all I had, and now because of you I don't even have that."
"Brave words Human" jeered the Dolphoid, pressing the weapon a little harder into Nobby's temple.
"Go on kill me, you've left me with nothing to live for. Even my dog hates me."
"No!" shouted Bill, "Don't". Randy turned his head to see Bill stood a couple of yards away, he had momentarily forgot about him.
"Oh, don't worry. Unfortunately for me, I need him alive." He swung Nobby around and pushed him in the direction of Bill. "Now get over there."
"Are you alright?" Bill fussed over Nobby as they moved.
"Yeah, although I'm not sure about the inside of my underwear." Nobby smiled to his friend. Bill found that Nobby's smile didn't affect him in the slightest anymore.
They reached the garbage compactor. Randy unlocked the fastening mechanism of the compactor door.
"What now?" asked Bill
"Inside" replied Randy.
"I thought you needed Nobby alive?"
"I'm not going to kill you, I just need you out of the way for a while, and seeing as these things are sound proofed.." He indicated the compactor, "..I figured that

you won’t be able to attract anyone's attention from inside. So when you are ready." he held the door open for them. Bill stood his ground.
"Not until you tell me what you are going to do." he said
"I am.. I mean the Human here has an appointment to assassinate an Emperor."
"No I haven’t!" Nobby exclaimed
"Not personally you haven't. Let’s just say you will be well represented." answered with a small chuckle. Once again he pressed the small control panel on his belt, almost instantly his face began to warp and change.
"How does he do that?" Nobby asked Bill
"Holographic suit."
"Of course, how stupid of me." replied Nobby, "Fuck me!!" he added as Randy completed his change.
"There," said Randy, now looking like Nobby
"Uh, that's horrible," remarked Nobby.
"That's you." Bill pointed out.
"No wonder I couldn't get a shag."
"Silence." demanded Randy, also sounding like Nobby, "get in there." With a threatening waggle of his laser weapon Bill and Nobby reluctantly moved, albeit slowly, into the gloomy and rank smelling interior of the compactor. Nobby shook his head, trying to grasp the situation; after all, it's not every day you hold yourself to gun point. Even though the compactor was fairly spacious inside, perhaps big enough to hold thirty or forty people, Nobby felt an unnerving sense of claustrophobia even before the door began to close. Just as the last strip of light began to narrow and disappear inside the cavernous area as the entrance was filled by the solid metal door, there was a heavy thud at the other

side of the door. This was superseded by the short, surprised shout of a male and the whoosh of a laser discharge, then another scream, this time definitely female. Bill moved forward quickly and pushed at the door, it opened a crack. The light that entered the chamber allowed Nobby to see what Bill was doing. He stepped up to the door and pushed, there was a slight resistance as they pushed, but it moved fairly easily. As soon as the gap was wide enough, Bill quickly advanced into the main disembarkment area. Nobby followed swiftly and almost bumped into Bill stood just outside the door. The Dolphoid was stood with another Dolphoid, this one female. Nobby seemed to recognise her but couldn't quite place where from. She was looking shocked, tears welling up in her eyes. Both she and Bill were staring at the outside of the door, just behind where Nobby stood. Bill looked at Nobby with saddened expression and then back to the area behind Nobby. He followed their gaze and turned to see what was drawing their attention. Nobby now realised what had caused the resistance when pushing the door open. Lying at the foot of the door in a slowly spreading pool of blood was Rambo.

" ..And then as we entered the Disembarkment area, Rambo spotted what he thought was Nobby lurking in the corner and went wild." Explained Jill to the Security chief. Also present was Nobby, Bill and the Doctor. “He ran forward and pulled at the lead so hard that it caused me to trip over the prone body of one of the security team and to fall down the stairs and lose grip of the leash. I heard a shout and weapon fire, but before I could pick myself up, I heard the hum of a transferral beam and all I could see was Rambo lying still. That's when Bill and Nobby emerged from the garbage disposal unit."

"Well judging by what I found in Rambo's mouth, I think Randy will be in need of some medical attention. There was a fair bit of flesh and material in there." said the Doctor, "it's a bit ironic really, considering the laser wound to Rambo is in the portion of his body. It appears to be becoming a trend."

"He will be alright though?" Asked Nobby, his uniform still covered in stains of dried blood from carrying Rambo to the sick bay.

"Yes, the vet says he will be just fine." replied the doctor. Nobby nodded but remained silent.

"I have been in contact with a President Blattchud." began the Chief, "he is the Emperors personal envoy. I told him of the suspected attempt on the Emperors life, and he is preparing a plan of action as we speak. As to what it involves I don't really know, but he wants us to be ready to leave the ship at any moment."

"What do we do until then?" Bill asked

"Wait I suppose, we are effectively prisoners on our own ship." said the chief with a subdued sigh.

"He's quite mad you know!" It was Nobby who spoke, "Randy I mean."

"Yes, that is why holographic suits were outlawed." replied the Doctor. "The energy field needed to create the holographic image has been known to affect the central nervous system and can cause acute schizophrenia and paranoia."

"Incoming message" announced the computer
"Who from?" asked the Chief
"President Blattchud."
"Put it on screen." the screen glimmered in to life and the image of a pale green skinned alien appeared, he was dressed in what appeared to be either ceremonial robes or robes of office. Unlike all the other members of the empire that they had seen to present, the President was thin and quite elegant looking. He nodded slightly at the ship's crew.
"People," he addressed them, "It is my duty to inform you of the Emperors untimely death at the hands of the assassin of which you spoke of earlier." His tone was flat and betrayed no emotion. The Chief stood and Nodded in return to the President.
"May I offer the sympathy of my crew and I at this sad time," he said. The President was unmoved by the Chiefs offer.
"Prepare to be boarded immediately." he said as the screen went blank.
"message terminated" informed the computer unnecessarily
"Looks like the waiting is over." said the chief wearily.

Randy moved silently down the narrow corridors of the palace, his holographic suit giving him the appearance of an imperial guard. He had tried to beam himself directly into the palace, but some unseen force field prevented that route. The nearest he could get was in the lower basement kitchens. He had made his way via a more or less central staircase that appeared to span all the floors of the building. He had originally chosen the guise of a maid and began to ascend the stairway carrying a small tray that held a wine decanter and a single glass. Unfortunately, this disguise had attracted too much attention from the guards he had come across, not curiosity but sexual harassment. It was after three close calls with horny guards that he decided to change tactics. He had noticed that all the guards he had seen were of low rank so he chose a slightly higher rank, knowing that it would deter conversation, but at the same time not drawing too much attention. If he chose too high a rank, he would have drawn plenty of attention. He stopped at the end of the corridor and used the small scanner on his wrist to check the area before him for life. The stairs were clear, but the upper floor had two life forms, one at either end of the upper corridor. This was the floor before the Emperors private quarters. He knew that the guards on that floor would be numerous and well armed. He needed to be cunning, he realised that he couldn't take them on all at once, it had to be divide and conquer. Randy adjusted the image on his holo suit back to the maid and made his way up the stairs. At the sound of the approaching, the guard turned to see one of the young serving girls from the kitchen climbing the stairs. He watched as her bosom bounced gently at each foot fall, and how her green skin shimmered in the light thrown from the suspended lamps. She stopped several steps short of the top and beckoned for him to come. Nervously he checked up the corridor to his companion, he signalled that he had to go and relieve himself. His companion nodded and gave an ok sign with his finger and thumb. The first guard turned back to see the girl disappearing around the flight of stairs. He checked his breath in his hand and began to follow the girl.

After a brief struggle, Randy slumped the lifeless body of the guard into a dark corner and altered the image of his suit to match that of the guard. He headed back up the stairs and towards the other guard. Moments later he too was lying still next to his companion. Randy returned back to the far end of the corridor and scanned the area ahead. He double checked the reading, readjusting the wave length, and checked again. There evidently weren't any guards in the corridor of the Emperors private quarters, he must like his privacy. There were several people in the central room of the apartments, about thirty metres straight forward. He checked the corridor for alarms and used his wrist scanner to jam the signal on two motion detectors. Cautiously he moved along the corridor, trying to ignore the voices in his mind that were driving him on telling him what to do. He knew they wouldn't be silent until he had completed his task. They never were. He reached a doorway to an adjoining room to the one he needed. The door was unlocked; swiftly and silently he opened the door and entered the room. He looked around and instantly fell to the floor and rolled behind a large wooden desk and crouched there holding his breath and listening. His scans hadn't shown that the large double doors that joined this room to the next were made of glass. As he had entered this room, he was in full view of the occupants of the next. There was no shouting or

running foot steps. No alarms rang, Randy remained crouched for a few seconds longer before risking a glance around the table.
He could see movement in the next room through the glass doors, but no one was near enough to them to spot him. Breathing again for the first time in a while, he relaxed and decide to take stock of the situation. He moved further behind the desk and sat on the floor. He instantly regretted the action and only just managed to stifle a scream. Randy switched off the holo suit and moved onto his knees. Tentatively he felt the wound on his buttock, inflicted earlier by the dog. His fingers came away wet with blood, the hypo spray he had administered himself to numb the pain and stop the bleeding was wearing off. He unclipped his belt and searched for the small medi spray holder. He found it and quietly unclipped the spray, as he held the tiny hypo he noticed the pronounced trembling of his hands. There wasn't time to worry about it now, a quick shot from the hypo spray would sort out the wound for now, and he could attend to it in more detail later on. The pain began to subside almost immediately.
Randy took stock of the situation, this room was unlit, the only illumination coming from the next room flooding through the glass. That was good as far as he was concerned. He would be able to move nearer the door without being spotted. He slid forward onto his belly and began a slow combat crawl towards the double doors.
Randy stopped about six feet away from the door and watched the movement beyond. There were five or six people in the room, none in uniform as far as he could

make out, and therefore probably no weapons. Just beyond the doors, Randy could see the back of a very ornate high backed chair. The people kept moving in front of the chair and bowing, Randy surmised that the chair was a throne and judging by the attitudes of the room's occupants, the chair was occupied by the Emperor himself. He reached down and felt for the control panel on his belt. It wasn't there; he looked down at his waist.
"Damn!" he whispered to himself as he remembered removing it to find the hypo spray. He couldn't risk going back for it, but he needed it for his escape. He planned to burst into the room disguised as Nobby, shoot the Emperor, and possibly a few others while he was at it. Flee the room disguised as one of the people he shot, make it back to the kitchens and use the mini transferral beam to get aboard his own ship and slip away silently. He looked back, but the desk and floor behind it was in shadow.
"Damn!" he said again under his breath. He would just have to pick it up on his way back. He had originally wanted Nobby to take the sole blame, that way there was a chance that the other Dolphoids would be released if they could convince the authorities that the Human had worked alone. Unfortunately, without the control module on the belt, the holo suit was useless. Killing the Emperor as a Dolphoid would probably mean that the rest of the ship's crew would be executed, but he had to stop the voices, and this is what they wanted him to do. He checked his weapon and rose to a crouched position and peered into the next room. He saw the figures of six people all sat on chairs in a small semi circle roughly six

or seven metres in front of the Emperor. Randy took a deep breath and steeled himself. He raised his weapon and aimed for the window of the door. With a whoosh and a crash, the glass shattered and fell. Randy dived through the opening, rolling as he landed back on his feet.

He aimed his weapon and swung around the throne ready to fire. He stopped dead, the throne was empty. Swinging round aiming wildly he fired several quick shots at the people still seated in the chairs. Nobody moved, Randy ducked behind the throne heart pounding wildly. A quick glance around the throne revealed that the chairs were occupied by dummies. Randy recognised a trap when he saw one. Moving swiftly he darted back into the other room, with intentions of grabbing his belt and getting out as quick as possible. Unfortunately for him, the room he had left empty was now chock full of armed guards, both Imperial and Dolphoid. He was knocked to the floor from behind, and restraints clamped to his arms. The lights came on, and Randy was dragged to his feet. The Dolphoid security chief stood before him.

"I am placing you under arrest for the attempted murder of the Emperor and the willful destruction of an entire planet and the perversion of the course of justice. I am handing you over to the Imperial authorities to be tried for the afore mentioned charges." the Chief said briskly.

"But how did you know I was going to be here?" asked Randy

"If you must know Nobby worked it out, we just had to wait." replied the Chief. The Chief nodded to his men who had custody of Randy, they marched him over to a group of large sweaty green skinned Imperial guards. As they handed Randy over he turned and glared menacingly at Chief.

"This isn't the last you have heard of me. One day you will regret this." he bellowed. He would have added more, but an overzealous guard grabbed him roughly by the scruff of the neck and dragged him off for a cup of tea and a beating.

CHAPTER SIXTEEN

"A toast to our guests." The chief announced to everyone gathered in the dining hall of the Traveller. He was stood at the front of the hall at a long table, Seated at the table were Bill, Jill, the Captain, a fully recovered Rambo and of course Nobby. The room swelled with the sound of clinking glasses and cheers. Nobby blushed, and Rambo basked in the adulation.
"As you may already know.." continued the Chief as the hubbub died down," Both Nobby and Rambo have decided to leave us and return home, as soon as it is finished that is." a small titter rippled through the crowd. It had been several days since Randy had been arrested and imprisoned and despite all the trouble he had caused, Nobby asked the President not to administer the death penalty. Instead Randy would receive extensive psychotherapy and counselling.

Rambo leaned over to Nobby and nudged his elbow.
"Er.. sorry for biting you and all that." he barked
"It's ok, I understand your reasons," Nobby replied with a smile. "How are you feeling?"
"A bit tender when I sit down, but not too bad," Rambo said with a painful wag of his tail. "Jill says you captured that fish fellow all by yourself."
"No, I didn't capture him, but I did work out how to capture him." Explained Nobby modestly. Both man and dog sat in silence, looking at each other for several long moments.

"Are you waiting for me to ask you how you did it?" enquired Rambo
"Yes."
“Oh, I see. How did you manage that then?"
"Well I'm glad you asked, because it was relatively simple, but at the same time brilliant." gushed Nobby enthusiastically
"Will it take long?" interrupted Rambo.
"No, so shhh!" replied Nobby. "Right just after Randy shot you, when you mistook him for me, he transferred off this ship and into the palace of the Emperor and sneaked into the Emperors private chambers. He then Killed the Emperor and several dignitaries who were discussing things with him. Randy then escaped and left us to take the blame. When the ship was boarded, and we were all arrested for aiding and abetting an assassin, we were taken to the palace dungeons and interrogated. After talking to a couple of the guards on duty and finding out several things about their planet I began to have an idea. Are you listening?" Rambo raised his head from his crotch area.
"Er.. yeah of course." he lied.
"Well, when I had worked out the idea in my head I asked to see someone in charge. I was taken to see some general or other, and I explained my plan. He got it touch with the President, and I was taken then to see him, and the rest, as they say, is history." beamed Nobby more to himself than anyone else.
"Who says that?" asked Rambo. Nobby regarded the dog for a moment.
"Er.. people."
"What people?" Rambo pressed

"I don't know. Anyway that is how I saved the day." Nobby stated with pride
"You haven't told me yet." Rambo pointed out.
"Yes I have, weren't you listening?" said Nobby
"You said you told your idea to the President, but didn't say what the idea was."
"I didn't?" Nobby seemed surprised
"No."
"Oh, well in that case here goes. The plan was this, I told the president that seeing as they appeared to have time travel capabilities, why not use it to capture Randy before he kills the Emperor, seeing as they now know exactly where he is going to strike and the such. The president was so impressed that he allowed the Chief to lead the team to capture him."
"No blood, guts and heroics then?" Rambo asked Hopefully.
"No."
"Bit of a crap story then," complained Rambo. Nobby stared at the dog incredulously.
"I helped capture the Dolphoid that destroyed the planet Earth."
"That's nothing; I almost got killed tackling him." The dog held the bald area of his rump off the chair as evidence.
"Only because you thought it was me." Nobby reminded the dog. Rambo tried to think of a really good answer to that statement but couldn't. He decided that instead of wasting his time arguing he would just bite Nobby instead. Or at least he would have if Bill hadn't shown up.

"Excited about going back home?" He asked them both. Nobby smile and moved over to allow him to take the seat between him and the dog.
"Yes and no. I will miss all this.." Nobby looked around the room, "But somehow I think space is too dangerous a place for me to play in."
"I thought it was all blown up and stuff?" Rambo interrupted, nudging Bills ribs gently for attention.
"It was." Said Bill turning to face the dog. Rambo cocked his head to one side.
"Has it been mended?" Bill laughed and stroked Rambo's head affectionately.
"I'm afraid not. Apparently, it was beyond repair, they are building you a new one."
"That's nice." Said Rambo, letting his ears be tickled.
"The Emperor was so grateful for not being dead, he offered to have a new one built," explained Nobby
"What about all the people?" Rambo said
"The Emperor sent his entire fleet back in time to the point just before the er..accident and put the whole area into a time stasis field. They were originally going to tow the planet out of the way, substitute it with an old broken planet, let Randy think he had succeeded, and then replace it later." Bill elaborated still scratching Rambo's ears.
"So why didn't they?" Nobby asked
"Well apparently they had a quick look around the Earth and found that it wasn't working properly."
"Not working properly?"
"Yes, according to the movers they found that the air system was clogged up and highly polluted, the water and cooling systems were not functioning within safe

levels. Also, the under surface lubricating oil layer seemed to have all but disappeared, they said you were lucky it hadn't seized up," Bill continued "so they ordered a new one built to the same specifications as the old one."
"Oh. I see." Nobby said untruthfully. "So, any Idea how long the new one will take to build?"
"About ten thousand years, it's a big job."
"What!!" exclaimed Nobby loudly. "Ten thousand years, I can't wait ten thousand years." he spluttered
"Calm down, they just went back in time and ordered it ten thousand years ago. In fact, it was delivered two days ago." re assured Bill. "Everyone from the old planet was successfully transferred the same day."
"Has no one noticed the difference?"
"They haven't had chance to yet." smiled Bill
"How come?" pondered Nobby
"Well as soon as the transfers were completed, the movers set the weather system on severe storm. Heavy rains, minor Earth quakes and landscape damage and all that manner of thing." Nobby's brow furrowed as Bill talked.
"Why on Earth would they do that?" he asked
"Well, basically any minor changes in the new planet from the old one can be blamed on the storms. Slight defects in landscapes and building will be considered to be the result of the storms, same with the new clean air and water, the storms will be considered responsible for correcting the systems. All in all, it is just a way off covering our tracks."

"I don't think I could ever get used to all this time travel business, it all seems very complicated." Nobby shook his head in confusion.
"And very dangerous," added Bill putting his hand on Nobbys shoulder. "I'm going to miss you, friend." A lump suddenly developed in Nobbys throat. He fought it down again.
"And I will miss you, but I don't really belong here. I didn't realise how much I missed home until it had gone," he told the Dolphoid.
"I understand, I love my work, but I miss home just as much."
"When will we arrive?"
"Early tomorrow," Bill answered sadly; He had grown extremely fond of the Human over the past weeks. By coincidence, Nobby felt the same way about the Dolphoid.
Bill held out his hand.
"It has been my pleasure knowing you Nobby," he said. Nobby looked at Bills proffered hand, he chose to ignore it. Instead, he pushed it to one side and leaned forward and gave Bill a hug. Bill wasn't sure how to respond, hugging wasn't a Dolphoid way of displaying emotion, but he soon got the hang of it.
"Some one's stopped Scratching." broke in Rambo. He was stood on the table looking at them both. Nobby and Bill separated from their embrace and both began to tickle and scratch the dog together.

Nobby sighed and rose from the settee. Once again he returned to the window, Mrs. Gardens from next door walked passed his front gate. She looked up and Nobby waved. She smiled and hurried on, she hadn't talked to Nobby since her dog had choked to death on his cat some years earlier. Nobby smiled to himself, he still couldn't get over how he was the only one on Earth that could explain all the strange things that had been going on. Why everyone in France suddenly ended up in Germany and vice versa. Why the Presidents on Mount Rushmore were in the wrong order. Why some rivers suddenly ran in the wrong directions, Why the Sphinx grew a new nose and where had all the pollution gone. The television was full of endless debates and discussions, a thousand and one people all with their own ideas and theories. Nobby had listened too many of them and read even more in the popular press, but as yet nothing had begun to come close. He looked towards the sky and wondered what Bill was doing, probably off somewhere charting another planet in some unknown region of space. He sighed and shook the thought from his head, that was the past, and it wasn't healthy to dwell. You fancy going for a walk Rambo?" he said. Rambo opened one eye and had a looked round to make sure no one else was in the room before he spoke.
"Are you going to let me have some time alone if we meet any hot bitches?" he asked
"Oh alright, but only five minutes."
"That's all I need." barked Rambo, he jumped to his feet and made his way to the door. Nobby put his coat on and reached for Rambos lead.

"You touch that, and you will never have children," growled Rambo. Nobby smiled and put his hands in his pockets.
"Come on then, lead the way." he chuckled. It was good to be home, or at least somewhere just like home.

The End, **or is it?**

Printed in Poland
by Amazon Fulfillment
Poland Sp. z o.o., Wrocław

50876736R00217